# AWAKENING THROUGH DREAMS

# United Kingdom Council for Psychotherapy Series

Recent titles in the UKCP Series
(for a full listing, please visit www.karnacbooks.com)

# AWAKENING THROUGH DREAMS

## The Journey Through the Inner Landscape

*Nigel Hamilton*

Series Consultants

Aaron Balick
Alexandra Chalfont
Steve Johnson
Martin Pollecoff
Heward Wilkinson

# KARNAC

First published in 2014 by
Karnac Books Ltd
118 Finchley Road
London NW3 5HT

British Library Cataloguing in Publication Data

A C.I.P. for this book is available from the British Library

ISBN-13: 978-1-78220-050-5

Typeset by V Publishing Solutions Pvt Ltd., Chennai, India

Printed in Great Britain

www.karnacbooks.com

*For my beloved Sarah, my life's treasure*

# CONTENTS

# LIST OF TABLES AND FIGURES

# LIST OF DREAMS

# ACKNOWLEDGEMENTS

I am deeply grateful to my wife, Sarah, for her immeasurably valuable contribution to this book. Her tireless dedication to working with me on it, together with her love and support, has made the book possible.

I thank the wonderful travellers of the "Travellers' Tales", "Ava" and "David", to Mary and all the dreamers whose dreams are included in this book. My particular thanks goes to "Ava", who has been instrumental in this work. As well as contributing her dreams and personal commentary over many years, she has painstakingly recorded my dreamwork sessions and teachings in Zurich and structured these into the manual for participants from which this book developed.

I am immensely grateful, too, to the CCPE staff members who helped in various ways with the production of the manuscript, to Dave Hiles and Janet Love who have given their precious time and advice, and to all those who have supported and inspired me along the way.

This book is only able to touch upon the breadth and depth of its subject matter but further information about the Multidimensional

Dreamwork Model and the Waking Dream Process can be found on the website of the newly founded Dream Research Institute (driccpe. org.uk). Training in this approach to dreams can be undertaken at the Centre for Counselling and Psychotherapy Education in London (www. ccpe.org.uk).

# ABOUT THE AUTHOR

**Nigel Hamilton** is the founder and director of the Centre for Counselling & Psychotherapy Education, London—a psychotherapy training centre and clinic established in 1984 that has grown to be one of the largest training centres for transpersonal psychotherapy in Europe. Nigel is a psychotherapist, lecturer, and teacher. He is also a professional member of the UKCP (UK Council for Psychotherapy) and the BACP (British Association for Counselling and Psychotherapy).

Originally a research physicist at the Massachusetts Institute for Technology in Boston, USA, Nigel has a particular interest in transformative dreaming and has facilitated dream groups and trainings in the UK and on the Continent for many years. Nigel has continued to develop the dream research that formed the basis of his PhD in transpersonal psychotherapy and has presented several papers in the UK and abroad via the International Association for the Study of Dreams (IASD).

Nigel is the UK Representative of the Sufi Order International and has an extensive background in Sufism, alchemy and guiding spiritual retreats spanning more than thirty years. He lives with his family in the Malvern Hills area of England and likes to play the bagpipes and ride his motorbike (but never at the same time!)

# UKCP SERIES PREFACE

*Alexandra Chalfont*
Chair, UKCP Book Editorial Board

*Philippa Weitz*
Commissioning Editor, UKCP Book Editorial Board

The UK Council for Psychotherapy (UKCP), holds the national register of psychotherapists, psychotherapists qualified to work with children and young people, and psychotherapeutic counsellors; listing those practitioner members who meet exacting standards and training requirements.

As part of its commitment to the protection of the public, UKCP works to improve access to psychological therapies, to support and disseminate research, and to improve standards, and also deals with complaints against organisational as well as individual members.

Founded in the 1980s, UKCP produces publications and runs meetings and conferences to inform and consult on issues of concern to practitioners and to support continuing professional development.

Within this context, the UKCP book series was conceived to provide a resource for practitioners, with research, theory, and practice issues of the psychotherapy profession at the heart of its aims. As we develop the series, we aim to publish more books addressing issues of interest to allied professionals and the public, alongside more specialist themes.

We are both extremely proud to be associated with this series, working with the UKCP Book Editorial Board to provide publications that reflect the aims of the UKCP and the interests of its members.

# PREFACE

## *My journey*

The story of my process of awakening (a lifetime's work) began in the summer of 1978. I was taking a break from my work as a research physicist to attend a week of teachings at the retreat centre of the Sufi Order International in New Lebanon, New York State. While I was there, I received a telegram from my mother many thousands of miles away to say that my father had been taken to hospital after a heart attack and that "he might not make it".

The following day, as I was walking up the mountain to the retreat site, I experienced a sudden onset of excruciating heart pain, accompanied by an alarmingly high heart rate. At first, I thought that I must be picking up on my father's pain and that I was having a heart attack myself. But then, the initial sensations were followed by the opposite extreme—my heart rate became abnormally slow and I began to speak and move as if in slow motion. A profound sense of oneness and bliss overcame me—what I later recognised as the opening of the energy centres in the heart and crown[1] in the realisation of transcendental consciousness (beyond all existential experience). I could see myself and my life completely clearly and impersonally as if from beyond this existence. This lucidity lasted for about half an hour and then disappeared as quickly as it had arisen, but remained as a profound impression for the rest of my life.

I longed to regain this state which had come upon me so easily but, to my deep disappointment, it did not return. I pursued it in the years of considerable inner psychological turmoil that followed through many difficult spiritual retreats and the disciplines of meditation, spiritual practices, and prayers in the Sufi tradition.[2]

It was not until the summer of 1987, following a painful experience of divorce, that I again felt the same pain in my heart centre, in the midst of a short retreat. This time transcendence did not follow. However, a year later, during a thirty-three day retreat, not only did the heart and crown centres open, but I experienced visions of light and the spiritual bliss of the freedom of my soul. Equally important, I had a series of profound dreams at the same time which led to the realisation that there was a link between my awakening to subtle levels of higher consciousness and my dreams.

From this point on, I experienced the unfolding transformation process in myself and observed the way in which my dreams were always a mirror of this. Throughout a period of over twenty-five years of annual solo retreats (of between twenty-five to forty days) I have recorded my dreams and visions as a central part of my transformation process.[3] What has been revealed along the way in a pattern of stages are the visions of several planes of higher consciousness, with each vision always following a dream that reflected the themes, qualities, as well as the landscape, of that plane of consciousness.

At first, I wondered whether my experience was entirely subjective, of value and meaning to me only. But by my working with, and guiding others over many years through the advanced stages of the spiritual journey, I was amazed to discover that the patterns of changes in consciousness as revealed in their dreams were similar to my own. It seemed to me that an underlying "inner architecture" or "landscape" of consciousness was being revealed during the process of awakening that was, perhaps, universally applicable and relevant to anyone wishing to go deeper into their psyche.

What encouraged me in my discovery (the essence of which can be found in the mystical traditions of the past) was that the "evidence" supporting my insights came from many sources over three decades as a psychotherapist and teacher at a psychotherapy training centre, as a dream group facilitator, as a spiritual retreat guide, and from independent individual dream records of the transformation process that have been forwarded to me. Collectively, this confirmed for me the existence of a structured process of change comparable to the one that I had encountered in my own experience.

This book is based on the insights that emerged and evolved from these sources and on my own long research project.[4] It is my attempt to describe a new model of consciousness transformation and a new psychospiritual approach to working with dreams which has relevance not only to dream research, counselling and psychotherapy, but to anyone on a journey of personal transformation and spiritual growth.

It is a journey of discovery and exploration where there are no absolutes, but what I do know with certainty is that dreams will always be at the heart of my own journey and a great passion of my life.

# INTRODUCTION

Who looks outside dreams; who looks inside awakens.

—*Jung, 1964*

Though it may seem to be a contradiction, it is through our dreams that we can awaken. Our dreams hold the key to our "awakening" and, by actively engaging with them, we can initiate and facilitate our own unfoldment. This book is about recognising this process when it occurs in dreams, and how to work with them in service of our growth and self-realisation. It is relevant to anyone with an interest in dreams, and psychotherapy practitioners working with clients who bring dreams, to recognise and support the unfolding process that is taking place within the dreamer. As such, this book is not meant to be a comprehensive volume on dream theory, symbolism, or interpretation. Instead, it deals primarily with the phenomenon of transformation, and opening to transformation, which is reflected in our dreams and initiated by them.

By transformation, I am referring to a change in a person which is felt on every level—in thoughts, attitudes, feelings, physical experience—and which impacts on all aspects of their life. The person undergoing transformation experiences a sense of their deeper nature and a more subtle level of self. This new awareness is the main indication that they are becoming more conscious of the spirit[1] within them and have begun to open to it. Such a transformation can, and often does, lead to a spiritual awakening in the dreamer.

Dreams are the ideal medium through which we can track and observe every stage of transformation, particularly if they are followed over extended periods of time. Tracking many people's dreams in this way over many years has resulted in the creation of a new multidimensional model of dreams and dreamwork which is applicable to dreams generally, whether overtly spiritual or not, or whether part of a series of transformational dreams or not. It is true that the multidimensional approach to dreams is particularly helpful to the dreamer who is experiencing psychospiritual transformation—a profound change in their sense of self that involves experiences of the non-physical or subtle realms—but it can be just as fruitful when applied to "ordinary" or "one-off" dreams as a way of understanding them at a deeper level, and in everyday psychotherapy practice as a way of facilitating and enriching the therapeutic process.

Jung's ground-breaking contribution to the subject of transformation, in particular his appropriation of alchemy as a metaphor for awakening, has given us a solid foundation upon which to build our research. More than half a century later, we now have a considerably larger database from which to draw than Jung did: detailed accounts of spiritual awakenings and of the dreams of people on spiritual retreats, or undergoing a spiritual transformation process in everyday life.

The research data which came from silent, solo, spiritual retreats and contributed to the model presented in this book provided real examples of dream sequences that clearly reflected the process of transformation in being uncontaminated by the impressions of everyday life. The retreatant's attention is focused on the inner life day and night, without any interaction with the outside world, apart from a daily visit by the retreat guide. Yet, solo retreats bring up psychological issues in abundance and with great intensity, in dreams and otherwise. These have to be resolved in order for the retreatant to progress. So it was that the model which evolved from this extensive retreat dream material, blended the psychological and the spiritual before being applied to the dreams of people in everyday life.

The model presented here, which is referred to as the *Multidimensional Dreamwork Model* (or multidimensional dreamwork), builds on

Jung's work in drawing on the psychological perspective, the alchemical metaphor for transformation and the wisdom of mysticism (in particular, the understanding of the inner levels of consciousness and their correspondence with the subtle energy centres of the body found both in Sufi and Vedantic mysticism).

By integrating these perspectives, a multidimensional approach to the process of human transformation through dreams has been developed which recognises the interrelationship of the psychological and the spiritual, and works with the mirroring body in service of both.

The intention and purpose of the book is to communicate this synthesis of perspectives and convey its potential value when applied to dreams, demonstrating how the approach works in practice and bringing it to life through real case material and examples. Whilst there are many ways to understand dreams, the emphasis in this book will be on the transpersonal model presented. As will become apparent, without this perspective, dreams become increasingly hard to interpret using other paradigms the further the dreamer proceeds along the path of awakening.

## Overview

In Chapter One, the purpose and power of dreams understood from a perspective which incorporates the spiritual is outlined. In introducing the *Multidimensional Dreamwork Model*—a multidimensional approach to dreams and dreamwork that recognises the psychological, the spiritual, and the physical dimensions of human experience—its fundamental premise that dreams, as an expression of the imagination, act as a "bridge" between matter and spirit, is explained. The essential structure of the landscape of transformation—seen as an intersection of the horizontal (time-based) process and the vertical (consciousness-based) dimensions—is set out as a map for the reader in preparation for the full description of the journey of transformation described in the chapters that follow.

In Chapter Two, the importance of the "bigger dream story" that is apparent when we follow dreams over time—the *Psychospiritual Transformation Process*—is explained, and the travellers of the "path of transformation", whose journeys illustrate this book, are introduced. The story begins with dreams of initiation.

In Chapters Three to Five, we follow the path of transformation from its start through unfoldment and its later stages (though, of course, there is no end). We explore the forms of the landscape of consciousness transformation—its planes and alchemical stages, and its symbols and signs—which are like the flora and fauna, the landmarks and the local characters of the journey. We see this landscape come alive through the journeying of our travellers.

In Chapter Six, "Special features of the landscape of awakening", we look at four distinguishing features of dreams of the landscape of awakening: light and colour, lucid dreaming, balancing through visionary geography, and the emergence of symmetry. These sections are based on ground-breaking findings that have emerged from research undertaken since the research project published in 2006 (Hamilton, 2009, 2010, 2011, 2012, 2013). These sections look at the significance of light and colour in dreams as a direct experience of spirit; direction and symmetry in dreams as a reflection of the balancing of psychic polarities taking place in the personality during the process of transformation.

Chapter Seven looks at the model in action and focuses on the importance of the body, both physical and subtle, in multidimensional dreamwork. The *Waking Dream Process*, an approach developed over years of practice in the field, which combines creative imagination, psychological understanding and healing, is described and exemplified, showing how we can track the dream through the body in the waking state and, in doing so, unlock its potential by revealing the guiding spirit within it. The appendix provides a quick reference guide to some of the most commonly occurring symbols in the transformation process.

## CHAPTER ONE

# The landscape of transformation

The external life is but a shadow of the inner reality.

—*Hazrat Inayat Khan*, 2010

## The purpose and power of dreams

What are dreams? Dreams can be bewilderingly obscure and transparently clear; they can linger to haunt us and slip from our grasp. They can be a source of creativity, inspiration, guidance, and puzzlement. Dreams have the power to disgust, shock, terrify, and warn us, but they can, too, enlighten us and lead us to the wisdom that is waiting to be discovered within.

There are many kinds of dreams. There are the mundane, everyday dreams which simply reflect the day's events. There are the symbolic dreams which mirror the inner state of our *psyche*,[1] including "shadow" dreams, nightmares, and recurring dreams. There are psychic dreams which predict the future, or tell us something about someone else or somewhere else, and dreams about the body which bear warnings relating to our physical health. Then there are the dreams which come from

1

the spiritual realms—dream experiences of light, higher consciousness, sacredness—that which is beyond the personal.

We know that dreams can be a mirror of our worldly impressions and our state of mind and inner psyche. In this way, we make our dreams. But, sometimes, dreams are so potent that they make us. Remarkable dreams show us the power and potential of dreams. The nineteenth century German chemist, Kekulé had a dream whilst researching the molecular structure of the chemical benzene:

> I turned my chair to the fire and dozed. Again, the atoms were gambolling before my eyes … My mental eye, rendered more acute by the repeated visions of the kind, could now distinguish larger structures of manifold conformation: long rows sometimes more closely fitted together all twining and twisting in snake-like motion. But look! What was that? One of the snakes had seized hold of its own tail, and the form whirled mockingly before my eyes. (Roberts, 1989, p. 75)

The archetypal symbol of a snake with its tail in its mouth is the Uroborus (Figure 1). On waking, he realised that the dream image was

Figure 1. Uroborus.

showing him that benzene's structure was a closed carbon ring. This breakthrough changed the world of organic chemistry, giving us an understanding of how organic carbon chains are formed.

J. B. Priestley's whole life perspective was transformed by the following dream:

> I dreamt that I was standing at the top of a very high tower, alone, looking down upon myriads of birds all flying in one direction; every kind of bird was there, all the birds in the world. It was a noble sight, this vast aerial river of birds. But now in some mysterious fashion the gear was changed, and time speeded up, so that I saw generations of birds, watched them break their shells, flutter into life, mate, weaken, falter and die. Wings grew only to crumble; bodies were sleek and then, in a flash, bled and shrivelled; and death struck everywhere at every second. What was the use of all this blind struggle towards life, this eager trying of wings, this hurried mating, this flight and surge, all this gigantic meaningless biological effort? As I stared down, seeming to see every creature's ignoble little history almost at a glance, I felt sick at heart. It would be better if not one of them, if not one of us all, had been born, if the struggle ceased forever.
>
> I stood on my tower, still alone, desperately unhappy. But now the gear was changed again, and time went faster still, and it was rushing by at such a rate, that the birds could not show any movement, but were like an enormous plain sown with feathers. But along this plain, flickering through the bodies themselves, there now passed a sort of white flame, trembling, dancing, then hurrying on; and soon as I saw it I knew that this white flame was life itself, the very quintessence of being; and then it came to me in a rocket-burst of ecstasy, that nothing mattered, nothing could ever matter, because nothing else was real, but this quivering and hurrying lambency of being. Birds, men or creatures not yet shaped and coloured, all were of no account except so far as this flame of life travelled through them. It left nothing to mourn over behind it; what I had thought was tragedy was mere emptiness or a shadow show; for now all real feeling was caught and purified and danced on ecstatically with the white flame of life. (Edinger, 1991, p. 129)

Following this sublimatio dream experience (sublimatio is an *alchemical operation* which we will encounter in Chapter Four), Priestly abandoned his agnostic position and was convinced, instead, of the presence of a divine consciousness behind all nature. The dream was a life-changing, transformative experience, so powerful was its effect on him.

In these cases of remarkable dreams, we can see quite clearly how important and life changing they can be. But what of more "ordinary" dreams, or dreams that we dismiss as making no sense or being of no relevance? How are we to best understand and make use of our dreams?

## A multidimensional approach to dreams

Most Western approaches to dreams are constrained within a psychological paradigm—they are viewed as psychological responses, the processing of the mind. Dreams, in themselves, are seen as "unreal"—a subjectively distorted version of "reality". Jung's invaluable contribution to our understanding of dreams and the transpersonal field was his recognition of the presence of an inner archetypal realm in dreams, beyond the personal and emanating from a universal consciousness. We owe a great debt to Jung in widening the horizon of our dream world.

Everything we imagine or create already has an existence as an *archetype*[2] or a mental template waiting to be discovered. Seen in this wider sense, *dreams are real*. Dreams are rich with symbols and signs, which are unique to us and also universal in their archetypal nature. Using a framework of symbols that we can recognise, they speak of, and take place within, another reality—the subtle (non-physical) realm— but their intensity can be as affecting as any experience in the physical world. What happens in our dreams has a reality beyond the mind. Something *does* die in our dream death; our dream tears *do* heal us; our dream spiritual experience *actually* connects us with an infinitely greater reality than the material and transforms us.

In the psychospiritual approach presented here, dreams are understood in all their dimensions—psychological, spiritual, and physical. The transpersonal perspective, which recognises the whole person— body, mind, heart, and spirit—and is, by its nature, holistic or *multidimensional*, allows us to do this. It sees the world and the people in it, not just as they appear, but looks into and beyond what is on the surface, beyond what is apparent. Recognising that things are not fixed and limited to their material form, the transpersonal allows for an openness to the possibility of change and transformation. It is essentially hopeful.

From a transpersonal perspective, our consciousness can be understood as having reality at different levels or in different realms. There is the level of our cognitive reality which relates to the physical world and is a reflection of our conscious *ego*. These are the thoughts we think, the opinions we hold and the personal constructs we have formed during our lifetime. Then there is our *personal unconscious*, containing the impressions made by our personal past, which makes itself known through many of our dreams. This is what Jung called the *little self* (Jung, 1991).

Then there is the more subtle mind level where we are connected through our imagination with the totality and a wider human consciousness beyond our own personal limits—the realm of the *collective unconscious* (Jung, 1970). Between the personal unconscious and the collective unconscious lies an interval, which we cross between waking and sleeping. When we dream, the little self is subsumed by the collective unconscious and a "subtle self" that is more fundamental to us than our identity or persona. In spiritual terms, this subtle self might be referred to as the *soul*. (In this book, the use of the term "soul" denotes this level of self.)

Beyond this, and at the same time, infusing all levels of consciousness, is the transcendental realm of spirit—an essence which permeates and animates everything else. Jung called this the *Self*. As our consciousness expands from the cognitive into the collective unconscious, the sense of self "thins out". It becomes more subtle and we experience our soul. This expanding and subtlising continues until we become aware only of pure spirit, free from any personal or little self. At this point, we are realising something of the greater Self.

In looking at dreams, we can find the spiritual in the psychological and vice versa (and access both dimensions through the body) when we realise that *our imagination, of which our dreams are an expression, is a bridge between matter and spirit*. What we call dreams are really a mixture of our worldly impressions and our individual spirit which is trying to speak to us through the metaphors and narrative of our dreams. In this way, the spiritual comes through the psychological dimension.

Dreams can show us something of who we are in more than one sense. We can see our character in dreams—that which has formed as a result of our experiences and life context—with its strengths and weaknesses. Dreams can also show us who we are in our essential selves— that which has always been in us and is uniquely ours. Dreams are a window into our inner life and, ultimately, our soul or essence. In this way, dreams are an expression of body, mind, feelings, and essence. Furthermore, dreams can take us beyond even this—to spirit itself, which is impersonal.

On the one hand, there is the undeniable truth of dreams in that the dream images and narratives depict the ways in which we limit ourselves psychologically. The psychological approach to dreams can show us how the mind has been caught up in our own mental illusions— worldly constructs resulting from painful life experiences and the need to survive. This helps us to understand our personal, inner, world better. When we look through the psychological "lens" at our dreams, most of them seem to reflect our inner world symbolically and, as such, they require "decoding" in order to understand what the metaphor of the dream means and how it applies to our life.

However, dreams are only relatively true when seen from this perspective only, because these images and stories cover up, or hide, our sublime, unlimited potential. A transpersonal perspective enables us to become conscious of the guiding spirit—a more profound, intuitive wisdom—hidden within the code of the dream, to awaken beyond our existential state and open up to our spiritual potential. In this way, the dream is seen as holding within it, not only the psychological aspects of a person but also a hidden, yet accessible, spiritual potential and wisdom. Even dreams that seem dark and troubling can be seen in a different light when viewed from this more inclusive perspective.

Our spiritual potential begins to be revealed when the key dream images are explored more deeply. In doing so, we go beyond the symbolic consciousness of the dreaming mind and our dreams become more transparent—"truer", in that they reveal more and more clearly what lies behind the dream and who we *really* are. Eventually, our dreams become visions of our deeper, inner self—our "soul nature". Much of our suffering comes from our inability to access and express this deeper nature. We live our personal lives on the surface, to fit in with the world around us, creating a false self. Our dreams point this out to us.

Dreams can act as a guide to show us the ways in which we can express our soul nature as well as the ways in which we deny it. In our dreams, our spirit activates our imagination and guides us as to where to go (in the dream), who to meet, what to encounter, how to find the resources we lack and nourish our hidden potential. In our dreams, we can discover the gifts and qualities in ourselves that will enable us to flourish. This is our hidden treasure and it is the purpose of dreamwork to lift the veils that cover it so that we can discover and manifest it. In life, we may be thwarted but, in dreams, particularly in working with a dream in the waking state, there is a way, and that way is in us.

By taking a fundamentally transpersonal view of dreams, we are able, not only to identify and appreciate the spiritual elements of our dreams (which may be hidden in what appears to be purely psychological material), but also to better understand and progress in the psychological dimension, which is inextricably linked to the spiritual. From this perspective, our psychology is a block, but also a doorway, to our spiritual nature. The spiritual is reflected in, and impacts on, the psychological and vice versa.

## The inner landscape

The research studies into long dream sequences involving profound psychological and spiritual transformative experiences already referred to led to the discovery that there is an inner architecture of consciousness—a universal, innate, inner "structure"—which is clearly reflected in our dreams. This structure is far from being rigidly defined, and yet there is enough evidence in the dreams to enable us to identify its existence. Indeed, what is referred to as the "inner landscape" in this book has been experienced and described as subtle levels or planes of consciousness (beyond the mind) by Yogis, Buddhists, Sufis, as well as Jewish and Christian mystics, for thousands of years.

What empirical evidence has shown is that, just as the body has a structure with many interacting systems (skeletal, muscular, neurological, lymphatic etc.), so the psyche has a complex form—a discernible, intrinsic structure. It is not just a melting pot of all the flotsam and jetsam of mind consciousness. It is predetermined but not fixed; it is organic and dynamic, growing and renewing itself constantly, just like the body.

Why is this so important? Because, when we understand the form of something and understand how its parts interact, we can better understand how it is changing, recognise the signs of "dis-ease", the signs of healing and know when it is reaching the pinnacle of its potential. When we have a map, we can find out where we are, where we came from and see where we are going. So understanding the map of our psyche, of our consciousness, has enormous implications for the work of human unfoldment.

The new model of consciousness presented in this book marries the principles of alchemical transformation (which heavily influenced Jung's work), the planes of consciousness (spoken of in mysticism), and understanding of the subtle energy centres in the body (the chakras of the yogic and tantric wisdom of Hinduism and Buddhism). It represents a new multidimensional perspective on the role of dreams in the transformation of human consciousness, and is based on the four key ideas about consciousness set out below.

1. Consciousness is multidimensional; that is, there are different *levels of consciousness*.
2. Consciousness changes from level to level during the *stages of transformation*, transforming the sense of self as it does so.
3. Consciousness expresses itself through *the imagination*.
4. Consciousness reveals itself through the body's energy centres—*the subtle dream body*.

## 1. Levels of consciousness

*Dreams can come to us from many different levels of consciousness* reflected in our inner world. They can mirror our ordinary, waking reality, but they can also transport us to subtler, archetypal levels of inner reality. The deeper we go into our inner world that contains different levels of the self, the more we realise that our inner experiences, our feelings, our realisations, are as important, if not more so, as the external world.

Six *planes of consciousness* are described by the Sufi mystics (Harris, 1981; Abt, 2004), the Kabbalah (Halevi, 1986), Buddhism (Norbu, 1992; Wangyal, 1998), Gnostic Christianity (de Nicolas, 1996), Vedanta (Misra, 1980; Etevenon, 2004), and Taoism (Wilhelm, 1962). These levels of consciousness constitute an inherent order of subtle spiritual steps or leaps of consciousness that the dreamer transits in the transformation process.

There is a mirror of this mystical knowledge to be found in modern science. String theory (a physical theory, incorporating both quantum mechanics and general relativity, which posits that the fundamental building blocks of nature are not point-like particles but one-dimensional strands called strings) suggests that, in addition to our four dimensions of space and time, a further six, inner, hidden dimensions exist. This enables string theorists to account for, theoretically at least, the emergence of our Universe following the "Big Bang".

Jung also recognised that different levels of consciousness were being accessed from stage to stage in the alchemical process (Jung, 1977). He refers, for example, to alchemical texts that use the symbolism of the planets to indicate the presence of the different levels accessed during the Albedo stage, but it is not clear that Jung ever investigated or developed this idea. In establishing a clear link between dreams and archetypal levels of consciousness, Jung's psychological process of individuation is enlarged to encompass a fuller sense of the spiritual dimension.

In looking at the transformation evident over a period of time in the dreams of hundreds of people, I noticed definable cycles in the process. When such cycles were compared, a pattern of ascent and descent in consciousness became apparent. The changes in consciousness proceeded in a, more or less, step-by-step sequence, with each level of consciousness becoming increasingly subtle. The sequence seemed to follow a similar progression as the dreamers accessed distinct levels of consciousness one by one, each characterised by a particular set of qualities. This was relatively unaffected by differences in the participants' age, gender, culture, and the degree of exposure to spiritual ideas, texts, or retreat.

The dream research showed that each plane or level of consciousness is experienced as a unique level of self. Furthermore, in order to access each level, personal psychological obstacles that bar the way have to be encountered and worked through before the transition can be made. The moment the dreams reflect a resolving of the issue, or a "moving on" from that issue, a change in waking consciousness and in the dreams that follow is experienced. The psychological barriers to each plane of consciousness experienced appeared to be directly related to the "pure", spiritual qualities of that level. The blockage or barrier seems to reflect a distortion of a quality that the inner self is struggling to express. Once the barrier is removed, the quality comes through more clearly and has a profound impact on the dreamer, such that the dream experience is grounded in life in the form of a new and enlarged sense of self. In this way, the psychological and the spiritual realms are inextricably linked.

"Ladder dreams"—the dreams which move the dreamer from one level of consciousness to the next—reflect the progression of consciousness and, in themselves, can transform the personality of the dreamer. We can see how the dreams change as the dreamer proceeds

Table 1.1. The six planes of consciousness.

| Plane of consciousness | Level of self | Attunement |
|---|---|---|
| Earth Plane | Physical Self | Physical body |
| Gross Mental Plane | Worldly Self | Mental body |
| Subtle Mental Plane | Creative Self | |
| Third Plane | Loving Self | Soul nature |
| Fourth Plane | Wise Self | Mixture of mind and soul |
| Fifth Plane | Sacred Self | Light body (soul) |
| Sixth Plane | Pure Self | Light body (soul) |

through the levels—from being concerned mainly with everyday life in the external world to mirroring the inner world beyond the personal. The impact of the psychological on dreams begins to diminish and disappear as we go further on the spiritual path until our minds simply become a mirror of our essence and spirit itself (as we will see on the journey of transformation of our dream travellers).

## 2. Stages of transformation

Jung was the first Western psychologist to point out that alchemy—the transmutation of base metals to noble metals—is a metaphor for the structured method of self-transformation which is applicable to all transformation processes, from the growth of plants to the unfoldment of the psyche (Jung, 1983). He saw *the alchemical model as a means of understanding the process of human transformation* as it reveals itself through dreams.

The research into the dream cycles of transformation processes has revealed a striking affinity with the four stages of transformation described in alchemy—*Nigredo* (the black stage), *Albedo* (the white stage), *Citrinitas* (the yellow stage) and *Rubedo* (the red stage).

In describing the subtlising of consciousness in terms of the alchemical stages, the journey begins with Nigredo. Our notions of reality, based on concrete, rational thoughts and beliefs, are shattered by the revelation of powerful feelings, unbridled instinctual forces and anxious thoughts. This leads us to what St John of the Cross refers to as a *dark night of understanding* (de Nicolas, 1996)—a confusing, bewildering interval in which we leave behind our worldly perspective and enter the world of the unconscious. After sufficient purification, the journey then takes off with an ascent—*Albedo*—through the planes of consciousness, beginning with an experience of the archetypal mind (Jung's collective unconscious) and, if we are ready, continuing on to an experience of the subtler realms and the deepest feelings (and light) of the soul.

Finally, we encounter what St. John of the Cross calls the *dark night of the soul* the *void* in Buddhism and *fanā* for the Sufis) where the "light of the soul" appears as *black light*[3] before it becomes transcendental light in the stage of Citrinitas (the *Truth Body* in Buddhism or *Hahut* in Sufism). This is the high point of alchemy—the marriage of our soul with spirit—or, to be more precise, the absorption of our consciousness in the experience of pure spirit. At this point, consciousness has no form; there is no separate sense of self. This is an experience of *oneness*[4] or what Jung called the *Self* (Jung, 1983).

The final stage of the process, *Rubedo*, is the descent of consciousness back down through the planes to the physical and concrete mental world. This descent is not experienced as simply being the reverse of the ascent in Albedo; it is the experience of unfolding of pure spirit as our state of realisation embraces our mental and physical bodies. At this stage, we retain some aspect of our consciousness of the purity and perfection of spirit within us, whilst at the same time becoming aware of the increasing grossness of energy and perception in the descent. Furthermore, the latter is experienced as an increasing sense of enrichment from plane to plane so that, upon reaching the physical plane, we experience unity of spirit, soul, mind, and matter.

These stages of transformation can be experienced in varying degrees of depth and profundity from person to person and at different times. Citrinitas, for example, will be experienced by most people as profound insight rather than as a marriage of soul and spirit or oneness. Yet, however the stages are experienced, they share the same fundamental characteristics.

Each stage always involves *purification* (in order to progress in the transformation); *marriage* (or the coming together of opposites); *death* which paves the way for *birth* (usually symbolising the beginning of the new stage). These "primary" *alchemical operations* do not necessarily come in this order, and they often appear repeatedly in the dreams. We could call these "mini-cycles", many of which can follow in quick succession within any of the four stages of the process.

The seven alchemical operations are the processes that take place during alchemical transformation and which promote and accelerate the process. They are the operations of purification: *solutio, calcinatio, sublimatio* and *coagulatio*—purification by water, fire, air, and earth respectively; *separatio*—separating the subtle from the gross in one's psyche; *coniunctio*—the marriage of opposites in the psyche; and *mortificatio*—death of the old self. These operations are clearly observable both in dreams occurring during the therapeutic process and as part of the spiritual quest, as well as in the challenges of waking life.

From a transpersonal perspective, the operations can be seen as the actions of our guiding spirit, helping us to achieve self-realisation. One could say that, behind these actions, is the ever-present divine guidance. It is the ultimate separatio of the subtle from the gross—the extraction of soul from matter within which it has become entrapped through the impact of the material world upon it.

Edward Edinger describes the significance of the operations as follows:

> After the prima materia has been found, it has to submit to a series of chemical procedures in order to be transformed into the Philosophers' Stone. Practically all of the alchemical imagery can be ordered around these operations, and not only alchemical imagery. Many images from myth, religion, and folklore also gather around these symbolic operations, since they all come from the same source—the archetypal psyche. (Edinger, 1991, p. 14)

In terms of the Multidimensional Dreamwork Model, the alchemical operations are of secondary importance to the alchemical stages.

Table 1.2. Alchemical stages, phases, and operations.

| |
| --- |
| *The alchemical stages* |
| Nigredo |
| Albedo |
| Citrinitas (the peak of Albedo) |
| Rubedo |
| *The primary alchemical operations (present in each stage)* |
| Purification |
| Marriage |
| Death |
| Rebirth |

(*Continued*)

Table 1.2. Continued.

| *The seven alchemical operations* | |
| --- | --- |
| Solutio | Purification by water |
| Calcinatio | Purification by fire |
| Sublimatio | Purification by air |
| Coagulatio | Purification by earth |
| Separatio | Separation |
| Mortificatio | Death |
| Coniunctio | Marriage |

## 3. The imagination

The approach presented in this book is based on the premise that everything in the physical, outer world has a counterpart in the non-physical, inner world and vice versa; the one is a mirror of the other. The two dimensions are interdependent, with each impacting on the other. *Our imagination acts as a bridge between inner and outer, matter and spirit* because the realm of the imagination is bigger than the physical or spiritual realms and contains both.

The role of imagination was explored comprehensively by Ibn 'Arabi, a great Sufi mystic, some 800 years ago, who maintained that our dreams (one of the products of our imagination) occur within an imaginal inner realm of consciousness between the physical and spiritual realms, an inter-world where spirit and form meet (Corbin, 1969). He quotes a revelatory moment that inspired the prophet Mohammed to declare: "In the imagination of the heart of my devotee you will find heaven and earth" (paraphrased version of the Hadith). In other words, when the aspirant's imagination embraces the spiritual path, then the heart opens up, revealing heaven and earth together.

Dreams are the product of the workings of our unconscious imagination, always acting as a mirror, not only of our outer world, but also of our inner world during sleep (Chittick, 1994). In expressing the inner landscape of our consciousness through our dreams, our imagination yields rich detail of this inner world in its images, sounds and felt experience. Imagination expressed in dreams, visions, or waking dreamwork can be more than just a mirror of our inner world; it can reflect changes taking place in our consciousness.

In this way, the more subtle mental and spiritual states, also called "planes of consciousness", can be revealed through our imagination.

Table 1.3. Different forms of imaginal experiences.

| *Imaginal experiences* |
| --- |
| Fantasy (using the imagination to deal with the limitations of life or project onto the world) |
| Constructive imagination (images are constructed in our mind from memory through concentration) |
| Creative imagination (images come through from a deeper, "awakened state", e.g., in meditation) |
| Dreams reflecting both personal, "collective" and impersonal realms |
| Psychic and lucid dreams (an "awakened state" beyond personal consciousness) |
| Revelatory visions (an "eyes open" experience, sometimes starting as a dream) |
| Absolute imagination (a non-dualistic visionary experience) |

When consciousness moves away from the limitations of the outside world and begins to turn within, our imagination becomes unlimited with the capacity to reflect, not only the personal, but also the divine.

### 4. The subtle dream body

According to the Vedantic and Sufi tradition there are seven chakras or *subtle energy centres* located in the subtle body (comprising our subtle *light body* and subtle body of the mind or *aura*). The Sufis call them *lataif*; they are *wheels of light* in the Vedantic and Buddhist traditions. In these ancient traditions, the biophysical-biochemical model of the body is superseded by the *subtle* physiology of the body. In other words, the origin of the body, its organs and function, is to be found at a more subtle level. In this way, it is the inner world that is the template for the human body and mind (Brennan, 1990).

These energy centres act as portals to our inner world, as well as giving out their energies to the physical body. Whilst the energy centres are the expression of our subtle body, they are nevertheless often experienced, or felt, in "physical" ways. During the transformation process, we may experience sensations that appear to be physical, whereas in fact they have nothing to do with the physical body.

In the same way that the physical body holds impressions of worldly experience at a cellular level, which can be accessed in therapy (using methods such as EMDR—Eye Movement Desensitisation and

Table 1.4. The chakras or energy centres.

| English terms | Correspondence in body | Related aspects of self |
|---|---|---|
| Base centre | Base of spine | Instincts |
| Sacrum centre | Pelvic area | Sexuality/creativity |
| Solar plexus centre | Below the rib cage | Power/sense of self |
| Heart centre | Between the rib cage | Emotions/love |
| Throat centre | Adam's apple | Expression/inner sound |
| Third eye centre | Central forehead | Seeing/inner sight |
| Crown centre | Top of head | Spirit |

Reprocessing—and bodywork), so the "subtle body" holds the psychic impressions of our dream world. Just as the physical body enables us to perceive the physical world, so *the subtle body is the psychic organ that enables us to perceive the world of dreams and beyond*. Furthermore, physical impressions have their counterpart in the subtle body and vice versa; any strong emotion in a dream will be felt in the waking state in the physical body. There is an osmotic flow between the two "bodies". In fact, there are many fascinating studies of dreams that show the onset of illness in a particular body organ long before any such malfunction can be physically detected (Mallon, 2000).

It is the subtle senses that we experience in our dreams that activate the energy centres in the subtle body. When a particular plane of consciousness is entered into during a dream, the energy contained within a particular energy centre is stimulated. Likewise, when an energy centre opens, our consciousness has access to the inner level of consciousness that the energy centre is linked to. Different energy centres correspond to different levels of consciousness. This has crucial implications for dreamwork. By working with the dream through the body, it is possible to access, not only the deeper level of the psyche, but also the level of consciousness from which the dream originates (see Chapter Seven).

*A new map for the journey of transformation*

By applying an understanding of levels of consciousness, the stages of alchemy, the subtle energy centres and the way in which the imagination binds all these together, we can begin to describe the richness and complexity of the transformation process. The time-based axis of the four alchemical stages (observable horizontally through the extended dream sequences) and the vertical axis of the subtle inner spaces or levels of consciousness (the transcendental dimension) are inextricably woven together in one "structure", which is experienced as a process of progression through the stages whilst ascending and descending (see Figure 2).

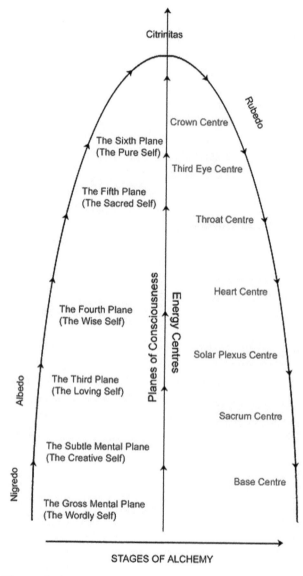

Figure 2. The Multidimensional Dreamwork Model.

The *Psychospiritual Transformation Process* describes the transformation of consciousness (expressed through the planes of consciousness and the subtle energy centres) over time (expressed in terms of the alchemical stages). In this process, we see the falling away of our ego "structure" to expose the innate, archetypal, inner structure of the emerging consciousness that lies beneath. The process, in this sense, is simply revealing something which is already there.

In this way, the process of human transformation through dreams is understood as a journey of consciousness through an inner landscape where the psychological, spiritual, and energetic dimensions are intertwined. This inner landscape represents a new map for understanding dreams and, in particular, transformation and spiritual awakening as they manifest in dreams, and is described and illustrated in the following chapters as we join our dream travellers on the path of transformation.

In drawing a map of the terrain of transformation for the reader—showing its "structure" and the richness of its forms and features (in Chapters Two to Six)—as well as providing tools for travelling through it (in Chapter Seven), the Multidimensional Dreamwork Model hopes to inspire an appreciation of the depth and breadth of this fascinating and compelling journey.

## CHAPTER TWO

# The journey of transformation

Trust in dreams, for in them is hidden the gate to eternity.

—*Kahlil Gibran*, 1969

## The Psychospiritual Transformation Process

I am calling the transformation process itself, as revealed and actualised through dreams, the *Psychospiritual Transformation Process* (*PTP* for ease of reference). It is only by observing and following dreams continually over long periods, in what may be called "extended dream sequences", that we are able to recognise the presence of a PTP in the dreamer. This is the bigger dream story. When we track the dreams of one person over a long period, we come to understand the dreamer's language and narrative and we can see how this story starts to change radically when awakening is underway.

When such a process of transformation is taking place in a person, distinct changes in their dream content and dream themes, in which we can see the newly emerging aspects and levels of the deeper self, become apparent. Often, particular kinds of unusual dreams or dream sequences tend to occur whilst we are undergoing a breaking down of the old or redundant personal sense of self. At the same time, the more

19

subtle dimensions of human consciousness start to reveal themselves in identifiable patterns. Dream studies of PTPs covering periods from several months to several years have shown these patterns.

Furthermore, there are other "awakened" dreamers who recognise these patterns in their dreams. Patricia Garfield, in her book *Pathways to Ecstasy*, describes her three year dream journey through several levels of consciousness, using the rings of the Buddhist mandala to illustrate each level. In her process, she also identifies key dreams that she associated with the four directions of this mandala: east, south, west, and north, symbolising the balancing of her psyche (Garfield, 1989).

Most books on dreams and, indeed, most dream research, are focused on either short dream sequences or single dreams (APA Journal, 1991). Whilst these have value in themselves, they miss out on the underlying narrative of our awakening consciousness. From the point of view of the PTP, it is like looking at a single vignette in a play, or a brief narrative that belongs to a much greater story, and expecting to understand its full meaning.

This is particularly true of single transformative dreams that have been lifted out of the context of a long series. If a single dream is looked at in isolation, it is likely that our insights into the content of the dream will be limited. If we do not understand or even know of the context within which the dream occurred (including the dreams preceding and following the "important" dream), we have little insight into what facilitated the transformative dream experience, or how such an experience can be grounded in a meaningful way in everyday life. Short dream sequences and single dreams act mainly as mirrors to the dreamer's inner world at the time of the dream, whereas extended dream sequences provide a broader context—the bigger picture of our inner life—and an insight into the nature of the changes in consciousness taking place in the dreamer at a much deeper level.

It is true that a single dream can be so significant that it marks the beginning of a process of transformation which is then reflected in subsequent dreams, as well as in change in the dreamer's personality over a period of time. A single dream can also be a significant indicator of the need for transformation and, if heeded and worked with, can initiate that process of transformation in the dreamer. In this way, work with a "landmark" dream may lead to a PTP which will be apparent in subsequent dreams, each having the potential for the unconscious and conscious transformation of the personality.

The Multidimensional Dreamwork Model is invaluable when a transformation of the human personality is taking place in the dreamer's inner world. It enables us to recognise the emergence of a new consciousness within the dreamer, infused with spirit, breaking through the habitual mental scripts that have dominated their mind world. The action of spirit is seen in dreams where the dreamer, free from the limitations of the personal perspective, can experience a higher dimension. The effect of this shift—the emergence of spirit—will cause a change in consciousness, a change which will impact on every aspect of the person's experience. Seen from this point of view, the purpose of dreams is to guide us in the transformation of spirit within.

Likewise, the multidimensional dreamwork approach has the capacity to facilitate and enhance any deep psychological transformation which, it is suggested, always has a spiritual component. Every psychological transformation frees up something of the spirit within. By recognising and honouring our experience of the latter in the psychological work, we enhance our psychological insights and realisations. By the same token, any spiritual transformation must incorporate the corresponding psychological aspects in order to be regarded as stable. It is important to ground our spiritual experiences by reflecting on their implications for the way in which we live our life. Whether dreams have an overtly spiritual connotation or not, they can have a profound impact upon the dreamer if a multidimensional approach is used in working with them.

In a profound transformation process, a kind of spiritual or consciousness awakening takes place which has significant psychological consequences. Such an experience can lead to far-reaching changes in values, beliefs, attitudes, behaviours, and possibly even, physical changes in the body. This has been widely documented (Maslow, 1971; Marlan, 2005; Wilber, Engler & Brown, 1986). The PTP can also cause a major shift in consciousness, resulting in a distinctly new sense of self-realisation. These experiences transcend the conventional psychological perspectives, interpretations and explanations. Indeed, Jung recognising that life's journey is, essentially, a spiritual one, introduced his concept of *individuation* to account for something deeper than the psychological healing resulting from psychological work and maturation.

Yet, we must acknowledge, too, that reaching high states of consciousness alone does not necessarily guarantee a correlating level of psychological maturity, which is why it is so important to ground our spiritual experience in this world. The mystical tradition of the Sufis, for instance, makes the distinction, on the one hand, between a spiritual state (*hal*)—an experience of a higher consciousness that is inherently unstable in that it does not result in a greater stage of realisation and could revert back to the old way of being—and, on the other hand, the progressive stages of spiritual realisation (*maqamat*), which have to be worked for and necessitate much psychological change in the process. Once a new *maqam* or new stage is reached, it remains stable and there is no regression. This is similar to the distinction between *states of consciousness* and *stages of development* that Ken Wilber has described with increasing clarity over the years (Wilber, 1986). Thus, it is important to make a clear distinction between isolated spiritual experiences, in a single dream or dreamwork session, and a profound PTP which can be tracked over long periods of time through cycle after dream cycle and integrated into the conscious psyche on every level.

Psychospiritual transformation is, in fact, an age-old process hinted at in rather cryptic terms in alchemical and ancient Sufi literature (Corbin, 1990), but it has never been described and exemplified through present daydream examples. Now the time is ripe to show a larger public how the esoteric wisdom of old can be played out in our own dreams. Today, there are many more people undergoing spiritual experiences in transformative dreams and this is reflected in the increase of public interest in such topics. It is hoped that this book will contribute to a better understanding and acceptance of these extraordinary experiences and, at the same time, show that the potential for transformation lies in our "ordinary" dreams too.

Three main sources of dream data are used to illustrate the inner landscape and journey of awakening. (As far as possible, the dreams are quoted in full, but some have been condensed out of necessity).

1. The PTP dreams of two dreamers—Ava and David (their pseudonyms)—spanning a period of approximately eight years.
2. Dreams drawn from a study of 1,500 dreams of people from different backgrounds during their experiences of a rigorous spiritual, silent, solo retreat; some were short retreats (five to ten days), some were longer (two to six weeks).
3. Dreams from extended cases of PTP in psychotherapy clients.

Permission to use the dreams in this text has been obtained and principles of confidentiality applied.

## Travellers on the path

David was referred to me early in 2006. He was suffering from a deep depression and sense of hopelessness that had not been shifted by the therapy he had undertaken. I was impressed by David's commitment to therapy and by his demeanour, despite his obvious desperation. I had an intuitive sense that we could work well together, although I had little idea of what would unfold or how we would both be tested.

I met Ava in 1999 at a dreams workshop I was running and started to review her dreams. Clearly, she was on the cusp of some kind of major transition in her consciousness. Ava paid particular attention to noting down the fine details of her dreams, as well as meticulously documenting the associated waking experiences in her consciousness, body, and perception, and shared these with me on a weekly basis over a period of ten years. As such, I believe this was perhaps a rare case of someone documenting a psychospiritual transformation resulting in something of what the alchemists of old called "alchemical gold", which referred to the spiritualisation of matter and materialisation of spirit.

My analysis and interpretation given in the "Travellers' Tales" is an amplification of the dreamwork that took place in their processes at the time. The stories of these two dreamers (in their own words below, and in mine in Chapters Three to Five) are wonderful examples of awakening through dreams.

### David's journey

In the seven years plus that I have been undergoing this very particular therapeutic journey with my therapist, many extraordinary and remarkable things have manifested or unfolded in our work together. I came to Nigel with already over twenty years of therapeutic work (in one form or another), as well as a serious commitment to meditation and the spiritual path. All of that previous work had been helpful and important, but the core of my difficulty in life, namely a schizoid complex, had remained ferociously intransigent.

This complex that had arisen in the first year of my life (possibly whilst still in the womb) amidst profound maternal deprivation occurred developmentally speaking before the formation of any thought or language and had seemingly been imprinted or "hard wired" into the very fabric of my being. This existential experience (a cold, empty state utterly devoid of feeling—a kind of living death) was split off from all conscious ego experience, which had formed on top of this profoundly weak and narcissistic foundation (a house of sand).

Accessing this archaic experience, being strong enough to face it, had proven to be extraordinarily difficult and had exhausted or defied all previous conventional therapeutic treatment (although it is clear to me that previous work had, in a certain way, cleared the way for what was to come).

Beginning therapy almost immediately catalysed a creative, therapeutic outpouring of material that has included many hundreds of dreams, as well as over 150 paintings generated from a profoundly dynamic and vital source. From the very beginning, the process of working on my dreams, of walking through the dream under the unerring guidance of my therapist created a subtle, but truly alchemical, effect on my ability to work with the schizoid condition. Relating to the dream, focusing on crucial elements within the dream as a bridge to the spiritual, whilst at the same time evolving a deepening awareness and understanding of the schizoid experience, has proved slowly transformative.

Going into the "heart of (my) darkness" has been, for me, an extraordinarily difficult, painful and exhausting business. The approach offered by Nigel, coupled with his wisdom and guidance, has given me the method and "tools" with which to work meaningfully with those elements of my psyche that lie beyond conscious experience, as well as giving me the fortitude and strength to confront those resistant elements that were so impervious to change and transformation.

## Ava's journey

Dreams have always played an important role in my life since I started to write them down as a young woman, but it took several life-changing events to guide me towards the spiritual path and make dreamwork the central focus of my life. It was only when my overly busy life had led me close to burnout that I was finally ready to take dreams seriously and look for answers in the inner world. While in a dream session in therapy, I had my first experience of overwhelming light in some other reality—a place of beauty and bliss. In coming back, I saw tears in the eyes of my therapist; she must have known then that I would have to go on without her. But no other guide was available and the door to heaven was closed again for me.

A few years later, I became ill and was given a six month leave of absence from my job as a language teacher. I retired for a whole winter to the quiet loneliness of a house high up in the mountains. In the small village close by, I encountered a Jungian analyst—a welcome serendipity as I had long felt the desire to enter more deeply into my dream world and the Jungian approach was the most advanced and fascinating path I could imagine.

During the seven year analysis that followed, my analyst encouraged me to work with my dreams using "active imagination" and was extremely interested in the reports of my imaginal journeys, all the while insisting that I needed to do this type of dreamwork on my own. In this way, I became more and more confident in my ability to enter into my dreams consciously. I began reaching that, almost forgotten, realm of light again. My dreams became more and more archetypal and mandala-like until, one day, I presented such a dream to the analyst and he flatly responded: "This is the end of your analysis. I cannot accompany you any further. From now on, you will have to find or create your own path through unknown territory". This came as a shock to me and I tried to argue with him, but he remained firm. I am deeply thankful to him now for throwing me out of the comfortable, but also limiting, nest of psychology and forcing me to fly on.

This flight was not easy. I was afraid of pushing ahead without a map or a guide. "The master appears when the student is ready," I had read somewhere, but it took me another couple of years to understand that being ready meant emptying my cup so it could be filled again. When my son left home for university, I found myself in an empty space. A time of prayer and meditation had come for me now, filled with the deep wish to find a guide who had walked the dream path before me. Having heard about spiritual guidance through dreams in other cultures and former times, I still doubted whether there was anyone doing this work here and now, or that they could be found.

I heard of a workshop called "A spiritual perspective on dreams" and I signed on immediately. It was the first workshop Nigel had offered in my home city. I was stunned in watching him guide people through their dreams using the Waking Dream Process, enabling them to access otherworldly places and find hidden treasures within themselves in the most unlikely places. It felt mysterious to me, as if he was performing magic, but it rang true. I sensed that he knew where people were going because he had been there before. He obviously had a map, and I felt an overwhelming desire rising in me to discover that map myself. To my surprise, he agreed to work with me on my dreams. Little did we know that this process would last for ten years.

Now that I was paying even closer attention to my dreams, dream recall intensified and I wrote down several dreams almost every night (approximately 1,000 dreams per year). Without close guidance and continual encouragement, I would have been lost in the maze of the alchemical processes, which appear quite impenetrable when you are in the midst of their very real impact. During the phases of darkness and emptiness, I needed reassurance in order not to lose trust in my spiritual path, which became visible step by step, dream by dream.

Then, a few years into the process, dreams of teaching appeared and, at the same time, people began asking me about their dreams. With the support of Nigel, I started offering dreamwork sessions and, now, spiritual dreamwork is my main occupation. So I have become a "language teacher" again, passing on my deep trust in the dream process to dreamers who are eager to learn the language of their soul. What could be more wonderful for a teacher than to serve as a midwife, bringing the inner knowing into the light?

There is no doubt that the journeys undertaken by these "travellers" are remarkable. Their dreams were unusually prolific and detailed (and far too numerous to include in their entirety). I have chosen to focus on some of these dreams in this book because they exemplify the role of dreams in psychospiritual transformation and their potency in the process of awakening. They show us what the path of transformation, as it appears in our dreams, can be like. We are able to follow them through the landscape of consciousness and see where the journey of transformation can take us.

I need to emphasise, however, that this book is not just intended for people who have been on such a journey, but for all dreamers—as a guide to transformation wherever we may be on the path and whatever is transpiring in our dreams. In being given a map by those who have explored the terrain as far as the eye can see and from above and below, we are better able to recognise where we are and where we might be going—remembering, of course, that every journey is unique and, in that sense, unknown.

## Dreams that initiate awakening

How does the awakening process begin and why? It seems that there are as many answers to this question of how and why a PTP begins as there are travellers on the path.

It may be that we are plunged into a serious life crisis which, in breaking our heart, breaks it open and initiates a spiritual transformation. It may be that a life-changing spiritual experience that occurs "out of the blue" or after many years of spiritual practice marks the beginning of the journey. For others, the experience of intensive solo spiritual retreat triggers a profound inner response. The process can begin simply when the longing for meaning and the desire to seek within are overwhelmingly strong and persistent. In all these cases, we are more attuned to our inner life than normal and more likely, therefore, to remember a profound dream or a series of significant dreams which reflect the stirrings of awakening.

In some cases, it is the dreams themselves that initiate the process of awakening. These dreams of initiation may be extraordinary, but for some, a commitment to remembering, recording and working with dreams in the waking state is sufficient to trigger, in time, a definite turning point when spiritual guidance begins to become apparent.

My spiritual quest began in 1978, following a significant spiritual experience of transcendence. Although this had made a powerful impact upon me, causing me to change the course of my life, I had no idea why it had occurred or from whence it came. I began to pay attention to my dreams and to undertake an annual spiritual retreat, guided in the Sufi tradition. By 1988, I was ready to attempt a long retreat.

The first eleven to twelve days were tough, frustrating, but I was determined to continue regardless. My dreams reflected my personal limitations. However, the next four days saw a change in my experience. I felt lighter, more focused, and could meditate for longer periods, free of personal thought. I felt sensations and pains around the heart centre and around the physical heart.

On day fourteen, I started to experience streams of inner light in my spiritual practices. The meditations became quite blissful. This phenomenon continued on day seventeen until I stopped to hold my breath, only to be startled by the impression of "someone" blowing air on my face. Only later, did I come to know what these "winds" were.[1] However, that night, I had a very significant dream.

### Soul, Mind, and Seeker

I am in the middle of a town square and spot a rather sad looking young woman sitting on a bench. I go over to talk to her. She is waiting for her beloved to arrive and, in the meantime, she had lost her luggage. So I volunteer to go and search for it and to find her bags. My search is aided by an older friend, acting as an experienced guide (he is an ex-detective). We finally find the luggage hidden in a river by the seaside.

On my return to the town square, I see a naïve looking innocent young man looking for the sad lady and I suddenly remember that she had been lured away by another rather dubious character. My guide reappears and we set off to a hotel where we suspect we might find the lady and her manipulative companion. On arrival, we discover that it is a gambling den. Nevertheless, I enter the place and discover both the luggage and the "dodgy man". I confront him and say: "You can't bargain for your soul".

Upon waking, it seemed that the woman represented my soul, or *anima*[2] (from the Greek for soul) figure, the "dodgy man" my shadow (my unacknowledged self), and the innocent young man was the seeker of my soul in unchartered territory. It is clear to see in this dream that, luggage found, the long journey of transformation was about to begin for me. Perhaps the luggage was a symbol of a treasure, yet to be revealed as well as my "stuff" which needed to be unpacked.

In the case of David, an extraordinary dream recorded long before he began psychotherapy with me foretold his journey of transformation and awakening through dreams. He called this dream the "big dream".

### Heaven and Hell

I'm in the Houses of Parliament listening to an intense debate. I sit and listen for a while and then decide to leave. I exit by a side door that takes me out into a wide, deserted street. I walk down the middle and, as I do, this quite extraordinary energy begins to manifest inside of me. It is awesome and overwhelming in its power. It comes from within me, but is beyond my ordinary mind, and has contained within it all the passions—ecstasy, terror, awe, intoxication, wonder, happiness—and so on. As I continue to walk down the street, the strength and power of the force builds and I take to the air and soar up into the sky. I take off, flying over the land looking down on the landscape below that has taken on a numinous quality that is magical and radiant in its display. I am filled with happiness—heart bursting with feelings.

… I rise and rise, gathering speed as I go, leaving the world far behind. Totally concentrated now, I push myself like a rocket and hurtle out of the earth's atmosphere into space. As I float there in space, I look up and there, in front of me, is a scene of such majesty and glory I can hardly behold it. In the centre, the sun and the moon are sitting side by side—their radiance extending far into space … Countless creatures and lights and colours of every hue are all manifest in this vast heavenly space. Celestial music is ringing out and I am in a state of pure rapture that builds and builds. Finally, a unicorn gallops across in front of the sun and moon and my heart almost bursts with the intensity of it.

I know I cannot stay out there in space and, after a while, I turn earthward and, holding my arms aloft (superman style), I begin the long journey back to earth. I feel all-powerful and am travelling at great speed towards the earth. I decide not to stop and crash into the earth, penetrating the earth's crust with ease. I travel down into the earth towards the earth's core. Suddenly, my descent begins to slow and I decelerate as I encounter resistance. There is a brief tumbling sensation and then I come to a halt completely encased and trapped inside a very peculiar honeycomb structure that holds me like a baby in a womb. I start to struggle and the sides of the structure, which are dry and brittle like old thick parchment paper, give way under my assault. I break my way out and find I am inside a small chapel with a simple altar and cross upon it. Next to the altar stands the tall elegant shape of a woman with her back to me. I am expectant and filled with longing that here is my soul mate that I am about to unite with, thereby becoming whole. The woman turns to face me and, instead of the beautiful, sentient woman I had (confidently) expected, I am faced with a woman that is incredibly sluttish and whorish in her appearance. I feel repugnance and am profoundly disappointed, beyond all words deep in my heart. (1991)

In David's dream, he is catapulted heavenwards to experience celestial wonders beyond the mind (which he will not encounter consciously until the awakening stage of his process eighteen years later), but because his psyche is out of balance, he is pulled back again to crash into the earth where he must first encounter his own unconscious feminine—the grotesque female figure. The inner wisdom of the dream brings him down to earth where his is born into his own struggle. (This is a case of *false sublimatio*, which we will encounter in Chapter Four).

As he worked with me on this dream, and those that followed, he slowly unravelled the psychological knots that had been crippling him. Following significant progress in healing the split in his psyche, he began to record profound spiritual dream experiences that accelerated his healing process. In this way, David's journey is a wonderful illustration of the role of dreams in making our psychological blocks available for healing in order that we might take the next important leap in consciousness.

Ava, having worked with a Jungian analyst for several years, sought my guidance in working with her dreams as a way of deepening and furthering her spiritual quest. This led to a series of deeply spiritual experiences in her dreams which became the focal point for her process of awakening. Ava's PTP is ongoing and has taken her through several complete cycles of dreams. The cycle that culminated in her awakening is described in "Travellers' Tales".

We shall now follow the journey of awakening from its inception using these travellers' dream journeys in Chapters Three to Five. In each chapter, the key elements of the "inner landscape" are described first, and the dreamers' journeying, which illustrates them, follows.

As with any journey, it is helpful to be open and flexible about what it might bring, even if it is not what we expect. The travellers' journeys do not always neatly fit the model (which, by necessity, simplifies what is a very complex process), nor should they. They are full of the richness and complexity of human transformation and awakening to spirit. We can become confused when we try to follow this mercurial spirit with our limited minds!

Whilst there are commonly occurring symbols at each stage (as set out in the tables of themes and features), we must always have a respectful sense of the individual expression of these things. As Jung himself says: "We need a different language for every patient" (Jung, 1963, p. 131). Having said that, whilst symbols are personal at the outset, they become more archetypal through the process (though the archetypes are often expressed in personal forms) and entirely impersonal at the apex of the process.

Also, the movement from one plane to another is not "cut and dried" in every individual dreamer; it is more of an organic ebb and flow through the process where mingling occurs at some points of overlap. It is akin to the developmental stages in children, where the child practises going to and fro between stages until they are confident enough to make the permanent shift to the next stage.

It is in the nature of journeys in the outer and inner worlds, that we sometimes experience the merging of one environment with another at border areas; we back-track because we have forgotten something or want to fix an important landmark in our memory; or, if we get lost, we just go round and round for a while. The journey in the inner landscape is just as personal and idiosyncratic. The aim has been to try and strike a balance between exemplifying the model for the reader whilst communicating the spirit of the dreamers' journeys through the landscape of awakening.

## CHAPTER THREE

# Beginning

I then begin to think that the purpose now is to let myself fall into
the abyss; that is what should be done.

—*David*, 2006

## The landscape of beginning

### The Earth Plane

As was explained in Chapter One, consciousness is multidimensional
and dreams come to us from these different levels of consciousness
which form the vertical axis of our "inner landscape". The first of these
levels of consciousness which has an influence on our journey of transformation is the *Earth Plane*.

Whatever our nature, the influence of this physical world is such
that most of our conscious time during the twenty-four-hour cycle is
taken up participating on this level. What we end up sensing and feeling impacts on our inner world, which is then reflected in our dreams.
Although as young children we often dream about and sense other
worlds, by the time we reach adulthood, our consciousness is grounded
in the physical world. Most of our dreams as adults, therefore, are

physical or worldly. In our modern age, the images that predominate are often artificial, man-made. They show the influence of our concrete, materialistic consciousness on our dreams and our sense of self.

We have been educated and trained to think rationally, logically, objectively. Whilst this facilitates efficient transactions with the world around us, it also suppresses our personal feelings, inner thoughts, intuitions, and our instincts. In terms of Jungian personality typology, we are subject to a bias towards extraversion—focus on, and absorption in, the world around us. Our dream images reflect the impact the world has made on us.

But what of our suppressed introverted feelings, thoughts and our "irrational" inner world? The predominantly objective consciousness which operates in the daytime makes a significant switch at night to a subjective consciousness. This is what is reflected in our dreams at the beginning of the transformation process, which sees our consciousness move from attachment to the external world to engagement with our subjective, inner world. The unconscious realm that was submerged under our concrete, mental functioning self now appears through images in our dreams.

What we begin to see in our dreams is the manifestation of a split between our inner and outer worlds. We see our rational thinking, our habits, preoccupations and attachments to the material world. Simultaneously, we start to see our hidden or repressed thoughts, feelings and instincts appearing in distorted ways in apparent contradiction to our conscious personality and perspective. Jung described the phenomenon extensively in his description of our conscious and unconscious worlds (Jung, 1983).

## The Gross Mental Plane—The Worldly Self

The mental plane is the level of the mind and can be broadly divided into the lower and higher mind—the Gross and Subtle Mental Planes, respectively. The level of consciousness we start to access at the first stage of the process is that of the *Gross Mental Plane* where our subjective, inner life is dominated by our worldly orientation and instinctual nature. Here, the mind is functioning at a lower, concrete level in its preoccupation with physical and worldly matters such as money, power, and sex, as well as feelings such as fear, anger, and desire. It is our contact with the Earth Plane and its impact on our consciousness (comprising our conscious mind and its counterpart, the personal unconscious) that results in the formation of what can be called the *Worldly Self*. Themes that often appear in dreams during the early stage of the PTP at this level of consciousness are set out below.

The tendency of the lower mind in dreams is to concretise aspects of our inner reality, which take the form of worldly metaphors indicating our attitude and mood state. In our dreams at this level, the lower mind manifests through images of artificial objects and manufactured items; the setting is often an inner city landscape, a shopping place, a train station, and so on. These specific images and scenes contain personal thoughts and associated feelings that the lower mind has generated through our ego, our experience of the material world. These thoughts and feelings translate themselves into pictures: if we feel sad, the correlating dream image is dark and gloomy; if we feel trapped, we are stuck in a small room. Concrete thoughts exist as discrete and autonomous entities in our dreams. They can be associated with past events, memories, and held-in feelings. In dreams, each thought becomes a character or aspect of the dream.

Table 3.1. Themes and features of the Gross Mental Plane—The Worldly Self.

- Instincts, e.g. violence, anger, rage, sexual seduction, greed, hunger, jealousy, envy, bigotry
- Worldly concerns, e.g. money, status, power, material objects, sexual desires
- Darkness, blackness, heaviness
- Death
- Mess, pollution, chaos, disorder, dirt
- Controlling/out of control behaviour
- Loss, sadness, despair
- Danger, destruction
- False self
- Shadowy figures
- Instinctual animals, reptilian creatures, black raven
- Proliferation of thought forms, e.g. swarms of insects, rats
- Illness and sickly body parts
- Learning difficulties
- Man-made environments, inner city
- Colours—black, brown, earthy yellow, artificial colours
- Healing images, doctors, hospitals

The corresponding mood of the Gross Mental Plane is dark and sometimes takes the form of nightmares. This phase can be experienced on retreat and in therapy as a time of boredom, frustration (with the restrictions of the therapeutic container and boundaries, or the retreat conditions and practices) and resistance to the process of transformation occurring in the body, mind, and emotions. Psychologically speaking, it is experienced as negative and sometimes quite depressing.

When we (as clients or therapists) encounter such feelings in waking dreamwork, we also experience a heaviness or sleepiness. It feels like wading through treacle or mud—a resistant, viscous feeling. When somebody is telling us a story that is lodged in the lower mind, or when somebody is depressed and the anger is suppressed, we start to feel sleepy as we encounter the grosser energy form. Working on these dream energies is psychically very tiring.

When the anger is expressed and the unconscious reality becomes conscious, however, there is release and the energy starts to flow again. It is very important to understand, here, the link between *energy, mood, and consciousness* and that, when we create a shift in any one of these, the other two are affected—they are interdependent.

A man had the following dream at the start of his retreat showing us something of the Worldly Self.

Omar Sharif

I see Omar Sharif and his accomplice. The accomplice is one-third-size and egg-shaped. He is in a water tank with glass sides. Omar Sharif leans on him. The accomplice is so small he suffocates under water. He is pulled out, angry and spluttering. He accuses Omar Sharif of being a ladies' man. O.S. denies this—it's just that he has to look after two gorgeous women! O.S. collects the women. His pride and joy is a red Ferrari which he drives to the house but bangs it against a wall. The windscreen breaks. Disaster—no possibility of mending it quickly. The one-third-size accomplice says: "Give me the Ferrari and I'll fix it"—and he will. O.S. goes off to ponder this—Is it a rip off or a bargain? Then my heart said to my mind: "Take it—it's a bargain".

The dreamer is angry and jealous of the ladies' man, Omar Sharif (the dreamer's image of a role he'd like to play). This figure, however, is rather superficial—he represents the false self. The accomplice, being the dreamer's suppressed side, gives help and guidance to Omar Sharif; that is, the offer of fixing or "correcting" the rather flashy red Ferrari upon which the dreamer's instincts and desires are projected. The guidance affirming the change in the dreamer comes from the dreamer's heart.

That there are two "gorgeous women" in the dream is important. The number two is the most frequently appearing number in dreams (von Franz, 1974). According to Jung, it signifies the conscious emergence of an unconscious aspect of the psyche as part of a balancing taking place in the dreamer's psyche, which, in this dreamer, is to do with the opposition between the persona and the authentic self.

A Freudian interpretation of this dream would focus on the red Ferrari as a symbol of the dreamer's repressed *libido*. However, when approached from the multidimensional perspective, the energy of the libido is seen in the context of the dreamer's unfoldment. In the case of this dreamer's PTP, this *drive* was transmuted into a series of powerful spiritual experiences which were then integrated into a whole self that was both sexual and spiritual.

### The alchemical stage of Nigredo

In Chapter One, it was pointed out that there is a striking affinity between the process of transformation in dreams and the four transformational stages described in alchemy—*Nigredo, Albedo, Citrinitas* and *Rubedo*. The first of these—*Nigredo*—will loom large at the beginning of the journey and can be seen quite clearly in our dreams. Much of psychology and psychotherapy is concerned with this stage, Nigredo—the sphere of the earth. In its themes, we can see quite clearly the overlap with the earth and mental planes described above; the two dimensions (alchemical stage and level of consciousness) intersect in Nigredo.

In alchemy, Nigredo or "blackness" is the rotting down of the old form that needs to take place in order for the transmutation of "base matter" to occur. This is the "black work" of alchemy. For our purposes, Nigredo symbolises the stage in our process when our psychological "stuff"—the way we relate to the world and to ourselves—is put into a container (therapy, retreat, or a period of self-examination) and "cooked" and cleansed until we can progress to the next stage in our growth.

In the Nigredo stage, the process manifests as the reactivation of feelings and memories held in the body. Our worldly identification is broken down to release repressed, unconscious forces. It is disappointing to be faced with the realisation that conscious attempts to counter these "scripts" and to repress old feelings have failed. We are forced to face the fact that we are still relatively unconscious of this buried material and of the powerful ways that our ego uses to defend itself.[1] Nigredo is a real threat to our egoistic self. Instinctively, we fear disintegration and loss of that sense of self.

It is a period of confusion, during which the client or dreamer is challenged to re-orientate their consciousness and turn away from the concerns for, and attachments to, the outside world, towards their inner world. Initially, this is experienced as darkness and an encounter with negative, shadowy figures and scenes in our dreams. We feel lost, sad, despairing, and empty. This emptiness is referred to in Sufism as the *barzakh* or interval between the external material world and the inner world of the soul. It is experienced when we turn within, away from the world.

At first, our ego reacts defensively in response to this illusion of emptiness, employing the instincts and its worldly attachments in its struggle to survive as an independent entity. It feels like we are regressing at this early stage of the process. We must wrestle with ourselves, our attachment to the body and the concrete thoughts and images associated with it. It is an experience of our limitations and the intoxicating mind-body prison which we have made for ourselves, separate and safe from the inner world. Ultimately, the soul longs to be free of such limiting conditions.

In Sufism, this reaction is described as the activation of the instinctual *nafs* or "appetites". In Buddhism, it is seen as our attachments to worldly pleasures, which are a distraction from the emptiness of our inner world. Freud saw it as the ego's struggle to contain instinctual forces for fear of their breaking out and being exposed to public morality; the instincts are seen as a threat to the ego.

The dreams in Nigredo are dark and heavy, carrying the feelings of fear, anger, envy, and desire within them. Themes of destruction, chaos, disorder, and sickliness of the body characterise our dreams. Images of aggressive men and women, animals and threatening reptiles appear. In alchemical terms, the soul is subject to, and constrained by, the power contained in those forms.

The mind can react by producing obsessive thoughts around worldly matters, objects, and concerns. This is typical in the retreat process. Dreams of swarms of insects or rats and similar creatures proliferate, symbolising our fears and the extent to which the ego employs thoughts as a defence against our unknown, deeper nature.

A psychotherapy client in Nigredo dreams that: "A teddy is stuck in the roof of my home; I pull it and shit falls out". Something "emotionally messy" in the psyche (the house or home is often a symbol of the psyche), related to childhood perhaps, is a block to a higher consciousness (it is "stuck in the roof") and needs purifying.

## Psychological blocks—Transforming shadow energy

Dreamwork from a multidimensional perspective is based on the understanding that it is our guiding spirit that is hinting to us, through metaphors, and sometimes even directly, as to the nature of our psychological blocks. These blocks are our defence mechanisms and have acted as protection in life, helping us to cope in spite of our wounds, our vulnerabilities and our weaknesses. But these blocks also limit us and stand in the way of our growth and flowering. Ironically, they can be the source of most of our own pain.

These blocks can be removed by psychological work on the self or, as is often the case, when we are forced to face ourselves at crucial turning points in our life—when our personal world is shattered and our defences are rendered useless. When one chooses, or is forced, to give space to the exposed vulnerability and emotion (of anger, fear, or loss), a new consciousness develops and, with it, a more mature and deeper sense of self. These psychological blocks can also be removed by working with our dreams.

We must first confront our fears of the shadow or darkness in our dreams and, in doing so, it is useful to differentiate between two kinds of darkness: darkness as a veil or protection (which we will encounter later in the journey) and darkness as distortion of light. At this stage of the journey, it is the latter that we usually encounter in Nigredo.

Freud showed us that distortions in our thinking and perspective arise through the presence of unconscious desires and motives which are driving forces that we are unaware of (Jacobs, 1992). This is shown in our dreams as shadowy figures, in nightmares, and in repulsive or ugly images. Once we become conscious of a desire or an intention, we can then use our will to act on it. Our confrontation with this kind of darkness is, in fact, a meeting or conjoining with our unconscious side.

In being born into this external physical reality, we learn to hold on to the externalised light to feel safe. In the process, we split off from the natural darkness of the womb that we had been accustomed to before birth and the light from which we came. We begin to fear that which we do not see as part of us—darkness—and our inner light. From the spiritual perspective, it is not surprising, then, that it takes a lifetime to realise consciously that we are, essentially, a being of light.

In confronting our shadow, we gradually become conscious of our light. In our dreams, it literally starts to appear, helping us to leave behind our fear. We realise that this darkness is really light that is obscured—distorted light. We develop confidence in our personality until, ultimately, we are convinced of our light. In coming to terms with and accepting our darkness, we are well on the way to succeeding in the battle to free ourselves from the frightening inner impressions that come out of the shadows of our minds.

The process draws out in us valuable qualities such as patience, courage, acceptance, and humility. Indeed, the so-called "dark" aspects of ourselves are simply distortions of a "seed" quality or element that could not be consciously and freely expressed. However, once confronted, the anger or envy reveals a purer quality such as truthfulness or aspiration. Furthermore, these qualities will now be able to express themselves more consciously through our personality. The hidden treasure in the shadow is our essence.

In our psychic work, there is nothing we need to be afraid of. The distorted images of our shadow will have no power over us when we uncover the hoaxes of the mind and remember our light. What we commonly call evil is simply the distortion in our minds of a natural spiritual impulse that has been corrupted—through our conditioning, through our greed, our fear, our ignorance, our narcissistic self-referencing, and our illusory beliefs.

As the blocks are removed one by one, a new spiritual awareness grows; the more blocks that are removed, the more profound the experience of awakening. A total transformation of the person's former perspective is then possible, wherein the subject begins to handle life and life's problems in a completely different way. What bothered us before no longer does so; what was frustrating is tolerated; what was feared is confronted. Furthermore, our compassionate understanding allows others to be themselves, warts and all.

It is a mistake to see the material world, the earth as a hindrance to spiritual progress or to deny the negative thoughts, feelings, and the body. The shadow has its role in spiritual development. Everything we know in the manifested world is a constant flux of that which is revealed (light) and that which is unknown (dark) and this is mirrored in the inner world. As Robert Johnson says: "The psyche spontaneously divides itself into pairs of opposites" (Johnson, 1986, p. 46). In our journey, we must learn to come to terms with and accept these fundamental opposites. Only when we do so will our potential to transcend the dualities of manifestation be realised.

## The alchemical operations in Nigredo

Besides the four stages of alchemy, there are also the alchemical *operations* that promote and accelerate the transformation process. The operations are active in the process whatever phase we are transiting and are reflected in our dreams. However, some operations are more likely to appear in certain phases, whereas other operations are present throughout the process.

In the stage of Nigredo, there will be:

- an experience of the psychological complexes we are stuck in;
- a purification process (usually *solutio* or *calcinatio*);
- the assimilation into our personality of a new pure quality, hidden in, and freed up from, the old psychologically distorted forms (*coagulatio*)
- a conscious conjoining with these relatively unconscious qualities as a new, more subtle way of being (*coniunctio*);
- a letting go or dying of an ego attitude or stage (*mortificatio*).

### The alchemical operation of solutio in Nigredo

One of the operations we are likely to encounter at the start of our journey is *solutio*. Solutio is one of the four purifying "actions", each of which is related to an "element"—water, fire and air and earth. As human beings, we are a complex form of the natural universe and, as such, these primary elements of nature are also part of our inner make-up. These elements hold distinct qualities. We experience them in ourselves and others experience them in us. Our elemental nature can be seen very clearly in our dreams (so, for example, a person with a strong water nature will have many watery dreams) and particularly in the PTP, which is characterised by the operations of purification.

Solutio refers to the dissolving of a solid in water, like a lump of sugar in tea. Solutio is connected to our water nature, which is flowing, creative, feeling, and relational. If water is seen as the bringer of life, then solutio can be seen as the regenerator of the life force in us, and as a potential awakener of the deeper soul feelings in our hearts. However, before solutio can take effect, we must be prepared to surrender to it.

Solutio is one of the most important alchemical operations in the transformation of the psyche and it can involve a radical purification. A dissolving of the fixed nature of our ego takes place in solutio—a dissolving of our opinions, beliefs, and ideas about ourselves, about others, and about what is important in our life. This is, of course, very threatening to the ego. We may find ourselves in the midst of a life crisis where everything we identify within our lives— our relationship, our job—is dissolving around us. It feels like life is falling apart and we are overcome with emotion. The "floodgates" have opened and, whilst it is very difficult to experience the pain, our tears are cleansing and purifying.

Joining a spiritual group or starting therapy can also evoke deep emotions, as our individual ego undergoes the experience of being dissolved and contained within a larger perspective, a larger spiritual consciousness (the spiritual teachings or community, or the therapeutic "container"). There is the story of the monk who was learning to meditate but was struggling, and his teacher said: "You're stuck. Go and fall in love." The monk protested, "But I'm a monk". The teacher insisted, "Go and do what I say". So the monk went away and fell in love. When he came back many years later, the teacher said: "Now I can teach you, because your heart has dissolved".

When solutio is operating, we are likely to find rising water and flooding in our dreams. It may indicate the conscious emergence of a wealth of feelings, or it could be a tsunami heralding a major reorganisation and awakening of deep and powerful soul feelings that will change our whole outlook on life. The Biblical story of Noah's Ark is such a powerful, archetypal solutio story because it represents a mass purification of our (inner) world.

The following dream is a powerful example of solutio in action. It took place at a time in the woman's life when life as she knew it had been swept away by a series of devastating events that came in quick succession.

### Surrender

> I am in my therapy session. There is something I don't want to talk about and I look out of the window. To the left is the sea and mountains. I notice that the sea is coming in and out quickly then, suddenly, the water comes up as far as the window in a huge surge. I move away quickly, knowing that it will burst through the glass. It does, and I am carried up the stairs. I *have* to surrender to its force—I have no choice. Everything slows down and I prepare to die. I am at peace with that.

She had no choice but to die to the old life and her dream reflects this death and purification by engulfing solutio.

Solutio is indicated whenever water appears in the action of the dream (not when it is simply present in the background). So a ceiling leaking water would be solutio, possibly indicating a need to cleanse the mind of its false or rigid attitudes. Typical images in dreams might be falling into, drowning, or swimming in, a lake, a river, or the sea.

One of the most profound and interesting aspects of solutio is its form in the *royal alchemical bath*—the meeting of polarities of soul and spirit. This is symbolised in dreams by bathing with a lover. In the alchemical texts, a king and queen, symbolising spirit and soul, are seen to be bathing in the royal alchemical bath. This is the symbol of the purification and removal of the veils between soul and spirit.

### The alchemical operation of calcinatio in Nigredo

Just as solutio was to do with our water nature, so *calcinatio* is the expression of spirit through the fire element in us. The tendency of the fire nature is to rise, expand and radiate. Psychologically, the fire in us enables us to assert and express ourselves, to be confident, truthful, courageous, and passionate. We can also use it in self-protection. Fire is the opposite of water. Its nature is light and heat. This is shown clearly in dream images of fire and light. As it contains heat, it can be very intense, dangerous. Fire needs to become safe before it can be made useful. It needs the earth element to give it a boundary.

As with solutio, calcinatio can be seen in a person's outer life, as well as in their dreams. An extreme form of calcinatio would be a terrible accident, like a car crash in which we are badly injured, or our loved one dies suddenly and we are consumed with anguish—that's the fire of calcinatio. It may be the fire of anger, or of grief, shock, or loss.

Calcinatio is the opposite of solutio, but the purifying effect is the same. Water cleanses and fire purifies by whitening and burning away what is dead and diseased. Furthermore, as with the other operations of purification, though the reality of such a radical breakdown is devastating, it can lead to a breakthrough. Purification by fire leads to the transformation of fire into light.

Typical fire element dream images are the sun, fire, burning, heaters or boilers, landscapes with red rocks in them, volcanoes or landscapes show evidence of volcanic activity (craggy rock peaks in mountains), images of violence, war, conflict, and anger. The dreamer's associations with the images should be explored alongside a treatment of them as symbols of calcinatio.

A woman has this dream at the beginning of a cycle of dramatic change in her life and perspective. The wise guidance of the dream is that salvation lies in staying with the fire.

### Fire in the Loft

I am told that work is being done on the building I am in and I have to go to the top floor. I go to a huge, dirty loft where a girder is hanging and then falls. Men come and set fire to the entrance of the loft. I go and get help and shout up to the people trapped in the burning loft, "Don't jump; save yourself."

## The alchemical operation of coagulatio in Nigredo

Coagulatio is related to the earth nature in us, which manifest in qualities such as solidity, patience, steadfastness, and endurance. It is the operation of grounding something, embodying it. If something coagulates in us, it becomes conscious, like a building block for further development. The term comes from the process of blending metals together in metallurgy. First, the metals are melted. When the mixture of the two is right, it is fixed (by "quenching"—dipping the mixture in cold water to harden it and make it adamant). This is coagulatio. It is the establishment of the right mixture and its stabilising in a body. Psychologically, it is the embodying of an insight, a new way of being in our personality. Spiritually, it is the embodying of our true inner nature, of grounding the most subtle aspects of our soul in everyday life.

Coagulatio can be experienced as descending—coming down to earth and grounding a new insight or experience; and also as ascending—moving to the subtle self and making the subtle world real for us. At this stage, it involves the incorporation of a quality emerging from the transformation of shadow energy. The movement is a bringing down into being. Birth or babies in our dreams are a sign that something subtle has coagulated, or been born, in our consciousness.

Coagulatio will often take the form in dreams of eating. Whatever it is that needs incorporating into the psyche is literally taken in through the symbolic action of eating. At the end of a retreat, a woman has this dream of incorporation.

### Fish Head

I am carrying a small baby. The baby wants me to remove the head of a raw fish so he or she can eat it.

### The alchemical operation of coniunctio in Nigredo

Coniunctio is the most important operation because it reconciles the opposites in us, which is the raison d'etre of alchemy. Archetypal opposites include: masculine—feminine, spirit—matter, dark—light, sun—moon, love—hate, and the marriage of these is the only way one may progress in the process of transformation. As soon as the polarities appear, there is a conflict which can only be solved if the opposites come together and are reconciled. At that point, the dream images connected with this conflict, will show a reconciliation between the two sides—like two enemies becoming friends, two parts of a puzzle coming together, two halves making a whole.

### Wedding

I am with my lover. He is standing. I am sitting next to a woman and immediately next to me is a brown-haired girl. She is drawn to me and tenderly rests her head in my neck—a lovely feeling. My lover is touched as he watches. He says: "We could have a white wedding and have it here on the mountain plateau with all these sympathetic people as witnesses". Then, the others and I watch him do a display. He lies along a pole, makes himself rigid then uses his strength, determination, and vigour to move himself with the pole from side to side, up and down.

This woman's dream contains the presence of the feminine (the woman and the tender experience of the girl) and the masculine (the strength and vigour of the lover's physical display). The suggestion of a wedding in front of sympathetic witnesses reflects the readiness for the marriage of masculine and feminine in the dreamer's psyche.

The operation of coniunctio begins with the union of "lesser" or "grosser" opposites, like mind-body, head-heart, dark-light, and culminates at the apex of the process in the ultimate conjoining of spirit and soul. The union of conscious and unconscious appears at this stage as a physical act of coniunctio. At every stage of the process, we will experience problems with opposites and we will have to go through the operation of coniunctio in order to progress. In fact, in every stage we will have to go through a purification, a marriage and a death. The purification exposes polarity and imbalance in us, the marriage brings the opposites together, and the death of our identification with some old aspect of ourselves allows us to enter the next stage, often symbolised by a birth.

## The alchemical operation of mortificatio in Nigredo

Mortificatio means death. In our dreams, it signifies the end of something; for example, it may be the end of a way of seeing, thinking, or experiencing life. As we complete each stage in alchemy—Nigredo, Albedo, Citrinitas, Rubedo—we must experience a death in order to move on to the next stage. In order to become a butterfly, the silkworm has to die. It has to go through a mortificatio transformation.

Of course death is the very thing that we are all afraid of. Even if our reality is unpleasant, we are reluctant to let go of it because death is more frightening. Sometimes, people who have been depressed for a long time don't want to let go of it because it's the only reality they know. Death is necessary. It will appear again and again in our dreams so we can learn to overcome our fear of change. If we want to take the spiritual path, we must be prepared to change; we must be prepared to die.

Typical mortificatio dream images are corpses, decapitation, being shot or stabbed to death. The dreamer is either the victim of mortificatio or its witness, in seeing another being killed.

The following dream from the beginning of a retreat shows the common association of calcinatio with mortificatio.

Conflagration

I dream of Celts with painted figures and faces. I am at a massive
fire ritual. People are being catapulted into the conflagration. In the
end, everyone is killed. There is a sense of revisiting a past event.

The following day, the dreamer made a transition to the next plane (the
creative realm) with the alchemical stage of Albedo heralded by the
image of the birth of a baby.

During this alchemical stage, the mind is caught up with the instincts.
By wrestling with the instinctual forces in Nigredo and, paradoxically,
accepting them as they are, we begin to transform the ego reactions
and free up the soul. The instincts become quiet because the life-force
is being withdrawn from them, and the soul experiences its first taste
of freedom.

Having accomplished the extraction of the soul from the grip of the
body (instincts) and the mind (destructive thoughts), we are more able
to be at peace with ourselves. (We will see this very clearly in David's
early dreams). Compared to soul consciousness, personal thoughts and
instincts are superficial, so we have to go beyond the dualistic mind-body
interface to experience the natural subtlety and beauty of the soul.

The challenge of this stage of the process is to survive the encounter
with the unconscious and to begin to master or contain the instinctual
forces. Unless the dreamer can do this, he or she does not complete
the transit to the higher mind and the subtler levels of self. Ultimately,
healing is the outcome of this stage of the process (in Nigredo, it is a
visceral experience), once purification and integration have taken place.
Completion of this stage will be reflected in dream images which are
more natural and balanced than artificial and worldly, and images of
healing.

## The lower energy centres

In Chapter One, the importance of the subtle energy centres in our bodies as mirrors of our developing consciousness was highlighted. It was
suggested that each energy centre corresponds to a particular level of
consciousness and alchemical stage. In reality, the relationship between
them is more complex, with energy centres and channels active at all
stages and levels. The lower energy centres which tend to dominate at

this phase of Nigredo and the concrete thinking of the Worldly Self are introduced here. Further guidance on working with the subtle body is found in Chapter Seven.

## The base centre

This is called the *qalab* (*latifa qalabiya*) in the Sufi tradition, meaning "mould" or template of the physical body. It acts as a grounding point between our physical and subtle bodies and is associated with the earth and fire elements. The Yogis call it the *muladhara* and see it as providing groundedness, strength, and stamina, and the capacity for survival in our psyche. This point of view coincides with that of the Sufis who see the base centre manifesting as the human tendency to become caught up in our aggression when threatened.

In working with the body during dreamwork, we will find that the descending direction in dreams (going down to the basement of a house for example) takes us towards the lower energy centres, including the base centre. Often sensations of heat (inner fire) are felt in the base of the spine and/or the legs. Similarly, tingling sensations can be experienced in the feet when the base centre energies are becoming active. The awaking of the energy centres in the PTP will often begin with the rising of the *kundalini* (or dormant fire energy) from the base centre at the bottom of the spine. This is commonly experienced as heat around the lower centres, particularly the base, and is often symbolised in dreams of awakening as a snake or dragon. The kundalini will be present throughout the process, once activated. In the "Travellers' Tales" that follow, we see the kundalini energy stirring in David's dream of a "multicoloured coral snake" (12/2008) in Chapter Four. Towards the end of the process (in Rubedo), the base chakra is activated again, indicating the grounding of the process in the subtle body. David's earthy "Elephant" dream (02/2013) in Chapter Five exemplifies this.

## The sacrum centre

This is called the *svadisthana* by the Yogis and the *latifa nafsiya* (*nafs* meaning desires) by the Sufis. In terms of the elements, it is associated with water and fire and is the source of our sexual drive (the fire of passion) and creative energies (water). As with the base, it is an important centre for the incarnating energies (that is, the descent of spirit) in coming fully into life.

In terms of imagery and dreams, this centre expresses itself through sexuality, creativity, eating, and sensuality. However, the dream guide has to learn to differentiate the expression of these desires of the ego from the subtler meanings that dream images of food and sexual union can convey. For example, food and sex images in the Nigredo stage of the alchemical process refer to physical ego desires; whereas, food and sexual attraction to others in the Albedo stage usually indicate an inner feeding of the soul and a conjoining with a particular aspect of soul consciousness, respectively.

When a lack of energy in these lower centres is detected in therapeutic work, working with the imagery arising from focused attention on the corresponding physical areas will help to ground the dreamer's consciousness in the body. This gradually strengthens the ego (by incorporating the unconscious aspects and energies contained in our instinctual nature), particularly if there were developmental problems in early life. If we think of development starting at the base centre at birth and moving to the sacrum centre in the first few years, then problems in these areas might indicate a developmental arrest in early life which is held there. This is shown in David's "Yellow Fish" and "Numinous Fish" dreams (12/2007 and 02/2009) and his "Bliss" dream (07/2009) in the "Travellers' Tales". In Ava's case, the sacrum opens up later in her process in Chapter Five in the "Emptiness" dream (06/2002).

## The solar plexus centre

This is called the *manipura* centre by the Yogis and is the seat of the ego which is underpinned by the sacrum (desires) and the base centre (survival). In Sufism, there is no solar plexus centre. Instead, they refer to the *qalb*, the personal heart, situated on the left side of the breast which regulates personal feelings.

In Sufism and Vedanta, the solar plexus centre is regarded as the sun and fire centre, and the centre of power in the psyche, enabling us to claim our individuality or "I-ness" in relation to others. Our ability to safeguard our boundaries stems from this sense of personal power which can also be expressed as assertiveness and domination. Aggressive energy can emerge from the lower two centres and influence the solar plexus centre. However, the energy of the solar plexus can serve a higher purpose than the little "I".

In dreams, the solar plexus centre shows itself through our personal dream cameos and themes. As these themes come up during the dream exploration, it is important to focus on the solar plexus centre, to see what images emerge. Similarly, when exploring a dream, if an image evokes a sensation around the solar plexus, then it is important to focus on it and wait until the effects of doing so are felt. Typically, negative sensations (which give rise to negative associations and images) eventually give way to a more balanced, or even positive, feeling (once the block or issue has been cleared). Opportunities for exploring and healing a fear of self-empowerment and poor boundaries will arise. The dream will reveal notable imbalances in the psyche and so it is the dream guide's role to spot, focus on and draw out the more repressed or emerging aspects within the imagery.

In David's dreams, the solar plexus energy is activated in the "Courtroom Rage" (08/2007) and "Suicide of the View" (09/2006) dreams, and strengthened in "Numinous Fish" (02/2009), "White Rat" (04/2009) and "Bliss" (07/2009) and the dreamwork on them. Ava's solar plexus was particularly active in "Spheres of Consciousness" (02/2002).

## Travellers' Tales

### David begins

We can follow this beginning phase of the journey through David's psychotherapy process. David, in his fifties, was divorced with grown up children. As a client, he was serious and intense, always well-presented and pleasant, but underneath was depressed. David was sensitive and idealistic and an experienced meditator in the Buddhist tradition. He was holding down a responsible and difficult professional position in which his good personal judgment was needed to resolve conflicts, yet there was a fundamental conflict within him—a split between his unworldly idealism and his more human, earthy side. One could say that he had a schizoid personality. At the beginning of his therapy, he was not conscious of the depth of his anger, could not assert himself, and was terrified of intimacy with people, particularly women.

David had all but given up hope of ever being free of his psychological afflictions. This was mirrored in my countertransference where I felt, at times, disappointed by the resistant nature of his schizoid mind and wondered if he would progress beyond his initial psychological successes. There emerged a pattern in our work in which David would move through distinct levels of resistance, as if we were peeling away endless onion-like layers of his defensive mind. Desperately painful feelings of meaninglessness would emerge at each "barrier" causing him to really struggle from session to session.

Then a dream would come in which some new element emerged (often in the form of an archetypal figure with whom we would engage using the Waking Dream Process), showing us what needed to be tackled next. David would connect with the image daily between our sessions, which gave him an immediate sense of relief and hope that he could progress further. He would start to feel better and then reach a "plateau" in therapy when he tended to focus on external issues such as work. Then, he would suddenly "hit" the depressive wall again as he encountered ever greater resistance to going deeper. In the latter stages of therapy, this cyclic pattern became less and less marked as he penetrated the depths of his defensive core. From that point on, David's ability to relate to people improved dramatically.

In one of David's first reported dreams, he undergoes a kind of death.

### Suicide of the View

I ascend to the top of a mountainside. I look out and am confronted by a vista of extraordinary beauty—natural and numinous in nature ... [There is] a sheer drop of many thousands of feet. A totally awesome sight and feeling ... I then begin to think that the purpose now is to let myself fall into the abyss—that is what should be done. I have the sensation of the ground beneath me giving way. A very strong wave of fear sweeps through me and I wake. (David, 09/2006)

At this point, several dreams had already contained the familiar theme of ascending a mountain, symptomatic, in his case, of his persistent tendency for the "spiritual bypass" in an attempt to avoid the messy and difficult stuff. Whilst reflecting on the dream, a voice in his head says "The purpose of all this is the suicide of the view". It is not uncommon for a PTP to begin in this way; a death-related image signifies the beginning of the death of the mind. Dream images of decapitation are common—the severing of identification with the conscious mind.

In the four days following the dream, and in a subsequent dream, David experienced contractions and spasms in his solar plexus. This is the first time that David's response to a dream had registered in the body; in this case, the solar plexus, where the sensations were experienced as a purely physical phenomenon. The dream shows the operation of mortificatio (in the falling away of his standing place—his "heady" consciousness) and initiates coagulatio in being the first step towards closing the split between mind and body, indicated by David's reaction at a physical level. In subsequent dreams, the therapist begins to act as a good mother figure, giving David a green (a colour often indicative of healing) liquid to swallow.

There followed a series of dreams showing the presence of the operation of solutio in which David's fears of intimacy begin to dissolve and give way to the possibility of being touched and held (at this stage in his process, by the therapy).

Foetus

I am lying on the floor … The feelings inside me are among the very worst feelings I have ever experienced—a very deep archaic agony, like a living death going on forever—a black hole in my soul … I am fervently hoping that Nigel does not want to come any closer to me … As he does, I curl up into the foetal position—hyper-sensitive, paralysed and deeply exposed … Ever so carefully, Nigel puts his arms under and around me and hold me to him … I become disconnected and take refuge in cruel doubting thoughts, a deeper place of isolation and hopelessness. (David, 04/2007)

This dream also shows the operation of coagulatio (in the containment and "holding" of the therapist). At this stage, however, David still takes flight into "cruel doubting thoughts"—his schizoid state (a fear of being intimate and of then being touched). Further coagulatio takes place through grounding in his body and later dreams show David being able to be held by his therapist, safely.

Running in parallel, several dreams showing the operation of calcinatio start the process of incorporating David's split-off fiery and angry energy into his psyche.

### Sword Fighting

I dream of my (deceased) spiritual teacher—a Rinpoche I used to follow. He kisses the cheek of a sour, angry woman and then collapses, shouting and bellowing like a madman. Suddenly, a younger, angry man appears and is confronted by the Rinpoche. My old teacher is having a sword fight with the younger, shadowy man. Their swords shine like numinous lights, flashing in the dark. The younger man leaps towards the spiritual master. The fabric of reality appears to tear open and he disappears inside the Rinpoche, who in turn disappears. (David, 11/2006)

This is the first sign of conflict in David's process. It is the battle between his conscious and unconscious attitudes—the spiritual (represented by the revered meditation teacher and the "numinous lights") versus the raging force deep within his psyche (symbolised by the angry woman and the "shadowy" younger man). At first, the one side infects the other as the Rinpoche takes on the anger of the older woman in kissing her, but then the spiritual dimension temporarily dispels the shadow (the angry, cynical, critical aspect). What is important is that the unconscious, out-of-control fiery nature is starting to be exposed.

Another calcinatio dream follows.

### Courtroom Rage

I am in a courtroom. My brother is trying to find me and is storming up some stairs. He rushes into the courtroom in an almost hysterical fury. The room is full of people and it is a foreign place for him so I am confident, for a moment, that he cannot find me. However, to my consternation, he knows exactly where to find me and rushes over with clenched fists ready to hit me in the solar plexus. I'm saying: "I'm sorry, I'm sorry", over and over again. I wake up to find my solar plexus region throbbing and pulsating. The dream leaves a strong impression. I feel this dream is close to some core truth about me. (David, 08/2007)

David's relationship with his brother was characterised by conflict and enmeshment. The rage in the dream brings to consciousness David's own split-off fury; partly with his brother, who he is still unable to stand up to, and partly with the feminine (his mother, as will become apparent later in the process). It is important to note the stirring of fiery energy in his solar plexus centre.

Later, David reported another calcinatio dream—a dream of a deeper part of himself which takes the form of a "dream within a dream".

### Magical Garden

I'm in a magical garden. A large dog appears, jumps up and bites my hand. I feel afraid but remember my therapeutic waking dream-work and relax. My fear dissolves and, at the same time, the dog lets go and starts to lick my hand affectionately. (David, 08/2007)

The biting dog in the "Magical Garden" dream can be seen as David's instinctual, fire nature. The lucidity of David's dreaming state enables him to bring self-awareness to his fear of his instinctual fire and over-come it. In doing so, his attitude is dissolved—solutio. The change in the relationship to the dream dog shows that he is beginning to trust his instincts and his fiery anger which, as a result, are instantly trans-formed. This will prove to be his protection later in the process.

Two months later, he has the following dream showing calcinatio, mortificatio, and coagulatio.

### New Family

I'm in a big house—private and detached ... I find myself in a large attic room. In the room with me are another male and an older woman. I appear to be in very serious conflict with this woman and the tension between us is at crisis point. The woman then pro-duces a silver pistol, points it at my head and shoots once at close range. The bullet, I feel sure, has gone right into the brain. I fall to the ground and tell my male friend I am going to die. After a while, I am astonished to find that, somehow, I am not dead ... The conflict has resumed and I become aware that the older woman is lying on the floor dead ... There is a lot of blood—her blood on the floor and carpet. I am in urgent discussion with the other male about what to do now, when we hear voices outside. I go to the attic window and look down.

There, at the front of the house, is a large black family, everyone animated, talking loudly. In the group are older and younger women (some very big and fat, one on crutches), children and menfolk. I realise that they have come to be shown around the house ... I go down and open the door. I explain to the family that the person they were expecting to show them round is very ill (pneumonia) upstairs in the attic and cannot be disturbed ... I invite them all in. I turn round to start the tour and the house suddenly looks very different inside—much bigger and grander somehow. I show the family, room after room—some huge with high ceilings and tall mirrors, whilst other parts of the house contain secret passageways and hidden little rooms. I keep thinking we must be getting closer and closer to the attic room, but we never do and the house just keeps revealing more and more rooms. I feel good and somehow unconcerned about the dead woman upstairs in the attic. (David, 10/2007)

In this dream, David is confronted, once again, by a negative female figure which holds his fear of, and rage at, the feminine (appearing as the "sluttish and whorish" woman in "Heaven and Hell" some fifteen years earlier). This dream shows his development since meeting her first and the death of the woman signifies the death of the old, negative anima figure, which paves the way for the appearance of the positive feminine. What also dies is the psychological pattern of being in his head (symbolised in the dream by the attic that recedes in importance).

The dream shows the development through the operation of mortificatio to a new state. After the death of the negative anima, David goes downstairs (mirroring the descent into his body) and a new family (he associated them with his repressed earth nature) moves into the house (his psyche) which grows larger and larger as the family explores it. This enlargement signals the opening up of his psyche.

Shortly after this, David dreams of meeting a beautiful young woman with a "serene, calm face" (11/2007). There is a strong attraction between them. They embrace and kiss passionately. This was the first time he could remember a conjoining with a woman in his dreams. We could see this as simply the sexual aspect of his Worldly Self, but also as another example of solutio in service of coagulatio, in the intimacy and grounding with the feminine in the dream. It is also the first appearance of coniunctio in David's dreams. Coniunctio in Nigredo is called the *first coniunctio* and is often symbolised in dreams as sexual union where person with whom we are intimate embodies the qualities with which the psyche is seeking to unite.

One month later, David had another calcinatio dream. He confronts his angry brother aboard a boat. His brother complains that David is not doing enough in relating to him. David tells him that he does not want to be so enmeshed any more and that he longs to separate out and be himself. This time, David is the angry one (12/2007). This kind of power struggle is a feature of dreams at the start of the process where the Worldly Self dominates and opposing aspects of the self are in conflict. In confronting his anger in the dream, David takes a significant step forward in overcoming a psychological block (enmeshment) and he feels stronger in having incorporated some of his fire (anger).

Shortly afterwards, David has a powerful solutio dream.

### Yellow Fish

I'm in a grand town house ... I walk out into the garden, turn to my left, and standing next to me is a beautiful dark-haired young woman. I know immediately that I want her. There is a deep and serious reserve in this woman's demeanour. Her unspoken message seems to be: "If your approach toward me is not perfectly natural, spontaneous and in harmony with my inner nature/beauty, you will not succeed in having me". I approach her, take her in my arms and kiss her on the neck. She takes my hand and leads me over to the chalet where I realise we are to make love. I feel overwhelmed by intoxicating feelings, but as we enter the chalet, I register that I need to urinate. I walk across the garden and over to the stream. I straddle the stream and look down and am surprised to see a drop of twenty or thirty feet down to the stream. The flowing water is dark, but very clear and cool.

Suddenly, I am startled by a rustling noise very close to me. I look up at the top of the bank and see a very large yellow fish wriggle through the undergrowth. It moves towards the edge and launches itself into space, falling gracefully through the air down into the water, closely followed by a second fish which has also appeared. I have a brief moment of apprehension, which vanishes as soon as the fish are in the water. I look down at them, marveling in their mysterious presence. Suddenly, without any warning, and with the merest flick of their fins, both fish disappear and vanish into the depths. I walk back to the chalet, lie down next to the woman and take her in my arms. (David, 12/2007)

We could interpret this dream merely as an expression of libidinous desire and sexual anxiety (a fear of impotency perhaps), but this would not do justice to its richness as a step on David's spiritual journey. The goddess-like woman is, in Jungian terms, David's anima (his soul in feminine form) and the dream context contains several qualities that would seem to be an expression of a higher consciousness—a "grand town house", "perfectly natural, spontaneous, in harmony with my inner nature/beauty". These things (as we will see in Chapter Four) represent subtler levels of consciousness that are waiting to be contacted and are making an appearance here in David's dreams.

But first, purification is necessary—thus the need to urinate (a yellow fluid). However, a yellow fish appears and magically wriggles through the undergrowth, leaps in the air and dives into the water. This action seems to allow David to regain his beloved. A solutio is achieved through the action of the magical fish—a spiritual symbol (Jung, 1983)—which moves from a stuck place (the undergrowth) to its natural habitat (water).

The fish symbolises a dynamic, conscious force (spirit) acting in the dream so as to purify the lower two centres. The yellow colour is associated with the lower base and sacrum centres (Gyatso Geshe, 1992). The solutio achieved by the fish appearing and diving back into the water again dissolves the tension in the lower abdomen (the disappearance of the dreamer's need to urinate). In his waking life, David suffered from a considerable tension (when he was anxious) located around the sacrum centre of his body from which he sought relief by compulsive masturbation. Using the Waking Dream Process with this dream, David begins to experience a lessening of this tension.

The process continues with another calcinatio dream in which David finally stands up to his violent brother.

### Defiling the Painting

I am with my brother and father in a restaurant. I walk outside to look at a large painting that is my creation. Suddenly, my brother appears and begins to defile the painting, walking away smug and satisfied that I am enraged. I challenge him physically because his pride, provocativeness and aggression are shocking and inflammatory. I do not back down. Taking a beating will not defeat me. My father does little to intervene and, when I ask for his help, he is ineffectual in reigning my brother in. (David, 02/2008)

A couple of weeks later, David records a dream in which he and his brother are reconciled (03/2008). More than wish fulfillment, this seemed to indicate that something of David's anger had been integrated into his consciousness.

Then, David has a dream of falling off a perpendicular cliff face through trees and branches. He falls a great distance until he hits the earth and becomes entangled with the roots of the trees. The scene becomes darker and more alien to him, but he is not afraid (03/2008). Here we have a fully developed coagulatio dream where he not only falls, but becomes entangled with the roots in the earth. In David's case, we can see that mortificatio comes in two stages: first it precipitates the dreamer's initial descent to earth, and then "knocks out" the old way of thinking.

Finally, David's transition to the next stage is indicated.

### Road to Heaven

I'm driving along following a woman who is in a car ahead of me. I am deeply and strongly connected to this woman. We start to drive up into the mountains and get higher and higher. We come out onto a ridge and reach a fork in the road. One fork goes down and returns to the lowlands where I live. The other way goes upwards and, as I look, I see the track goes way up into the sky, almost like a vast bridge, but completely natural, not man made. I know I must go back down, but resolve to follow the woman right up to the very top, then come back down. So I follow until we reach the very summit of the track. The view and the atmosphere up there are paradise-like. I call to the woman to stop, indicating that I must turn round and go back. She stops and gets out of her car. I rush to meet her and we kiss passionately and say goodbye. I turn and go back down the track all the way to my house at sea level. (David, 03/2008)

This dream indicates the partial conjoining (coniunctio) of the opposites in David's psyche—the spiritual and the earthy. In the dream, the woman is the guide and David is the alchemist. The fork is the key image connecting the split between spirit and matter, heaven and earth. In the union of David and the woman, we have an indication that the split within is beginning to heal.

As such, it signifies the end of the Nigredo phase in David's acceptance of his instinctual nature. It seemed at this stage in David's process that he had experienced a significant degree of integration of his anger into his conscious awareness and was able to experience intimacy to a limited extent for the first time. He had overcome his fear of the negative, archetypal feminine in his psyche. The schizoid and rather innocent self had become more earthy and worldly, substantiating and strengthening his ego. The bodily sensations that accompanied the dreams indicated a gradual "downward awakening of energy" from the head ("Suicide of the View") to the solar plexus ("Courtroom Rage") and then to the sacrum and base centres ("Yellow Fish"). Also noticeable, is the alternating in the dreams between the operations of solutio, calcinatio, coagulatio, and coniunctio (meeting the beautiful young woman) and culminating in coagulatio ("Road to Heaven"). Clearly, the latter operation was the most important development thus far.

Psychologically speaking, David had grappled with his shadow and was beginning to become conscious of his dependency on smoking and masturbation as defences and distractions from his deep, existential anxiety and painful feelings of isolation. David was strong enough to be able to proceed to the next stage of the process, Albedo, and this last dream with its invitation to ascend shows his readiness to do so.

## Ava begins

Ava, in her sixties, is a highly intelligent woman of what one might call "fine" sensibilities. She is a lover of music and the arts and is married with one grown-up child. She began her dream process actively when she was about fifty years old after many years of spiritual searching. I was Ava's dream guide for the period of her journey described here, but Ava was always very much at the "helm of her own ship", as it were, and her journey continued on without me.

In Ava's case, the Nigredo stage begins with the theme of death in a dream. Ava starts her process from a clearer and more spiritually transparent position than is usual. In contrast to David, the themes of love and beauty are prominent from the outset. Instead of having to work through layers of difficult psychological material, Ava has fewer (and less) serious issues to deal with.

This very first dream, which Ava presented to me at a dream workshop, seemed to come from the mind level.

### The Famous Writer

A man is on a hike over a hill. He is a famous man (a famous writer) and photographers are always taking pictures. When he notices them, he puts on a sad and serious face and makes his chest stiff and ugly. He has told me that he wants to kill himself. This makes me feel my love for him and see his beauty ... "I love you, I love you, you are so beautiful, you know, when you smile and when you don't keep your chest so tightly upright. Ah, how beautiful you are!—I know. I am ready to let you die if that is what you really want"—I am even willing to help him. There is a subterranean river there, into which I push him. Somehow he is wrapped in a yellow blanket, his dog is running around. But at the bottom of the hill, in the café, he is still sitting there, the famous writer. This way to die would not have been the right way. He seems a little disappointed, almost angry that it didn't happen. And he died only seven years later. (Ava, 11/1999)

Ava encounters her *animus* figure (the beloved male figure, representing her inner spirit, who will appear many times in her process). He is suicidal and puts on a show of sadness when he becomes aware of being seen. Ava loves him and tries to mirror his beauty back to him, which he has forgotten. Once again, we see the colour yellow appearing in Nigredo indicating the activation of the lower centres, which are also symbolised by the "subterranean" river.

Although it could not be recognised at the time, this dream is a foresight of what is going to happen in the following years. The "famous writer", a mind aspect of the dreamer that cuts her off from her soul nature, wants to die in order to be transformed. The dreamer is ready to help him die, but the time is not ripe for this experience. However, death is a classic indication at this stage of the desire for inner change. The reference "and he died only seven years later" was not understood and soon forgotten by the dreamer. But in fact, exactly seven years later, in 2006, the death of this dream figure finally did happen, brought about voluntarily by the dreamer, and coinciding with Ava's profound spiritual awakening.

### The Persecutor

I am invited into a castle where the son of the house persecutes me. First, it looks like a game, but then becomes serious when I try to hide and he goes to fetch a rifle. I hide in the kitchen, telling the cook that I love her ... The man comes in and sits down on a bench. I sit very close to him and, all of a sudden, I see how unbelievably beautiful he is. I say, "Do you know how beautiful you really are?" This was the magic word—it makes him find all his self-confidence. I kiss him sensually. I know that he is not dependent on me now and does not need to persecute me any more. (Ava, 12/1999)

In waking life, Ava did not suffer from any such persecution complex. The persecutor in this dream seems to represent the conscious attitude of her concrete mind, which, in reality, can be critical and demanding. But from her unconscious side come the themes of love and beauty. "Beautiful" is the "magic word" and her love for the man transforms the persecutor who holds Ava's sense of inadequacy and need for perfection to sustain a good sense of self. The dream awakens Ava's self-confidence so that the conscious mind does not need to persecute her with doubting thoughts. In the coniunctio of the qualities of love and beauty, the conscious and unconscious opposites are being reconciled.

### Imprisoned

We are a group of people, all wearing old-fashioned clothes from the nineteenth century, going on a walk. A man forces us, at gunpoint, to be his prisoners. We have to continue walking as if nothing had happened. Life goes on. The whole village is now imprisoned, but we always return back there from our work and receive food. We find our valley very beautiful, although it is really quite narrow, and that our houses are beautiful, although they are just old huts. I am taking liberties, like kissing a man wildly. I would like to go to the city once. He allows me to go. I drive a huge truck, then come back as promised. Somehow we have all quite forgotten that we are prisoners. (Ava, 01/2000)

In this dream, the distorted aspect of the animus is once again threatening and dominating. The lower astral plane takes the form in this dream of a rather dull prison camp, but it is also comfortable ("we receive food"). In it, the dreamer is convinced of its beauty and even forgets it is a prison camp at all. Being so used to the Earth Plane, and often not even believing that there could be any other reality, we tend to turn a deaf ear to the soul feelings of imprisonment and a longing for more space, more light. Out of fear (the man with the gun)—the suggestion of attack always presupposes fear—"we ... continue walking as if nothing had happened".

But this dream can also be seen as hinting at the higher planes to come in that, once again, the ideal of beauty predominates in the dreamer's mind and Ava seduces the threatening man in order to gain freedom for herself. It is the soul's desire to break out into freedom ("I am taking liberties") and something is, indeed, freeing up in her mind. The mind is allowing love to emerge and coexist consciously with her thoughts. Though she is not yet truly free, it is an auspicious sign that she has a "huge truck," a very sturdy vehicle, to drive her in and out of her "prison".

The predominant alchemical operation at work in these first three dreams is solutio as love dissolves the critical attitude of the mind and Worldly Self. A celebration follows.

### Celebration

I am taking part in a celebration out in nature, in a large meadow close to the woods. I have been chosen to be the carrier of the central symbol so I am wearing a wonderful costume, all in green ... I am very tall, shining green ... A child leads me along a path to the right of the meadow with the crowd. All of a sudden, the sun comes through and everything is shining, especially my green dress ... I think that we should certainly take some pictures as long as the sun is still shining. I ask the child, "Do you have a camera?" Yes, but it is a little farther on and only has a black and white film in it. "That's too bad, but run and get in anyway ... I want to first take a picture with the 'inner circle' and me, and then with all the people". (Ava, 01/2000)

The dream goes on to describe the beauty of the landscape and ends with Ava positioning herself for the photograph in front of a round house between a bifurcating road "in all my shining green beauty" and is encouraged by the photographer to "be natural".

As a result of the solutio operation of the previous dreams, Ava allows herself to be photographed as her authentic, natural self (in contrast to the inauthenticity of the man of "The Famous Writer" in front of the cameras). She is more confident now, radiant with beauty. The theme of beauty underpins the dream—in the scenic beauty and her own. Indeed, the natural landscape of a meadow and the prominence of the colour green are indicative of the emergence of the Third Plane of consciousness and the Loving Self (see Chapter Four).

Whilst the insufficiency of the black and white camera film suggests that there is more work to be done, it seemed that the split between Ava's soul nature and her critical mind was being healed as she moved through the process. Her central positioning for the photograph at the bifurcation of the road is perhaps symbolic of the healing of the split, but might also represent the unification of heaven and earth in a larger sense, as did David's fork in the road of the "Road to Heaven" dream. The dream indicates the emergence of the spiritual dimension and, as such, signifies that Nigredo is drawing to a close. However, further mental purification is necessary before entering Albedo.

### An Existential Question

A male guide figure is staying at my house. A caterpillar crawls around and then flies, so I put it outside. I move a plant; this exposes a heap of ants. Again, I get rid of the ants. Now my guide is in the middle of the room asking if I have a housekeeper. I am not clear as to why he asks this; I ask him: "What is the use or sense of teaching literature?" I embrace him and ask him earnestly: "How do you solve this?" (I explain I had begun to find my job meaningless it was more to do with intellectual development in the students, so I resigned from it.) I woke up with the blissful feeling of love, and at the same time disappointment, because he is not open to me. (Ava, 01/2000)

The caterpillar might symbolise the untransformed prima-materia, in worm-like form, that is yet to be transformed, and the ants might be the constant thoughts and questions. It is a special caterpillar because it flies, but Ava doesn't recognise this magical figure in the dream and tries to get rid of it. She is focused instead on drawing out her dream guide, but he remains silent and impassive except for asking her if she has a housekeeper—hinting at the need for purification and transformation.

In a dream that followed, Ava undergoes a final purification of the mind by eating a healing potion to "clear her head"—a mixture of red and white flowers from a bush that blooms in a compost heap (a wonderful symbol for the putrefaction of Nigredo). This leads to a dream of the baptism of a child, signifying, perhaps, a process of rebirth in which a larger, spiritual self is reborn. The coniunctio dream that followed would seem to indicate the union of opposites in Ava's psyche.

### My Second Wedding

Today is my wedding. I am wearing a fire-red gown under a thin, white, wedding gown. It is beautifully floating down my body. I am in a beautiful hotel with a wonderful entrance hall … We go down a spiral staircase. Down there I will meet P whom I am marrying for the second time. (Ava, 02/2000)

The colour symbolism in this dream seems particularly significant. The fire-red gown is hidden under the white gown. It could be seen that the fiery quality in her personality, symbolised by the red gown, is becoming more conscious. The white gown seemed, with knowledge of Ava, to symbolise the gentler, loving side of her, the side which appreciates beauty and love. In this light, the marriage would seem to signify the coming together of both aspects—the inner marriage with her animus (the first marriage was a worldly one). The gown and the hotel are both beautiful; she has incorporated a sense of the beauty of her being into consciousness.

For Ava, Nigredo and the plane of the Worldly Self begins with mortificatio (the death of the critical and imprisoning attitude) and ends with a celebration and a wedding. The existential threat of the first dream is transformed now that she is confident in the beauty of her being. The repressed libidinal feelings expressed in "The Persecutor" and "Imprisoned" are transformed into an open, loving self-acceptance. The cognitive, critical attitude gives way to self-confidence.

## Summary

In both stories, the psychological blocks of this first phase of the journey start to give way to the dreamer's deeper, emerging soul nature. This is more obvious for Ava, but even in the case of David, the spirit in him, which is split off from his mind and body, starts to speak through his ideas and fantasies of spirituality, and his first glimpse of "paradise" in "Road to Heaven". His soul nature, the anima, has already taken on a more positive form by the end of Nigredo than it had at the beginning.

In our travellers' journeys, we see in their dreams common themes of death, conflict, the tension of opposites, followed by healing and a sense of opening up. There is the first appearance of light and colour present in the darkness. Our travellers had to begin their process by encountering the instinctual energies of the lower energy centres, to purify them, so as to extract the "spirit" or subtle energy within. This process is necessary before their consciousness could "rise" in the next alchemical stage of Albedo.

## CHAPTER FOUR

# Unfolding

You learn to fly here.

—*Ava*, 2000

## The landscape of unfolding

### The Subtle Mental Plane—The Creative Self

When we speak of the *Subtle Mental Plane*, we refer to a mental realm which is relatively free of the limitations of the material world. Our narrow-minded, concrete and rational thought process gives way to a more open, expressive, and spontaneous state of mind. This higher mind is free to explore its own nature, which is abstract and creative, and what lies behind that nature—spirit. We can see spirit coming through at this level most clearly in creative genius. This level of consciousness can be called the *Creative Self* and reflects the transition from the lower to the higher mind.

Dreams are the inner manifestation of the dual influences of the physical and spiritual realms, which predominate in varying proportions, depending on the stage of the journey. At this stage of the PTP, transpersonal consciousness begins to appear more strongly, loosening the grip of the physical and worldly impressions upon the mind. The consequence is that the mind is partially liberated from concrete thoughts and can be more imaginative and receptive to the spirit of inspiration. It operates in a more subtle way and is attuned to the inner world. The Buddhist tradition refers to this experience as the beginning of *clear mind*, when the "light of the mind" is freed from the grosser worldly forces (Norbu, 1992).

In this state of the higher mind, we are receptive to the archetypal forms that reflect a subtle, collective level of reality (Jung, 1983). In this sense, the Subtle Mental Plane has a reality which is independent of the mind (unlike the Gross Mental Plane which is a mind world of our own creation). These archetypal forms rarely descend to our concrete, rational mind in the waking state and, when they do, they are either experienced as overwhelming to the ego (if fragile), or as inspirational.

The dreams of the Creative Self begin to show these archetypal motifs, together with an increase in colour and light (Hamilton, 2006). The Sufis maintain that, in this stage, our minds have the potential to mirror the light of the soul; that is, the colours and light, the landscapes and the archetypes in the dreams are reflecting something of our soul nature (Chittick, 1994). The "heavy" tone of the Worldly Self is replaced by clarity and a "lighter", more positive atmosphere. The instincts are quieter, tamed now, and the thinking function is emphasised. Creativity comes in the form of new ideas, a visionary sense of new possibilities, insight and, with this, excitement and joy.

Table 4.1. Themes and features of the Subtle Mental Plane—The Creative Self.

---

- Clarity of mind and of the dreams
- Creativity, new ideas, insight
- Laughter, joy
- Celebration, carnival, festival
- Mythological imagery, e.g. mirrors, the moon, dragon, unicorn
- Appearance of the magical—people or creatures with special powers
- Flying, birds flying
- Snakes
- Travelling to the Orient, going north, Eastern figures
- Creative performance, e.g. theatre, films, fashion, TV

---

(*Continued*)

Table 4.1. Continued.

- Talents and interests—artistic, musical, literary, sporting
- Famous people
- Beauty of architecture, design, art, and music
- Beautiful objects, treasures, e.g. antiques, sculpture, jewellery
- Dramatis personae, e.g. the trickster, the guide, psychopomps
- Being clever and showing insight, lacking insight
- Life scripts, perceptions
- Mind activities, professional work situations, learning
- The number three, number four or multiples of four
- Large, tall, new or beautiful buildings and cityscapes
- Colours start to appear (particularly green in nature)
- Healing images

In the Creative Self, dreams represent the first crude attempts in our consciousness to apprehend the intrapsychic forces and qualities of our subtler, inner world. We begin to connect to deeper and more meaningful aspects of ourselves, beyond the mundane conflicts and problems of our everyday life. Artificial, as opposed to organic, objects may still appear in our dreams, but they are not underpinned now by instinctual forces and symbolise something deeper in the psyche than our attachment to the world.

Our inner wisdom speaks to us in our dreams at this level through guide figures, dramatis personae and magical beings, who play their part in resolving our inner conflicts and helping us progress.

### The Crab

There is a competition to catch the "biggest" fish. My brother leads a group of people who have acted in a drama club ... to catch the fish ... My brother and his team capture the largest King Crab ever caught in the world in the deepest part of the sea ... Someone eating the crab says: "This meat is magical. It's the best meat in the world."

The Creative Self themes present in this dream are the presence of the magical and the artistic world represented by the dreamer's brother who leads a theatrical group. The crab meat is "magical ... the best in the world". Here, we are reminded of Jung's observation that the archetypal figure often has a "magical" quality (Jung, 1983). The crab represents a basic spiritual consciousness in the dreamer, which evolves later into that of a fish in her dreams.

Our dreams at this level begin to show the quality of beauty as our first encounter with the divine. Ibn 'Arabi understood that, in a psychospiritual transformation, the transcendental or spiritual aspect first appears through our imagination as beauty (Corbin, 1969). We saw this theme of beauty emerging in Ava's transit through Nigredo and culminating in her dreams of a celebration in nature and wedding. Celebrations and festivals seem to signify a ritual marker of change, and the transformation of negative mental patterns is often indicated by healing symbolism (e.g., hospitals, doctors).

Blocks to the Creative Self come from our habitual thinking and mental scripts about ourselves and our life. Typical psychological issues that arise on this level are questions about whether we are good enough, loveable, or beautiful. Issues around gender—an inadequate or confused sense of our masculinity or femininity—often arise. These themes appear in the narrative of our dreams, but once they are worked through, our consciousness changes and our dreams become less personal and clearer. We begin to tap into the archetypal realm. A fresh perspective opens up and new, or even great, ideas are revealed. The dream landscapes are more expansive; we are going to a place beyond our personal view.

The dreamer's new perspective may be represented as a kind of treasure or a new skill. Flying typifies the activity of this plane—the ascent of our consciousness—as the following dream from a psychotherapy process shows.

### Flying High

I am flying—going higher and higher through physical barriers, like roofs. It is mind over matter. I am travelling in a north-easterly direction.

The dream describes an experience of breaking through barriers in the ascent as the mind rises above body. The reference to the "north-easterly" direction seems to confirm this upward movement of consciousness towards spirit; the North symbolising the crown centre and the East symbolising the soul (see "Visionary Geography" in Chapter Six).

The colour green starts to make its first notable appearance at this level, indicating new growth. Jung saw the appearance of the green-leafed tree as "The Philosophical Tree" (or the *Tree of Life*), symbolising our life spirit (1983). The following dream image, showing a resurgence of life force in the dreamer, occurred in their Creative Self phase.

Green Shoot

A plant grows from seed. It has a thick green shoot that surges upwards before my eyes with incredible speed and power.

When considering numbers as metaphors, the number four appears regularly in Creative Self dreams, signifying the completion or establishment of this level. The number four has been used in many religious traditions as a sign of completion and Jung interprets the appearance of the number four (in terms of the quaternity)[1] as a significant step towards individuation or the development of the Self. The number three also appears, signifying the emergence of the transcendental (von Franz, 1974). The numbers three and four appear in all the higher levels of self, but they are likely to first appear in the Creative Self (as exemplified by the "Good Friday Snake" dream in Chapters Six and Seven).

## The Third Plane—The Loving Self

The *Third Plane* of consciousness is marked by a shift from a creative to a more idealistic attunement, characterised by the qualities of love, harmony, beauty, and innocence. The Third Plane is epitomised by the Elysian fields in Greek mythology—a classical depiction of the heavenly and idyllic. At this level of consciousness, there is something angelic coming through in us, once the psychological barriers to it have been overcome. A deeper part of ourselves is being accessed—the *Loving Self*.

In contrast to the artificial, man-made world (of concrete thoughts) reflected in the dreams of the Worldly Self, the Third Plane is defined by natural beauty which is simple and unspoiled (virginal), and harmony, often indicated in dreams by an expression of love or receptivity. Ibn 'Arabi refers to the "beauty of form and harmony, and the overflow of languor and tenderness and mercy in all things characterised by them" (Harris, 1981, pp. 43–44).

Table 4.2. Themes and features of the Third Plane—The Loving Self.

* Innocence—babies, children, young animals
* Virgin-like, unspoiled, simplicity, naturalness, nakedness
* Beauty (particularly beauty of nature)
* Gentleness, gentle animals, e.g. deer, kitten
* Light, transparent, moonlight
* Receptivity, feminine, heartfelt beauty
* Grace, elegance
* Joy, enthusiasm
* Harmony
* Love, lover, beloved figure
* Natural, idyllic landscapes, e.g. meadows, fields, rolling hills, the sea
* Soft pastel colours, green in nature

The retreat dream research showed that the consciousness coming through dreams at this level is more subtle than before. There is a sense of optimism and light. The qualities behind the dream scenarios of this level express something of our deeper soul feelings and longing for a more beautiful, harmonious, and loving life.

Children appear in our dreams in the Third Plane, particularly young children and babies. The innocence and playful energy of children reminds us of what we have forgotten in ourselves. The soul speaks as a child in our dreams because our essential nature is intrinsically innocent.

The theme of beauty is seen in the form of nature and of people; imagery is feminine, often expressed as graciousness or elegance. Whilst there is a beauty to the creative works of the mind in art, mathematics and so forth, in the Third Plane, this beauty is more embodied, felt, and expressed through relationships. The dreams of the Subtle Mental Plane often feature beautiful creations, such as grand buildings or priceless objects; whereas the Loving Self favours the simplicity and beauty of nature, and a deeper, more natural way of being.

Nakedness (a lack of clothing or transparency of clothing) often represents this simplicity in dreams. Reflective light and moonlight (not direct sunlight) symbolise the receptive, feminine aspect. Joy and enthusiasm in dreams reflect the mood of this level.

In the following dream, the dreamer moves from the level of the mind into the Third Plane sphere.

### Oasis

> From the city, I take a path which opens out onto an oasis of beautiful garden—green and water between stepping stones. At the bottom of the garden is an acropolis (a pinkish colour stone) and, beyond the boundary, London EC1.

The presence of "stepping stones" might be a reference to the stepping stones of the journey, of which this is one. The pinkish acropolis is suggestive of something from a higher level of consciousness than what might have been found in the city, and the Eastern region beyond the garden is a glimpse, perhaps, of farther spiritual realms (the East symbolising here the spiritual, as opposed to the worldly West).

If, at the level of the Creative Self, the issue of self-love has not been addressed, it surfaces in the Loving Self dreams, which show us where we are limited in loving ourselves and others. This is the psychological block to the Loving Self. We can discover, at this stage, that the very qualities that are important to us (that, previously, we sought outside of ourselves) are to be found within. We experience these qualities in their essence in dreams at this level of self. When we recognise that the source of what we long for lies within us, we are no longer compelled to project our needs onto our partners.

The following dream illustrates how the psychological can block access to the Loving Self.

### Beautiful Field

> I am travelling on a train, with my mother sitting on my left side. I look out of the window to my right into the countryside and see an exquisitely beautiful field of flowers. This moves me very deeply. I then turn (left) to my mother to point out the view and, as I turn to the right again, I see that the field has now been covered with debris and refuse, blocking out the beautiful picture.

This male client suffered from a difficult mother complex—feeling guilty about separating from her and angry at the same time. The dream shows the influence of this psychological issue; the veils over the beauty of nature momentarily lift, but then reappear. The moment he turns to his mother, her influence comes back in and the beauty of his own nature, symbolised by the field, is obscured.

Most experiences of this Loving Self level are fleeting in comparison to what precedes it (the inspiration of the Creative Self) and what follows (the trials and tribulations of the Fourth Plane). There is usually a quick transition from the Third Plane to the negative phase of the Fourth Plane in our dreams.

### The Fourth Plane—The Wise Self

The *Fourth Plane* is a challenging, sometimes frightening, level of consciousness to journey through. Our most important (and intransigent) psychological issues come up during the transit through this plane, which contains two aspects: conflict and conflict resolution. The level of the Fourth Plane seems to be located in the middle of the vertical axis of the psyche as it were, midway between the worldly, creative and loving planes below it, and the sacred, pure and transcendental levels above.

The negative phase of the Fourth Plane is often experienced as being similar to the dark period of the Worldly Self in Nigredo. In Nigredo, however, we are simply encountering our unconscious desires and instincts; whereas, in the Fourth Plane, we see very clearly the effects of our dominant mental outlook on our hidden, unconscious, essential or soul nature, and the conflict between them. Our dreams show us how deeply our worldly attitudes have penetrated our inner world. We are shocked by the discordance between our distorted mental attitudes and our natural disposition—a dichotomy causing us much suffering.

In the first "phase" of this plane, one of the most prominent themes is conflict. The deep inner struggles within the psyche are revealed through our dreams—the archetypal battle between dark (the shadow of the distorted mind) and light (the soul). In alchemical terms, it is inevitable that the polarities that exist in us must meet each other in order to unite, and it is in the Fourth Plane that we become aware that this is the struggle, the test.

In many cases, the Fourth Plane transit in dreams begins with a conflict or a war between two sides. The story of the Fourth Plane has been told through the ages in mythology and our modern day epics such as *The Lord of the Rings* and *Star Wars*. In the Ramayana epic of Hinduism, Rama battles with the demon king, Ravana (who could be seen to symbolise the mind), aided by the monkey general, Hanuman (representing the instinctual), for the return of his beloved Sita (Rama's soul). First, Rama must obtain the cooperation of Hanuman (his engagement with Nigredo) before Sita is restored to him, having undergone a Fourth Plane trial by fire to prove her purity. The hero's encounter with danger, battles, and finally, triumph, is the archetypal struggle for the authentic self, for inner truth.

A host of negative dream themes feature in the first phase of the Fourth Plane transit as the conflict between the two sides (the Worldly Self and our soul nature) are played out, as seen in Table 4.3 below. The theme of judgement and the law seems to act as a metaphor for unresolved conflicts and a lack of balance in the psyche. When we are in this phase for what may be a long time, there seems to be no end to its hellishness.

In terms of the elements, the Fourth Plane is related to our fire nature. References to hell in the Bible and the Qur'an are effectively describing this fiery, conflicted aspect of ourselves (Edinger, 1991). Fourth Plane dreams speak to us of our fire nature and show us what our soul is experiencing as a result of the dominance of the mind, which has co-opted our fire nature into a distortion of our true selves. If we are unconsciously angry or lack fire in our outward personality, images of fire and angry people appear in our dreams. Dream motifs such as explosions, firearms, burning buildings and cooking often feature, all of which seem to suggest the awakening of a fiery nature in the

Table 4.3. Themes and features of the Fourth Plane—The Wise Self.

*Negative phase: Dark*

- Conflict, war, battles, military themes, and figures
- Weapons, e.g. guns, knives, bullets
- Danger, violence, criminals, torture
- Deviousness, manipulating truth
- Ugliness, drugs, addiction, sexual distortions
- Suffering, despair, poverty, imprisonment
- Anger, explosions, fire, thunder, lightning, cooking
- Control/loss of control, being willful
- Accidents, crashes, fast cars, speed
- Law, trial, justice/injustice, authority, police
- Mental illness
- Challenging landscapes, e.g. deserts, wasteland, ravines
- Colours—red, red and black, red-orange, orange, greenish yellow, sickly pink

transformation process. The clash between our mental attitudes and a deeper, wiser, inner self is revealed and we wake feeling troubled.

Dream images in this plane typically make use of colours like intense red-orange, red and black, sickly yellow-green and sickly pink. Classically, these colours give way to green, silver, and gold later in this phase—the alchemical metaphors for purified soul and spirit—in preparation for the Fifth Plane, where the soul realises its own nature, seen directly as light (Khan, 2003; Thurston, 1990).

Typical Fourth Plane dream landscapes are dramatic and challenging with vast horizons. They can be Savannah planes, open fields, or hot, dry and desert-like terrains. Ravines, gorges, and chasms, like the Grand Canyon, symbolise the split in the psyche between light and dark. Volcanic and mountainous landscapes indicate that an "inner fire" is awakening and emerging.

Psychological blocks—Transforming distortions.

Distorted thinking and attitudes act as psychological blocks to the Wise Self (as described in Buddhism's *six realms of samsara*—the six distortions of human nature) (Wangyal, 1998). They arise because our psychological or mental attitudes (shaped by the past and our experiences in the world) distort the pure expression of our nature. Unconsciously, then, our soul suffers because it is confined to experiencing the world through a distorted mental lens (our assessment of life) instead of being able to express its more natural disposition. With the distortion dominating, we experience feelings such as shame, rage, hatred, and power intoxication, which are alien to our true nature.

Our desire for success and even our ideals can distort our perception. This type of distortion comes about when we override our feelings and compassion for others. We become egotistical and willful, creating suffering. Hitler, Stalin, and Mao Tse-tung were extreme examples of distorted idealism and will. Acts of terrorism are another example of fanatical beliefs superseding conscience and human feelings. Distortions of the will are not so easy to discover in ourselves. Our guidance has to be relentless in showing us this kind of darkness through our dreams in the Fourth Plane, until such time that we consciously try to transform it.

The distortions of the Fourth Plane centre around a number of qualities, all of which are expressions of fire. When they are out of balance, they form part our psychopathology or what Jung called the shadow (Jung, 1981). Distortions can arise from an excess of a quality, but also a lack of it. These key qualities and their distortions are set out below.

Table 4.4.  Distortions of the Fourth Plane.

| Pure quality | Distortion | |
|---|---|---|
| **Power** | | |
| + (too much) | Domination | Dominating for one's own selfish purpose, misusing power to have control over others. |
| | Aggression | Power which is destructive and harmful. The fire nature is recklessly out of control. |
| - (too little) | Weakness | A false sense of powerlessness within, a victim mentality and inability to make things happen. |
| **Mastery** | | |
| + | Willfulness | Imposing one's will regardless of the circumstances or feelings of others. |
| - | Incompetence | A lack of mastery of the self, being ineffectual and unable to fulfill one's potential. |
| **Truthfulness** | | |
| + | Ruthlessness | Prizing the truth above compassion and understanding in a way that is heartless and unfeeling. |
| - | Dishonesty | Evading and manipulating for one's own selfish purpose. |
| **Idealism** | | |
| + | Self-righteousness | In pursuing an ideal such as justice, it becomes one-sided and imbalanced, leading to intolerance of other people and viewpoints. |
| | Fanaticism | A distortion of faith where one's ideal is inflexible and rigid and becomes hatred and bigotry. |
| - | Amorality | A lack of faith or belief in anything, being unprincipled, permissive. |
| **Passion** | | |
| + | Drive | Pushing oneself at the expense of balance and at a cost to others. |
| | Sexual distortions | Being driven and taken over by the sex drive such that judgement and sensitivity are clouded. |
| - | Indifference | Not caring or feeling (the psychopath), being unmotivated and apathetic. |

In our dreams, the distortions most strikingly take the form of personifications which are exaggerated to ensure that they have our full attention! These dream characters can be welcomed as guides because they show us what is needed for balance. They may have too much or too little of a quality and be a mirror reflection of who we are at that time (albeit in caricature). If, for example, our need to control dominates our deeper feelings for our loved ones, dream images will depict willful, selfish characters that show little capacity to relate.

Or, they may embody something we do not recognise in ourselves at all—an aspect that we have completely disowned. A man in psychotherapy who was a pacifist could not relate to the warmongering general who appeared in his dream until he encountered him in the Waking Dream Process and discovered that he held a powerful part of himself that was denied.

If harnessed consciously, our distorted fire nature can be transformed. With patience, compassion and determination, fire turns into the light of illumination and inner wisdom. Alchemically speaking, purification by fire (calcinatio) is seen as the most radical purifier. Perhaps this explains the presence of the fiery imagery found in Fourth Plane dreams which results in a higher energy state—a "stepping up" of voltage and power that is needed in the ascent of the levels of self.

The level of the Fourth Plane seems to challenge us to manifest the pure (fire) qualities behind the distortions. We find that the qualities needed to balance the distortions of fire relate to the other elements: so compassion, and the capacity to relate are water qualities; discipline, tolerance, and humility are earth qualities; perspective and seeing all points of view are air qualities.

Once the Worldly Self has undergone a fiery purification and the distortions have been transformed, the second phase follows during which the conflict between the mind and soul is resolved, leading to a greater sense of inner balance—the *Wise Self*. Spirit begins to emerge as the grip of the mind weakens. We discover how to be authentic in the world, in connection with our inner conscience, our soul. In a sense, we could see this transit through the Fourth Plane as the journey of individuation.

Our dreams will tell the story of this coming together of opposites in us. David dreamt that he and his brother sit on "opposite sides" of a table to reconcile with one another before embracing. This is a very

Table 4.5. Themes and features of the Fourth Plane—The Wise Self.

*Positive phase: Light*

- Conflict resolution, coming together of opposites
- Acceptance, ending resentment
- Crucifixion/resurrection, rebirth
- Celebrations, rejoicing
- Truthfulness, directness, openness
- Faith, self-belief
- Power, flying, ascent
- Mastery, overcoming tests, sporting accomplishments
- Acceptance of loss of control, surrender of personal will
- Wisdom, compassion
- The sun, the triangle shape, lion/lioness
- The number four
- Mountains, green savannah landscapes
- Colours—blue, green, gold, silver, golden yellow, black and white
- Healing images

clear symbolic representation of reconciliation of the opposing sides of the psyche.

Positive fire symbols such as the sun, the lion, and triangular shapes (often in the form a mountain) indicate the positive phase of the Fourth Plane. Finally, symbols of completion will appear in our dreams, such as resurrection, surrender, gold, and the number four.

Signs of having overcome our test in this plane are often shown in dream images of sporting or physical prowess, which seem to be metaphors for successfully overcoming personal limitations. Flying is a theme as it was in the Creative Self, but this time as an accomplishment, along with a sense of self belief.

Learning to Fly

I am learning to fly. It is very hard, but I have a huge sense of satisfaction when I do it. I realise that faith is the key and I show others.

A retreatant had the following dream towards the end of the Fourth Plane transit.

Split Open

In a graveyard, there are groups of bodies waiting to be buried, indicated by their orange wrappings, and other older people who have died naturally in the last few days and so are priority for the special burial ... I travel with a priest in a car. I ask him if he remembers me from years ago when I had an injury (my leg was in plaster). He does not. Then there is a violent struggle between us and I try to hide ... He strikes at me with a stick on the forehead. I hit him back harder and he is split open. A yellow substance oozes out. He goes to hospital.

The mortificatio images of death and burial seem to symbolise parts of the dreamer's self, old and not so old, that have died and are being put to rest. Reference to a past injury might signify a wounded aspect that wants to be remembered. The central image of the violent struggle can be seen to represent the vanquishing and purification of the mind through the blow to the forehead and the splitting open to release the "yellow substance" (the sun yellow of the Wise Self) which leads to healing (Medically related imagery after a phase of conflicted dreams suggests that an aspect of the psyche has been healed). This substance in the dreamer has the potential for transformation into the alchemical "golden light" of intellect and wisdom (de Jong, 2002), perhaps through activation of the third eye centre hinted at in the dream.

Although the journey through the Fourth Plane can be a long struggle with inner conflict and distortions, it ultimately leads to wisdom—a balance between compassion and truth. It is only in working with our inner "demons" and discovering their true purpose that we can become wise. We surrender our mental constructs and discover the divine power within us in the truth of ourselves. In closing the gap between who we are now and who we want to be, we will need to listen to our inner guidance, but also to employ our will in manifesting wisdom in life.

The key to this transformation lies, above all, in the quality of compassion. In opening the heart, we balance the fire with compassion, which leads to wisdom—the "gold" of spiritual knowledge.

## The alchemical stage of Albedo

The ascent through the Subtle Mental Plane, and the Third and Fourth Planes of consciousness takes place during the alchemical stage of *Albedo,* which continues all the way through the Fifth and Sixth Planes (as we shall see in the next chapter). As with Nigredo and the lower planes, we see the overlap between Albedo's themes and its corresponding planes of consciousness.

Albedo is the white state, symbolising the light of the soul. In Albedo, we become aware of our soul through the subtlising (the refining and purifying) of consciousness. As Nigredo was the stage of blackness and descent, so Albedo is the stage of light and rising. In Nigredo, we had to deal with the conscious effects of body and mind on the soul. In Albedo, the soul's longing overcomes the mind-body complex and the soul begins to feel freer and less weighed down. The inner space is cleared and the ego "thins", allowing the soul to become apparent.

In Albedo, we still encounter the effects of mind on soul, but as we become "soul-conscious", we have a truer sense of ourselves. Something shifts in us and we are no longer in the grip of our egoistic (angry, resentful, afraid) feelings. We experience instead the soul's emotions: a longing for the sacred, beauty, purity, innocence, and a deep heart connection, and this is what comes through in our dreams. These are the qualities that characterise our experience of Albedo. It is a return to our original state.

We enter a stage where our consciousness is now relatively free of the impact of the world and we let go of our attachment to body. Our focus is withdrawn from life and we begin to be aware of, and attend to, our inner life and our dreams. It is in Albedo that the ascent of consciousness through the planes takes place and where, in dreams, we sometimes meet the landscapes of the soul.

Each landscape has a different attunement because it symbolises a different plane of consciousness or level of self. In reality, pure or complete representations of the planes are unlikely to appear in people's dreams. During a PTP, many people will experience the planes of consciousness simply in terms of different feeling tones. In some cases, Albedo will be experienced only through one or two planes; typically, the Subtle Mental and Third Planes. Later on, months, or even years later, the higher planes will reveal themselves. In other words, we access deeper and increasingly subtle levels within ourselves as we progress in this ongoing transformation process. As we do so, we become more subtle.

The influence of the external world wanes, revealing a proliferation of archetypal images of the subtler levels of self in our dreams. The images we might expect to find in dreams at this level are archetypally feminine, to do with ascending, expansion and "other-worldliness". The moon is an alchemical symbol in dreams signifying the receptive nature of this phase, the feminine and the rising of our consciousness (the moon is above the earth). A dreamer described a typical Albedo dream setting: "I am in the 'ideal' bedroom I created for myself when I was a teenager. The room is peaceful and lovely, full of moonlight, white shutters. The air is soft and fluid, like water".

The following dreams from a woman on retreat show something of the nature of Albedo.

### White Dress

A young girl shows me that she has made a pattern out of white lacy material for a dress. This can be adapted to make any dress. Once she has the template, there is no need for any further fitting.
    The next night.

### Dancing

My daughter wants to go through all my music tapes. She specifically wants music for dancing. There's going to be a party.

### A Call is Answered

It's a beautiful day and I'm sitting by a shallow river of clear running water, my feet in the water. I have a stick in my hands which I hold like an old primitive instrument, slowly and rhythmically beating out a sound on the bottom of the river bed. To my surprise, I hear a similar sound coming from upstream, as if a call is being answered. A baby water pig appears, very shyly at first, then, as I sit there quite motionless, it comes to my feet and lies on its back. Very gently, I pick it up and put in on my lap. I feel quite overwhelmed and graced.

The dream themes are beauty, purity, celebration, creativity, and harmony; all of which are themes of the Subtle Mental and Third Planes and thus belong to the ascent in Albedo. The "template" is the establishing of a new fineness and beauty in the dreamer (the white lacy dress). The encounter with the magical baby pig brings a gift of grace.

The appearance of babies, children, and young animals in our dreams usually indicates that Albedo has been reached and is also a sign of something subtle being born (coagulated) into our personality. As we shift our consciousness to the inner life, we identify less with our earth body until, in time, the subtle consciousness is established *in* us. We can feel it. We have begun to sense our subtle body (or light body) and can tune into this consciousness, not just during meditation, but in everyday life.

A woman in her sixties presented these dreams while on a dream workshop which show this process in exemplary form.

### Baby

I see a baby dressed in light blue. It is wrapped in plastic. I take the plastic away so the child can breathe. There is a second plastic cover around the head of the baby; I remove that too. I can immediately see the effect.

### Bread

I see three pieces of bread in front of me. They are triangular and white. I am offered these breads three times.

The baby signifies a new consciousness that is being born in the dreamer—a young and innocent, angelic aspect, but shrouded in plastic. This plastic wrapping (an artificial, mind-created object) must be taken away for the baby to breathe. When this action was repeated using the Waking Dream Process and the dreamer was able to hold the baby to her chest, she was deeply touched and reported that she could feel a heart connection between her and the baby. She stayed in this deep experience for quite a while and then proceeded to re-experience the second dream, eating each of the three triangular white breads, one after the other. Three triangular white objects being offered three times would seem to be symbols of the transcendental wanting to make itself known. The symbolic eating of the breads established the subtle self in the dreamer and led to an experience of the heart opening and abundant light.

The success of this operation is seen in a dream two days later when she stands alongside the queen in the court of the royal palace.

Royal Baptism

> I am together with the royal family. There are four children. Two of
> them are about to be baptised. I am participating. We are standing
> in the court of the royal palace. The queen and her sister are giving
> speeches.

The dreamer is now ready to contact the queen in herself and maybe
even hold a public speech from that inner space, indicating a significant
change in her self-image. There are four children now, four being the
number of completion. The baptism is not quite completed yet, but it is
under way.

The freedom that the soul experiences at this stage is often
expressed in dreams as flying or creatures that fly. Healing-themed
dreams refer to the psychological healing (of the mind) that takes place
in Albedo.

## The alchemical operations in Albedo

In the stage of Albedo, there will be:

- purification—by fire, water, and air—occurring naturally in ascent
  through the higher planes (*calcinatio* becomes more intense; *solutio*
  is equally prominent, further dissolving our attitudes and ideas in
  increasingly subtle ways);
- a separating out of our soul consciousness from the body and worldly
  identifications (through *separatio*);
- the increased subtlisation of consciousness in the ascent through the
  planes (*sublimatio* promotes this);
- *coagulatio* as something is born in us;
- an increasing sense of conscience (our spirit).

### The alchemical operation of separatio in Albedo

*Separatio* is concerned with separating, dividing, and differentiating.
This operation enables the separating out of our soul consciousness
from identification with the body and the associated worldly consciousness. Typical alchemical dream images for separatio are knives,
swords, and cutting tools. A classic alchemical separatio is described in

the Bible: "His winnowing fork is in his hand, and he will thoroughly cleanse his threshing floor. He will gather his wheat into the barn, but the chaff he will burn up with unquenchable fire" (Matthew 3 verse 12).

Often, separatio goes together with mortificatio. Death is the separating agent; that is, a dream in which a person's mother dies, or is killed by them, might indicate that they have been too close to their mother and need to separate. The mother in them has to die so they can mature autonomously. In the dream, the actions of mortificatio and separatio help the person to begin to separate out. Whilst anger in a dream can indicate an inability to contain or transform our fire, anger in a dream such as this could be our fire nature acting positively in protecting the self and helping us to individuate.

The following dream shows the shattering of the dreamer's mind through the operation of separatio. In this case, the ruling principle of the father as the basis of her thinking and beliefs is annihilated.

### The Cleaver

A little girl and her father are on a fishing trip … The little girl is busy trying to keep up with the man's impossible and endless demands. She is getting exhausted, and I wonder how long she can keep doing his bidding. Finally, she has the courage to say to the man: "You will recognise me!" In response, he grins malevolently … and picks up a large cleaver with a massive, shiny, silver blade … I look on horrified as he raises the cleaver in his right arm … The cleaver goes into the girl's head to her skull.

Using the Waking Dream Process with her therapist, the dreamer realises the impact of the negative masculine within.

I feel the cleaver as my mind—its incisiveness and analytical quality that can break up large bits of chaos into manageable pieces, like a butcher with meat. I feel the sadistic and judgmental nature of this mind as well. I also recognise the passion and power, the anger and the grief.

The following dream was recorded at the beginning of a retreat.

### My Book

I had to choose which work I was going to do and was creating an office space for this. My work was to rewrite the Materia Medica ... so that only the authentic parts were kept. This was to be my book. It seemed like a very big task and I interviewed people that I would employ to help me with this job.

The separatio operation in this dream is subtle. This dreamer will recover a more essential and truer part of herself through tackling a big mental task—writing "my book" by separating out "only the authentic parts" of a classical text. This is separatio on the level of the mind— clearing the mind.

A woman in psychotherapy experiences the transforming effect of separatio, together with solutio, calcinatio, and coagulatio in her dream.

### Boat Journey

I have a sense of needing to go on a journey so I take a small boat in the quay and leave life behind. I am aware of the lapping water and the physicality of the rowing. I am contained by the boat and the water; I am part of nature, in it. I am aware of the expansive-ness of the horizon in one direction and look back to the land to my right and have perspective on it. I need to be separate. I don't want to be called back. I see the harbour at night. It is attractive, twin-kling with lights, but I'm not sure I want it. I dally with the idea then continue to row out to sea to an island on my left side. It has a small wood in the centre and a sandy beach at the edge. I build a fire with sticks near to the water. It is dark now and I have a feeling of rightness in the dark with nature, experiencing myself in relation to the universe. That's all there is—a very private, intimate rela-tionship with God and the universe. I am crying. I cook bread and fishes on the fire as dawn breaks. I am in the boat again and eat some of the food in the morning light. I take some home to nourish the ones I love.

This dreamer leaves the activity of her worldly life behind on the right side (the active masculine), separates out from it and, in doing so, finds what she needs in the island on the left (receptive, feminine—a sense of her soul) where she engages in a transformative ritual that incorporates several purifying alchemical operations. She is cleansed by her tears and the sea (solutio); fire (calcinatio) is transformed into the light of the dawn; and she incorporates her new, greater sense of self and relationship to the divine in the eating of the food (coagulation) with its religious reference to Christ's miracle of the loaves and fishes. This dream facilitated the separating out of soul consciousness from worldly mind through the actions of separatio and purification.

### The alchemical operation of sublimatio in Albedo

*Sublimatio* is the alchemical operation that allows our consciousness to rise and expand, liberating us from the limitations of our personal viewpoint. We are free from the psychological complexes and confusions that our minds get caught up in and able to see the bigger picture. Our dreams may bring us a fresh insight through the action of sublimatio so that we can see our issues and problems from a higher perspective. Suddenly, there is clarity.

The air element is the most subtle, most difficult to grasp and the most changeable. Its subtlety is reflected in our intelligence, in our wit and in our understanding of the nuances of life. Unlike earth, water, or fire, it cannot be easily seen, unless it takes the form of fog or clouds. In dreams, our "heavier" thoughts in depression may appear as clouds; confusion, as fog. The air element is unpredictable; it can express itself as wind, storm, stillness, and clarity. In dreams, each symbolises a different state and a different degree of purification. When the air element is clear, perspective is possible and the imagination opens up to insight and realisation—the most important qualities that come through this element.

Typical images of sublimatio in dreams are: flying, birds flying, ascending into the sky, ascending in a lift, looking down from a great height (from a tower or a mountain, for example).

### Lesser sublimatio

We experience a *lesser sublimatio* in our dreams when we rise (literally) to a certain point and then can't stay in that place; fear sets in or some outer event compels us to descend again. We get a glimpse of where we might be going, but more purification is needed for us to pursue and sustain that higher state. In this way, a lesser sublimatio indicates the limits of the dreamer's current consciousness. Subsequent sublimatio dreams may help us to gain sufficient insight into our issues to enable us to progress in the transformation process.

The following retreat dream shows this process of rising and descent. A woman was disappointed to have a dream of killing and battles towards the end of her retreat. Further purification of her fire nature was needed. However, in a subsequent dream, she has a lucid sublimatio experience—an ascent of consciousness (climbing ladders) to a higher state in which she understands the significance of the first dream—before there is a humbling descent.

Ladders

I am at a house party. I need to climb ladders in the house to find my coat. There are more ladders than before. I go up them into more bedrooms that are still and white to fetch my coat. Whilst I am there, I realise the significance of the previous dream is to do with transformation. The weapon I used in the battle is a laser light from my third eye, pinpointing issues with deadly accuracy. So I am rather pleased to have made sense of my previous dream in this dream. I come back down the ladder, but need to slide myself through the slats, getting rather stuck around my breasts. There is much laughter as I explain to the hostess that I am not really seriously stuck, but love to do this kind of silly stuff as it helps people to lighten up and laugh at life's situations, bringing more joy into life.

Sublimatio has brought lightness, joy, and laughter, now that "heavy" issues are clearing. Note that the place where she finds her new insight is "still and white". This is a new plane of consciousness which she is allowed to glimpse, but cannot inhabit yet. It is important, though, to recognise that higher level of self, so that she can become more and more familiar with it in working with subsequent sublimatio dreams.

A special case of sublimatio, called *false sublimatio*, is a rapid ascent followed by a crash landing. Typical images would be flying and then crashing; standing on top of a tower that collapses; climbing a mountain and falling down, and so on. When we go "high" prematurely in a dream without integrating any insights, it means that the sublimatio operation has failed. False sublimatio is what we call "spiritual by-pass" in psychospiritual terms: a person manages to escape into a fantasy spiritual experience that is not embodied before, inevitably, coming down again into reality. David's dream of "Heaven and Hell" (Chapter Two) exemplifies a typical false sublimatio.

In some cases, this can be very damaging to the psyche and even lead to psychosis. It can happen if a person is not ready for transformation, or if they are unstable and trying to induce sublimatio by intensely repetitive practices (such as certain forms of meditation, dance, drumming). They quickly take off, but crash back down. In the Waking Dream Process, it is very important to proceed slowly and stay with the dreamer's experience, tracking it in the body to keep it "real". This avoids inflation and the corresponding downfall.

*Greater sublimatio*

In a *greater sublimatio* operation, we not only cross the interval from this world into the mind world, but then continue on our journey into what is behind the mind world. Sublimatio enables us to ascend to a point where a soul conscious state, free of the mind, can be accessed. There takes place, in effect, a purification and subtlisation of consciousness and, once we experience that inner subtlety, we never forget it. Even when we come back to the waking state, our consciousness has changed permanently. Thus, the greater sublimatio is associated with a transformation process that leads to a profound spiritual awakening (as described in Chapter Five).

*The alchemical operation of coagulatio in Albedo*

There is an alchemical formula which describes the two aspects of coagulatio: *the spiritualisation of matter* and *the materialisation of spirit*. At this stage in the process, coagulatio occurs as part of the spiritualisation of matter. The spiritualisation of matter means that the spirit that had been congealed in matter is freed from that constraint. It is no longer solid; it's fluid. This is the realisation and coagulation of the subtle (or light) body. In other words, something of spirit is born in us. In the "Boat Journey" dream, the dreamer coagulates her experience of spirit in eating the bread and fish. The same principle imbues the Christian sacrament of the Eucharist with its meaning. In the Roman Catholic tradition, the bread and wine *become* the body and blood of Christ through transubstantiation.

The opposite—the materialisation of spirit—means the subtle spirit becomes embodied in matter. It incarnates into the physical world. This is the alchemical model for coagulatio: First, consciousness becomes more subtle in its ascent (in Albedo); later, when consciousness returns to the world (in Rubedo), spirit and realisation is grounded in everyday life. So, coagulatio is like a coin with two faces.

### The heart centre

This is the *anahata* chakra in Vedanta which holds the capacity for love, relatedness, openness, and cosmic consciousness. In the Vedantic tradition, it is related to the air element. In its shadow aspect in the Buddhist tradition, it is the centre of jealousy, the inability to share— the illusory impediment blocking the experience of pure heart consciousness.

In Sufism, the qalb, located at the left side of the breast next to the physical heart, is regarded as the human, feeling heart. Whilst it registers our intimate feelings (pain, sadness, and longing), it also has the capacity to open beyond our limited self to a greater sense of intimacy with the divine, into transcendence.

The bodily experience of the opening or stimulation of the heart centre energies is initially registered through the sensation of tingling in both hands and arms, which are the psychic extensions of the heart centre. This centre is associated with the sense of touch—reaching out to touch others, to relate and express our feelings through our hands. Pains in the centre of the chest can also accompany the stirring of these energies. These are not to be confused with symptoms of a physical heart attack, which also include difficulty in breathing and feeling sick. Retreatants often report physical burning sensations in the solar plexus and heart centre when transiting this level. The burning is not physical, but psychic.

Dreams connected to the heart centre often contain deep feelings of longing, sadness, grief, and love. When a dream is being explored, the sensations in the hands, arms, or heart area are significant and should be focused on in the dreamwork. In doing so, we connect with the heart centre and to our deeper self, our soul. The heart centre is notably active in David's "White Horse" and "Centaur" dreams (02/2009 and 02/2012) in Chapter Five. In Ava's case, the stirring of the heart energy begins at the start of her process, but by Chapter Five, in "Death by Poison" (10/2005), it is clear the heart centre is fully open.

## Travellers' Tales

### David unfolds

Albedo begins for David with an alchemical dream of "a sacred object that ... is black and oblong with strange white crystals running through it. It is impossibly heavy ... and weighs down on my hand like a force of gravity". This is, perhaps, a symbol of the emerging soul: the white crystals within the overall blackness and weight of the "base matter" yet to be transformed. It is always spirit that initiates the stage of Albedo and, in a further dream, a dragon is the initiator.

#### Green Dragon

I walk across a grassy knoll and down into a wooded glade. The trees are spaced apart and the sunlight is streaming through the foliage. There are beautiful flowers growing and my mind is drawn out into the nature around me. I feel happy and uplifted ... I am delighted to be close to the sea and head down to the beach ... As I come to the beach itself I find I am emerging from a big, dark cave ... There, arising out of the water, is a huge sea snake ... As the snake emerges out of the water onto the beach, it metamorphoses into a huge green dragon ... Its skin is many hues of emerald and green, and its mouth and tongue are bright red. It exudes power: seething, writhing energy—beautiful, fierce and alien. (David, 04/2008)

The central image of the dream is the green dragon, which is a magical creature of the Creative Self. Something of the Third Plane may be "sitting behind" the dream (as indicated by the beautiful, natural setting), but it is always the central image that is most significant and indicative of the level of consciousness. This is the archetypal, alchemical dragon, symbolising the untransformed fire aspect of spirit (de Jong, 2002), which has the colours of spirit: green and red—life force and sun force (fire energy), respectively.

In David, the dragon is the symbol of the fire energy that needs purification and transformation. The raw energy of the lower energy centres (the "huge sea snake") is transformed into the dragon, which can fly and be free from the entrapment of the physical body (thereby facilitating sublimatio in Albedo). It "exudes power" but is, as yet, "alien" and will prove to be a significant force in David's PTP.

Over the next month, a number of dreams confirm the passage through Albedo. In one dream, David is in India with his spiritual teacher and a Jungian therapist looking to acquire land (perhaps to establish a base for his psyche). In alchemy, travelling to or being in the East (for a Westerner) symbolises the search for the soul—the quest of Albedo (Jung, 1983).

### Robert Mugabe

I'm visiting a therapeutic unit for profoundly disturbed children ... the energy is chaotic, confused and innately aggressive. However, I feel no fear; I am relaxed and friendly as I walk around ... Then I rest ... I seem to be on the edge of a precipice. I can hear a large volume of water flowing quietly over the edge beside me. It is falling a very great distance. I decide to "let go" and ... allow the water to take me over the precipice. I fall ... I feel I am going deeper and deeper into myself ... Then I am somewhere in some very distant land in the mountains ... in a huge mountain-top palace. There are thousands of rooms ... filled with beautiful Buddhist treasures. In one room, both monks and Westerners on retreat are chanting and praying.

Then I am ascending to the very top of the palace, to the uppermost rooms. I am ushered into a room that has a glass ceiling, very bright and spacious. There, lounging on the couch is Robert Mugabe. His skin is just like a lizard or snake—dry, smooth and shiny. He is wearing very expensive clothes ... elegant, but also very ugly. He exudes corrupt, cold power ... I find myself meekly running around serving him ... I manage to take my leave and start walking down the stairs to the lower levels ... Mugabe calls down to me from the top of the stairs. He asks me if I am coming to the theatre performance that evening ... I am flattered and can't find a way to say no. I turn away and immediately castigate myself for allowing myself to get caught up in a situation that I do not want. (David, 05/2008)

The therapeutic unit for profoundly disturbed children hints at the impact of David's early life on his state of mind. When the scene changes to David's familiar refuge—the mountain-top retreat—we discover the central image of the dream: Robert Mugabe (with his snake-like skin)—a "trickster" of the Creative Self. The reference to the theatre performance confirms this. David lacks power in himself and is mesmerised by Mugabe, acting in a servile way in seeking the recognition from him that he longed for from his father. Clearly, David is being shown by the dream that he needs to develop a stronger sense of self and the capacity to stand in the truth of it. Mugabe holds all David's split-off power. By saying "no" to the Mugabe aspect of his mind that tyrannises, David can begin to reclaim this power and strength of his psyche. Though this dream symbolises a distorted aspect of David, it is no longer hidden. The shadow has emerged and taken form, and can now be confronted.

Almost immediately, David has the following dream.

### Perfect Landing

I've been in a plane crash. I have survived and find myself on a second plane. We are in the air but in trouble. The pilot (a woman) is looking for somewhere to make an emergency landing ... Down the plane comes with the pilot gliding the plane in to make an absolutely perfect landing onto the runway. (David, 05/2008)

In reviewing the two dreams together, it appears that David still has a tendency to "ascend" before dealing with his inner unconscious forces—the spiritual bypass or false sublimatio. In the earlier part of the Mugabe dream, we see the action of solutio as he "lets go" into the water. He descends and goes "deeper and deeper" (into his unconscious) where he finds himself ascending again "to the very top". Here, he cannot avoid meeting his shadow who is waiting for him. In the second dream, the first plane crashes (reminding him of the danger of ungrounded mental fantasy), but the second plane, helped by the feminine, makes a "perfect landing". He has come to earth in a successful coagulatio.

Then, he dreams of his mother at a dinner gathering.

### Mother

Sitting at the head table in the head chair is my mother. She looks like a little sparrow sitting in such a grand chair, but as I lean forward and kiss her in welcome, I recognise that she is sitting there by right ...

Although physically she appears weak and insubstantial, her energy, life force, spiritual drive, is anything but weak. It is strong and indomitable.

Later, David is in a kind of museum room with valuable antiques for sale.

> Then, I look over to the other side of the room and my therapist is with me. I tell him about the events of this very dream (a dream within a dream) … He says very strongly: "He is dying in the place of your mother". I have a feeling that something to do with the mother archetype has happened. On waking, and for the following day, the subtle sense of something deep having taken place continues. (David, 06/2008)

Notice the "dream within a dream" (the beginnings of lucidity in David's dreams) and the setting of "valuable antiques", which could signify the discovery of treasure within. A healthy mother archetype is, at last, being established in David's psyche in place of the false self who is "dying" (mortificatio). This was made possible by the therapeutic dreamwork in Nigredo and up to this point, which helped him to: contact his anger (symbolically held by his brother) and the power within it; begin to heal the split between body and spirit; and develop his inner feminine, receptive aspect. In doing so, David completes the first and most important stage of development of the inner self-mother relationship. In David's outer life, this resulted in a significant shift in attitude towards his mother and he expressed this in a painting.

David had taken up painting at the start of the therapy, but his paintings, whilst expressive of his inner psychic conditions, showed a rigidity of structure and form during the Nigredo stage—a reflection of his carefully guarded state of mind. However, now Albedo had begun, this rigidity gave way to a movement and flow in forms, and the use of vibrant colour. This seemed to signify a creative phase in his therapy which lasted up to the point of his dreams of awakening (Chapter Five).

The level of the Creative Self ended with a dream where David celebrates with Bruce Springsteen (a creative artist and positive male figure for David) and a "special vintage wine" that tastes like "nectar, beyond description—very happy feeling". Bruce Springsteen seemed to represent a new, positive aspect of David that was emerging and his drinking of the wine is both a celebration and a ritual "imbibing" of spirit.

The following two dreams touched on Third Plane themes. First, he dreams of two "very beautiful women", one of whom is mother to a small boy who is playing nearby. David embraces the boy.

### Little Boy

He stays in my embrace and our energies seem very much in communion with each other. He is a lovely little boy and my heart goes out to him. (David, 06/2008)

In the second dream, David is in bed with his ex-wife.

### First Flush of Love

I'm in bed with B. The play of thoughts and feeling between us are as in the first flush of love—joyful and intense where every choice seems exhilarating and liberating at the same time ... All of it is so playful and pleasurable. (David, 06/2008)

We could see the latter dream simply as a wish fulfillment dream relating to David's ex-wife, but we can also see the dreams in the context of the Third Plane themes of the child, the lover, harmony, joy, and the activation of the heart. In embracing the boy, he is now in touch with a more innocent and healthier, inner child.

Two dreams follow—"Death of my Mother" and "Death of a Foetus"—both of which seem to symbolise a letting go of the unconscious attachment to mother, and are examples of separatio dreams in Albedo that go hand in hand with mortificatio.

Finally, in this transition from the Loving Self to the beginning of the Wise Self, David has the dream, "Arising from the Depths", where he is released from a "subterranean" chamber "deep down on the ocean floor" (his deepest heart feelings). He rises to the surface and flies over the countryside of his childhood (sublimatio). He encounters "strange creatures" which would seem to symbolise instinctual aspects buried deep in his psyche. The dream brings up feelings of "loneliness and isolation" which he is then able to work with as part of the transition.

A very different series of dreams begins with a confrontation with a cruel, inner aspect—marking the entry to the Fourth Plane.

### The Psychopath

I'm in a very large building with many rooms and many floors. We hear a commotion in another room and, as we enter, we see a man and a woman. The man is strong, handsome and charismatic, but I can see by looking at his eyes that he is a very cruel, vicious psychopath. The woman is beautiful, but weak, and appears to be under this man's power. He has been beating her, but our intervention stops him and, as we confront him, we tell him to get out … I am determined to confront and deal with him once and for all. (David, 07/2008)

David is now conscious of a much deeper rage towards the feminine in his psyche. In the Creative Self phase, he only touched on this issue in himself. The establishment of a positive, inner mother takes place at the level of mind and he is conscious of this. However, in the Fourth Plane, he experiences the roots of his mental attitudes; that is, the deep rage that fed the negative thoughts. In this dream, David becomes conscious of just how dangerous these feelings are and he begins to confront his inner psychopath.

Changes in attitude, attachments, and beliefs experienced in the Subtle Mental and Third Planes are relatively superficial in the PTP compared to the shift that takes place in the Fourth Plane. To effect a significant change at this deep level, requires a major reconstruction of the psyche, without which the old attitudes are likely to resurface in the mind. A breakthrough to the Wise Self requires a complete rebuilding of our inner, mental framework.

Shortly after, David dreams that he ascends a ladder to the top of a building, which is "under construction", in India. This gives way to a scene of a young boy "clambering over bombed-out ruins". The feeling tone of the scene (typical of the first phase Fourth Plane) is one of "loneliness and deprivation". Deep soul feelings emerge around his devastating experiences of emotional neglect and physical isolation in early life.

The following month, David dreams of his therapist massaging a painful tension in his upper back, neck, and head (indicative of the activity in the upper energy centres). He says: "His touch is very gentle, almost feminine, but it also contains real strength". The tension disappears and he meets a woman "who very much wants to engage with me". It seems that the healing touch in the dream has helped David to engage with the feminine.

This was followed by another dream, set in his early life home town, in which David wins a very important competition and receives the first prize of a pedicure given by the world's top pedicurist!

### The Pedicurist

I'm led out into the middle of the stage and am presented with a beautiful, square, wooden box. I open it and, lying in purple velvet, there is a display of silver instruments. Alongside, are many small bottles/containers filled with potions and ointments of many colours and hues. Then the world-famous pedicurist makes his entrance, strides up to me and congratulates me on winning such a special prize. The pedicurist has black skin but with a very curious, green radiance. He is outgoing and dynamic ... Slowly, if a little painfully, we strike up a dialogue ... Then I ask him what will be the benefit from the pedicure ... It will change my life, he is saying; it will have profound transforming qualities. It is a truly wonderful gift for which I should be very thankful ... The display of prepared potions looks beautiful and I recognise that the knowledge involved is secret, hidden, and esoteric. (David, 08/2008)

This dream was the first of a series of healing and purification dreams that lead to a turning point in the Wise Self where David overcomes his fear of touch and his rage against the feminine. The central image is the pedicurist, who is a healing figure (his "green radiance" is a sign of this), with, we should note, a special interest in feet—most important for David's grounding! There are Wise Self motifs of silver (instruments) and the square box (the number four signifying completion), and the colour purple together with the "esoteric" may hint at the Fifth Plane to come.

At this point, the fire element in a series of calcinatio dreams became more and more intense as the operation developed. In one, David is with his father and brother and a "huge barn of cathedral-like proportions" is "burning furiously with flames ten/fifteen feet high" until "the whole, entire edifice is an inferno" and "comes crashing down with anyone inside killed". This is the burning away of an internalised mental "edifice" (or the ego structure, to put it another way) until nothing is left. It is important to note the presence of the father and brother, who were often symbols in imagery arising in the therapy of a cold, unfeeling self-criticism (particularly in relation to David's own masculinity). This dream seems to be burning away the psychic impressions of such criticisms. Such an intense fire was also needed to break down the barrier in David's psyche that suppressed his anger.

In one of the later calcinatio dreams, a house is ablaze with fire, but this time he feels compelled to rescue the people inside: "two beautiful boys with big eyes—one a baby, the other a toddler, both holding each other in their arms". He brings them to safety but "the building burns and crashes into ruin". Here, he salvages an innocent, pure part of his essential self from the ruin of his ego construct—the part that is needed for his onward journey.

David dreams again of the family home; he is with his son with whom he has a good relationship, and his ex-wife and other children are inside the house.

### Torrent

The windows of the house are open, light shines out ... Suddenly, there is a thunderous roar and, all in a rush, comes a huge torrent of water careering down the storm channel ... The water plumes and fountains causing great spurts of water high into the night sky ... Finally, water rushes in through the roof and ceiling and comes cascading down through the interior of the house. Soon there is nothing to be done about it with water rushing through and immersing everything. (David, 08/2008)

This purification is by water, dissolving David's painful memories of his lost marriage and family. This dream shows the development of solutio in David's process since "Yellow Fish" in Nigredo—the "torrent" signifying a radical change taking place in his inner world, and a healing and cleansing of family issues in his process, heralding a new flow of energy in his psyche.

The two purification processes culminate in a complete coniunctio with the feminine in a landmark dream where the deep, cold, empty core of David begins to come alive. He dreams of making love to a beautiful young woman whom he meets on a train. At the point of coitus, he wakes up and spontaneously finds a point of strong meditative concentration: "The deep place in me that is cold and empty feels different. The vibration of life, vitality and warmth pulsates in the emptiness". The dream seems to suggest that, as a result of the coniunctio with the anima figure (his soul nature), he is beginning to penetrate the core of the schizoid condition. The "cold and empty" place in David can be now be warmed and revitalised now that his soul passion (the fire of the Fourth Plane) has penetrated this mind space.

Not long after, David dreams of a large building that houses an Olympic-sized swimming pool. A young girl is competing in the final of an Olympic event. He cheers her on as she forges ahead and wins by a narrow margin. She is presented with the gold medal on the podium and then runs to David and is affectionate and loving as though he is her father. His partner, who is next to him, is beautiful and looks calm and serene. David feels so happy to have the two of them with him.

Here is the Fourth Plane theme of accomplishment. The young girl may be connected to his memories at boarding school at the same age where David failed to succeed in physical games and meet his father's expectations. The girl, however, can be seen to represent more than this—symbolising some emerging aspect of his soul nature that has overcome early, painful, negative impressions. David's anima is now stronger and the "gold" of the process is in sight.

Later in the same year, David has a sublimatio dream that begins in a luxury yacht on the River Thames. He realises that "this is not an ordinary boat" as the vessel takes to the sky and flies over "a vast and strange landscape"—pools covered in green seaweed and "huge fissures or canyons". In a valley far below, he sees signs of a "lost civilisation … derelict houses and dwellings … the people long gone". Suddenly, he registers that his therapy has finished and he won't be seeing his therapist again. He begins to cry and is inconsolable. The day after the dream, David was very emotional, crying for no reason. At the time of the dream, David experienced a number of "power failures" in outer life: the car alternator failed, the boiler broke down, the transformer blew up.

In this dream, David experienced something of the landscape of his psyche and the pain of his soul (the "lost civilisation", the "fissures" representing the deep divisions within him that have yet to be reconciled) and a fear of loss of his therapist. These things are the obstacles that block David's path and the power that lies within. The green, watery pools are, though, a positive sign, which, as an embodied experience in the Waking Dream Process, was an uplifting feeling.

In November 2008, David dreams of crossing a border through customs where "the atmosphere is strict, military even". His passport is stamped with a two month visa and he is allowed to proceed to "enter somewhere where I need to go". Our traveller seems to be entering unchartered territory in himself.

Then he has the following dream.

### Serial Killer

I'm driving along a country road. With me is a close friend—someone I have known for a long time. He is a trusted and liked member of my family, as well as the wider community ... As we drive along, we come to where a tree has fallen across the road blocking our progress ... I see the naked corpse of a young woman in the ditch ... She seems no larger than a play doll now and I watch as my friend tosses her aside with evil, callous and brutal contempt. Instantly, I "know" that she is a murdered prostitute and that my friend is the killer, and that this is not the first time he has killed ... Suddenly, he rushes at me intending to kill me in order to get by me ... I head-butt him with the top of my head, right in the centre of his face. The impact knocks him out cold. I feel glad that I have stood up and stopped him. (David, 11/2008)

Early feelings of rage and contempt for his addicted and dependent mother had plagued David for most of his life, leaving him cut off, isolated and unable to relate to others. In this Fourth Plane conflict, David has at last confronted, head-on, the deep-rooted aggression and cold brutality towards himself, his feelings, and women, that has always tortured him.

The final dreams of the Fourth Plane mark the turning point in the struggles with his now conscious distortion. David dreams of a "multicoloured, coral snake" which rises up his leg and enters his body through his anus. It remains inside him. Here, he would seem to be incorporating the base centre energy which is no longer split off and retroflected. It might, or might not, be an indication of the first stirrings of kundalini energy. (In the context of the awakening process, snakes can represent kundalini rising and also the untransformed instincts). In another purification dream, David is in India again with his brother.

### Dark India

We drive out into a vast, cathedral-like space that is strange and alien in character … It is a truly huge, cavernous enclosure. The walls and roof are totally black with smoke and dirt of endless generations of activity. There is no lighting apart from fires here and there … Multitudes of people appear to be living in this dark, foreboding and lost place … I watch as long lines of people all pushing brooms start to push a big pile of rubbish together towards a far wall. (David, 12/2008)

It seems like a return to Nigredo, but the discovery of a "cathedral-like space" in India is suggestive of the clearing out of a newly exposed, but more natural, psychic structure that will reflect David's soul nature more appropriately, preparing him for the awakening to come. The cathedral motif has previously appeared in a more disguised form in David's dreams and will occur again in the next phase.

In a classic Fourth Plane dream, David dreams of an archetypal battle between two gladiators who fight to the death. One embodies the qualities of light; the other the qualities of darkness. Just as darkness appears to be victorious, he hears a call in the distance. "Suddenly, high in the sky comes floating a huge warship amid much cheering and joyful cries … This is a ship that was thought destroyed and lost with all crew killed, but by some miracle has now returned and, with it, some great emptiness or sorrow has been healed".

These healing dreams seem to represent David's conquering of his mental distortions and arrival at a more reconciled place in himself—the Wise Self. Light has triumphed within him, opening the way for the ascent of spirit.

Finally, David has the following mortificatio and calcinatio dream, which constitutes a ritual preparation for a new, inner journey.

### Sarcophagus

Sitting opposite my therapist is a young, handsome black man. There are preparations for a ritual in which this man is to take his own life—a transition to a life beyond … My therapist then hands him a saucer which has on it some grey paste-like matter … This is the poison that will bring about quick and painless death … I see for the first time next to him a large sarcophagus-shaped object with strange markings all over it … Looking back at my therapist, I see he is holding an iron-like object that is glowing with red hot heat. He proceeds to burn or brand marks into the surface of the sarcophagus (the surface melts rather than burns) whilst repeating alchemical phrases and words … He sears a thin line right across my palm. I took up and see a woman has also entered the room … He proceeds to brand her palm too. (David, 12/2008)

David and his anima have their process "fixed" and "hardened" in this final alchemical action of branding the hands, which, in the mystical traditions, are expressive of the heart centre (Khan, 1982).

In the dream that marks the end of the Wise Self, David is on a "cross channel ferry" when he sees a "huge storm approaching rapidly from the East" turning the ocean into a giant "centrifugal" whirlpool—"we are completely at the mercy of the elements". He watches with fascination as the ferry is thrown to the edges of the whirlpool and onto solid ground. There is rejoicing—"a miracle has happened". In this final surrender to the elements, David survives the stormy course of the Fourth Plane, which has been like a "churning" of the self. The rejoicing in the dream marks this point in his process. The mental scripts that inhibited and crippled his deeper, more authentic nature have been cleared so that the beauty, power and radiance of his soul can emerge consciously. The reference to the East is suggestive of the direction of his ongoing journey. A new series of dreams begins.

This phase marked an important turning point for David as his most intransigent depressions lifted, and relationships at work and with family improved as he became more extraverted. Sitting with him, he seemed to be in a more balanced state; the earlier desperation had been replaced with something more robust and solid. David was really engaged with the dreamwork, which had become a central focus in his therapy.

## Ava unfolds

Ava's dream, as follows, is a bridging dream, which facilitates the transition from one plane of consciousness to the next (in this case, from the Worldly to the Creative Self).

### The Walk

I am walking through the woods with a group of people, including my husband (P) and son. To the left, there is an old dilapidated house where an artist used to live. Between the trees, strange round sculptures are hanging, like car tyres. I point this out to the others. We walk along a narrow path and come to a little village—only a few houses. It seems to be empty. On the first house, I see a sign indicating that a writer used to live here and that he wrote a novel about the suicide of a girl who had lived in this village ... Then we come to another house, quite colourful, round. Then, the church. It is very special because it has a roof made of braided fabric—white canvas. I hope my son wants to have a look at it, and he does, so we all enter. Strangely bright light ... Then I tell my husband and another man to jog back and get the cars; that's what they do. (Ava, 03/2000)

The first part of the dream has a rather heavy atmosphere—a "dilapidated house", an abandoned village. An artist and a writer are mentioned (creative people typical of the Subtle Mental Plane), but they are dead and their artwork is not very appealing—sculptures like tyres, a novel about a suicide. There is an air of stagnation, of "no future".

But there are positive signs even from the beginning: they are in the woods (a natural environment) and children are present (always an indication of something growing). These elements evolve in the second part of the dream. They come to a colourful, round house. Colours are almost always a sign that something is opening up, and the roundness of a circle (the most symmetrical form) is suggestive of a new balance in the dreamer. The church, with its white roof and the bright light inside, is suggestive of Albedo and the potential for awakening to come. These subtle attunements are evidently quite unconscious in the dreamer at this point of the process; she is still very much involved in earthly concerns. So, rather than staying in the bright light, she has the men jog back to get the cars, which are worldly symbols.

The metaphor of flying often characterises the start of the Albedo stage, symbolising the dreamer's transcendence of their imprisoning inner world and movement towards something more subtle in themselves. The following dream combines this theme with the pleasure of learning—another typical Creative Self theme. In the Worldly Self, the theme of learning might involve fear of exams, not knowing what to study for, feeling incompetent and so on, but once we move to the higher mind, creativity really takes off and being able to fly is a metaphor for the ascent in consciousness (sublimatio in Albedo). The iron steamroller seems to act as an earthy ballast for Ava's ascent.

### Flying

I'm in a beautiful hotel, close to the sea. You learn to fly here. The teacher shows how to do it: he flies through the air, making turns, rolls. I can do it too; I feel free and happy. I land softly on the water … Back in the hotel, my father is there too. He thinks that flying is dangerous. I say it is not dangerous because you are fastened to a steamroller—a huge rusty brown one made of iron, and that is fastened to a helicopter. Now a child is flying by. The child is not fastened to anything, but under the clothes I see plastic pants filled with air. I find that a little risky, but maybe it is possible for children … The teacher says: "The course is finished for you, you can do it alone". He is working with those who still have trouble flying. So I will go flying again on my own. (Ava, 03/2000)

The expansiveness of Ava's environment, the imaginative teaching device, the helicopter for ascent are all elements that point to the level of the Creative Self. Note also the ingrained attitudes revealed by her father's comments—the restriction of the mind. A child is present in the dream, symbolising the emerging innocence of Albedo and the Third Plane.

The following dream indicates the Albedo stage in Ava's PTP in the motifs of white, birth and healing. Just before this birth dream, during the culmination of the Nigredo stage, she had a dream of marriage (in outer life, she had been married for many years), which is quite common around the transition from one stage to the other—coniunctio completing one stage; a birth beginning the next one.

### Pregnancy

I am pregnant. The embryo is only a few centimeters long. I am in the forest. I see large, white funnel-shaped flowers—they grow under the trees. I should be in bed. The doctor said the opening for the baby is not big enough—I have to go back to the hospital. A young male nurse says: "Don't let them take your baby away!" I say: "No, I don't want that. But if they say it cannot come out at all and they will have to cut me up later, that is not good". There is a doctor who specialises in such cases. I want to see him. He comes, without a white apron. He says it will be all right, but that I should stay quiet. I am allowed to leave the hospital. (Ava, 03/2000)

The dream suggests an unconscious fear in Ava about the birthing of the new self, yet the dream promises it will be successful. Ava's request for the specialist "without a white apron" might refer to a need for the reassurance of her dream guide in the process of her "labour" and "delivery". The following dream confirmed that the Albedo stage was established.

### The Famous Pianist

A young woman—a famous pianist—is staying with us. She can play everything, always by heart. I admire her very much … Once she plays a very funny trick: she programs a musical piece on the typewriter. Then she plays the piano, suddenly lifts her hands up and the music continues, played by the old mechanical typewriter. But it is only a very short piece (the programming is much too time-consuming). Everybody is laughing about the surprise. I almost don't dare talk to her. I would like to be able to play like her, but unfortunately, she has no written notes that I could play since she is playing everything by heart. (Ava, 04/2000)

Although there are man-made motifs (the typewriter and programming), the Creative Self is present in a famous person (a pianist), artistic talent, the funny trick, and the desire to learn. The atmosphere is light and enjoyable; humour is a feature of this plane. Ava is eager to play like the famous pianist but still believes she needs written notes for that. She is not used to accessing the Creative Self at this point, and so it is not easy for her to let go of this limiting belief and to tap into the higher ground of creativity freely. The emerging musical talent is a metaphor for her emerging subtler nature and the key is in the heart.

In these two dreams, an "inner guide" is present—a flying teacher in the first case; the young woman pianist in the second—confirming the establishment of the Creative Self. The theme of music (a thread running through her process) continues in the next dream, but is now set within a new context.

### Circle of Love

I'm in my college again. The students receive me with so much love! I come into the classroom; they have written welcome greetings on the blackboard. A girl is reading the text out loud. They are so happy that I am back after a year of absence. I go to the back of the room, sit down and all the students sit in a circle around me. They tell me that they remember having once gone to the opera with me. This warms my heart. We will do it again. I ask them if they know the "Magic Flute" by Mozart—No—So we will go to see it. A life without knowing the "Magic Flute" makes no sense. I wonder if I should sing a melody from that opera for them but I don't dare. I feel so surrounded by love. How could I not have noticed that before? It is a circle of love. (Ava, 05/2000)

This rather idealised picture of unconditional love between students and teacher is characteristic of the Third Plane and is one of Ava's solutio dreams in Albedo. The students portray innocent youth; they speak of the opera (a symbol of beauty and harmony), which warms the heart of the teacher; they form a "circle of love" (suggesting wholeness and harmony). The "Magic Flute" appears at this point in the process as a wonderful metaphor for the journey of purification and transformation in the Fourth Plane, where the protagonist undergoes initiation rites, trials by fire and water until, at last, with the protection of the magical agent—the flute—wisdom and light triumph over the forces of darkness. It is a story set in a land between the moon (Albedo) and the sun (Citrinitas), which, in alchemical terms, we might say is where Ava is heading. "A life without knowing the 'Magic Flute' makes no sense" is a deep insight.

One more element in this dream is significant in the light of later developments in Ava's dream life. Although she knows the melody, she is hesitant to sing it out loud. This theme repeats again and again until, finally, several years later, Ava steps in for the primadonna and publicly sings the leading role in an opera. Evidently, this can only be appreciated in hindsight, but it is important to pick up on such details, trusting that what the dreamer does not dare to do now will someday be accomplished.

The following two dreams are drawn from a collection of twenty in the Fourth Plane. They are only three weeks apart and show the rapid resolution of an inner aspect.

### Burning Rage

P and I are walking along a path ... A wild horse comes from the opposite direction, pulling a wagon with people, but it acts in a crazy manner—jumps into the air with all four legs. This could be dangerous if you get too close ... But P immediately wants to "help". I have a feeling he wants to put on a show. He has a red hockey stick with which he wants to drive the horse on the path. A dog also seems to be running around, maybe other animals. Somebody says: "How stupid that this guy is being so self-important". I have a feeling he will be injured and, a little later, the man who was driving the wagon comes and says that he is lying on his back, hands up, but that he is not seriously hurt ... A woman orders the horse to stand still and it obeys immediately—so it wasn't a wild horse after all ... I call P, then find him lying in a very narrow dog kennel. I go down on my knees to look in, shaking both fists in powerless, burning rage, shouting: "Stupid, stupid, stupid!" He says he is not seriously hurt, but how can I get him out of this kennel? (Ava, 06/2000)

Here is the Fourth Plane power struggle in this calcinatio dream. The horse (often a fiery symbol) and other animals (representing the instincts perhaps) are out of control, and this leads to accident and injury for the man who is showing off, and "powerless burning rage" in the woman, who is arrogant and judging. There is quite a distortion of the personality evident in both its male and female aspects. The woman who tames the horse signifies a wiser aspect of the dreamer who has understood the nature of the horse. Psychologically speaking, the mind, symbolised by the masculine, is unsuccessful in trying to control the wild, fiery horse with yet more fire (the "red" stick). He is unwise in trying to exert his will and power over the horse and ends up in a "very narrow" and demeaning place (the dog kennel). Ava's suppressed anger comes out as "powerless" outrage at this behavior. The dream shows Ava the inner conflict between masculine and feminine and its limiting effect.

In the subsequent dream quoted below, there is, in contrast, a beautiful resonance and cooperation between masculine and feminine. Balance has been achieved. Rather than calling the man stupid, the woman asks him for help in a rather delicate task.

### Shining Gold

A big, dark man (I cannot see his face), is kneeling on the floor, fixing a bracelet on his arm. This reminds me that I would also like to wear my fine gold necklace. It has a sort of fastener with a little ring that is difficult to close by myself. So I ask him to help me. As I pull on the fine necklace, I realise that it is intertwined with a heavy golden necklace, and both of them are stuck in a kind of treasure chest. I open it and find a handbag made of pure, shining gold … On opening the handbag, the two necklaces are free and the man can now fix the fine one on my neck. (Ava, 07/2000)

The "gold", which is the prize for the difficult battles in Fourth Plane, makes its appearance. We are moving into the positive phase—the Wise Self (the jewellery worn around the neck also prefigures the Fifth Plane to come). Notice the detail that is repeated in both dreams—"I go down on my knees to look in" and a big, dark man "is kneeling on the floor." Repetitions in dreams are never coincidental and can be very helpful in tracking developments in the dreamer. In this case, kneeling is associated with anger and rage at the masculine in the first dream; in the second dream, however, the kneeling man is engaged in the finely skilled action of putting on a bracelet, which facilitates her own adornment. The "Shining Gold" dream leads to a coniunctio—the man puts the golden necklace around Ava's neck.

This coniunctio image is one of several dream experiences that open Ava to the passage of the Fifth Plane. Many dream events are needed to really achieve a balance between the opposing forces in the psyche. This is a major task, and it can take years, but every time an accomplishment is shown in the dreams, we are encouraged on the path. This is the "gold" we find again and again.

Ava's intellect and her, hitherto neglected, feeling nature were, at this stage, coming more into balance in herself and her life. The dreamwork was awakening a desire in her to pursue the spiritual path more deeply, though she would continue to be challenged in subtle ways as to the influence of her will and mind in this journey. Separatio in Albedo was showing itself in Ava's increasing introversion as she separated from the world (and her marriage to an extent) in order to go more deeply into her process.

## Summary

Of our travellers, David starts off from a "lower base". He has considerably more work to do on himself in order to get past his mind and go deeper. Ava, although she started her quest much earlier, has less psychological baggage to deal with. As a consequence, her mind is a little more "open" and clearer. Her guiding spirit, so to speak, can break through more easily.

David's journey to this point has been one of confronting his psychologically crippling issues in order to access the subtler levels of his inner world. He has also needed to establish a good mother archetype within. Once this had been achieved, he was able to go deeper to contain and transform his deep rage towards the feminine. Jung's view is that, as in alchemy, our relationship to nature and to the feminine is the relationship to our soul (Jung, 1983). At this stage of David's process, the gradual healing that is taking place is enabling him to be more in his body and appreciate the value of touch and intimacy with the feminine.

Ava's journey to date has seen a very clear awareness of each plane— the Creative Self, the Loving Self, and Wise Self. Her struggles with the shadow side, particularly in the Fourth Plane, have been relatively uneventful. Psychologically, she has focused more on balancing the masculine (mind) with the feminine (feeling). The heart centre seems to have been the most active energy centre.

Both David and Ava have shown evidence in their dreams of progressing through a succession of levels of consciousness, each showing to the dreamer themes and qualities unique to that level. In the case of David, the individual planes are less clearly differentiated because his dreams are heavily overlaid by his psychological issues at this stage. Nevertheless, the movement from instincts (Nigredo), to mind (Albedo) and spirit (Citrinitas and beyond) is very much apparent in his dreams.

## CHAPTER FIVE

# Awakening

The white light appears ... I just remember the light and the peace it brought me.

—*Ava*, 2003

## *The landscape of awakening*

### *The Fifth Plane—The Sacred Self*

Thus far in Albedo (in the subtle mental, third, and fourth planes), we have seen an increasing emergence of soul consciousness as the dominance of the mind lessens, and yet, the mind is still a force to be reckoned with. It is only when we reach the last two planes of consciousness in Albedo, that we have entered the realms of the soul. The first of these is the *Fifth Plane*.

This plane is concerned with the search for our own divinity, our "hidden treasure"—that in us which is pure light. At this stage of our process, we begin to access our "inner light", which, according to the Sufi traditions, is the *light of splendour*—the divinity of our being. The imagery of this level differs from that of the preceding levels of consciousness; rather than emanating from the mind (personal or collective)

111

only, it is also experienced in visions or dreams as an intensely bright, white light. In the classical mystical traditions, all personal thoughts and images disappear. The Tibetan Buddhist tradition refers to this as *luminous mind*—a very subtle level of consciousness in which the mental imagery begins to radiate a deeper, subtler light lying beyond it. This is a preparatory step towards the experience of *clear light*—a non-dualistic state of consciousness beyond dreams (Wangyal, 1998).

Of course, during our journey as seekers we are tested in our faith; typically, during the Fourth Plane transit. There comes a point at which we fall into an empty space, like a waste land; we experience an existential nightmare that we must live through, until such time that the light of this inner space is revealed to us. During the PTP, most dreamers start to experience the luminescence of objects in their dreams in the second phase of the Fourth Plane transit as the soul's light begins to break through.

At this level of the Fifth Plane, the soul's light is expressed in dreams as qualities. When our inner world is dominated by the light of the mind, it expresses itself in our dreams (in the Creative, Loving, and Wise Self) in images of objects, people, and scenarios. The light of the soul at the level of the Fifth Plane, on the other hand, shows itself through qualities of splendour, sovereignty (majesty), peacefulness, sacredness, and innocence. The main purpose and effect of the dream images is to convey the qualities or vibration of the soul's inner light.

As we become conscious of the spirit in us, we become increasingly attracted by the sacred. This may take the form of the spiritual path of prayer and spiritual practice, or it may be a sacred path in relationship or community. However we define it, this is the level of the *Sacred Self*.

Table 5.1. Themes and features of the Fifth Plane—The Sacred Self.

- Sovereignty, majesty, magnificence, splendour
- Palace, court, grand buildings
- Sacredness—sacred rituals, prayer, worshipping/glorifying
- Ecstasy, a sense of awe
- Temples, churches, holy places, pilgrimage, going to the East
- Holy men/women, priests/priestesses
- Peace, retreat
- Finding treasure, mining for ore, jewellery (worn around the head and neck)

*(Continued)*

Table 5.1. (Continued).

---

- Innocence, e.g. children, angels, cherubs
- Hermaphroditic/androgynous figures
- Secrets, esoteric knowledge
- Intense white light, sword of light
- Concerts, music, singing, the voice, communicating
- The number four, mandalas
- Landscapes of forests, abundant greenery, gardens
- Colours—purple, green, turquoise, peacock colours (gold/blue/green)
- Healing images

---

Inner sovereignty is commonly communicated through dream imagery of royalty, the archetypal king and queen, and a sense of majesty. Splendour and magnificence are also expressed in our dreams in the form of beautiful, ornate temples, places of worship, cathedrals (as we see in David's story) or, if the religious aspect is not so emphasised, palaces or grand, majestic buildings. A retreatant describes a typical dream scene: "I find myself in the upper part of a huge basilica—a domed building or church. I walk down and through the central part, which is full of religious artefacts".

In the Sacred Self, there is an increasing sensitivity to the sacred, religious, and angelic aspects of ourselves—a longing to connect with spirit, without and within. This theme of sacredness is expressed through dream images of spiritual worship and ritual, churches, prayer, temples, holy men and women, and through an intangible sense of the subtle worlds.

A common theme found in the Sacred Self is looking for, and finding, treasure, or mining for ore. Here, one is reminded of the famous phrase from the texts of the Hadith Qudsi in Islam: "I was a hidden treasure, longing to be known", implying that divinity is a hidden treasure in all of us, longing to be experienced consciously. This is reminiscent of Maslow's idea of the higher potential in the psyche (1994). Perhaps this is the treasure we are unconsciously apprehending—that which outshines our limited self-image.

Along with the sense of sacredness and majesty comes the theme of peacefulness—a complete absence of conflict and discordance. This kind of peacefulness is found on retreat and in the great forests of nature, and is in contrast to the intense conflict and inner struggle of the Fourth

Plane. The presence of young children in Fifth Plane dreams reflects the innocent aspect of this level.

The landscapes of Sacred Self dreams are beautiful gardens, which symbolise the beauty of the soul—the *garden of the heart* in Sufism (Bakhtiar, 1991)—or vast areas of greenery, particularly big forests characterised by tranquility. Trees in dreams are often tall and shaped like praying hands; the taller the tree, the more transcendental is its quality. Occasionally, the landscapes may show the quality of the Fifth Plane in the form of majestic mountains.

Finally, there is the theme of communication and knowledge that is "secret" or esoteric. Mystical writings speak of "the world of dignity and serenity and firmness; the enigmas and the secrets" (Harris, 1981, pp. 43–44). The voice, often singing, expresses an inner, soulful feeling in Fifth Plane dreams. The beautiful, rich colours of the Fifth Plane reflect something of the splendour of this level—a culmination of all that has gone before. This stage of the journey is also characterised by an increase in lucid dreaming and symmetry in dream images (see Chapter Six). Dreams sometimes become visions (where the image is seen in waking consciousness with eyes open).

The following dream from a woman's retreat process exemplifies many of the themes of the Sacred Self: "splendour"; purity; light; holy people and places; a sense of awe; music and communication; Fifth Plane colours, including greenery; and healing. The strong heart feeling of the dream (the loving presence of the spiritual teacher, healing through love) characterises the spiritual quality of the Fifth Plane and differentiates it from the more impersonal nature of the plane of consciousness to come, of which the purity of the Virgin Mary is a sign.

### Virgin Mary

I saw the Virgin Mary and felt her pure, sweet and healing energy. I stayed there for a long time and then saw a very tall figure of light with a big sword of light (pointing downwards) behind her. I knew that this was Melchizedek and I was very much in awe. Then, my spiritual teacher was there and I felt held by his gentle, loving presence. He led me to a kind of court—a place of splendour, a palace in colours of gold, purple and green … There was music and story-telling and an atmosphere of celebration, generosity and spiritual wealth. My attention was drawn to a darker place, where

I saw a monk, holding a wounded person. He held a lamp in one hand and had a light in his heart. He told me that the way to heal is to bring light into darkness and to kindle the light in my heart. He led me up many, many steps into brilliance and light and a landscape of nature, greenery and Greek temples. He showed me plants with which to heal people. I felt great love ... Passing through the temples I had a taste of the heavenly music of Bach. I heard very loudly in my head one of my favourite pieces—"Jesu, Joy of Man's Desiring". I felt the magnificence and strength of that energy.

In *Pathways to Ecstasy*, Patricia Garfield encounters archetypal figures in her dreams entitled "Peacock", "Pale White Cherubic Child", and "Branching Woman" (a woman with a majestic crown of branching horns like an antelope) at this stage of sacredness and light in her process. She places these dream figures at the sacred centre (the fifth point) of the Buddhist mandala that she was using as the template for her process (Garfield, 1989).

The main psychological block to the Sacred Self lies in problems of self-image. The experience of divine splendour at this level brings a flawed sense of self into sharp focus. In this dream, we see this in the form of a "wounded" person. Typically, the seeds of poor self-image began in childhood, and so, when we first encounter the level of the Sacred Self, images of emaciated, hungry or injured children, or other forms of woundedness appear in our dreams. Self-healing through love and nourishment is needed before we can experience the angelic innocence that was our birthright.

The qualities of the Sacred Self may show themselves, initially, as distortions. For instance, one can value sacredness in life to the extent that it becomes a kind of sanctimoniousness and prudishness that has an oppressive effect on people around us. An inflated sense of our own greatness and "specialness", spiritual or otherwise, is also a distortion of this level of self. Similarly, one can become so peaceful as to be indolent and lazy. Nothing in life is worth struggling for when we can meditate, go on retreat or simply sit around doing nothing. As ever, our dreams will show us our distortions in a form that is impossible to ignore!

Often, in mid-life, we find that we have identified with an ideal, but over the course of time, its meaning to us has been eroded. Since our sense of self is identified with the ideal, our self-image is threatened and we may feel hopeless, even suicidal. Our soul suffers. We have lost touch with our core being and the impulse is to self-destruct.

The challenge of the Sacred Self is to go beyond our identifications to a place in ourselves that is eternal—our original light. On finding that the light, showing itself in our dreams, is, in fact, an even greater light than that of our human aura, we realise that our limited self-image has obscured our own splendour. What we thought we were—our old sense of self—is stripped away. The veil of the mind has to be torn aside in order to reveal what lies behind it.

## The Sixth Plane—The Pure Self

The passage through Albedo concludes with the most subtle level of consciousness—the *Sixth Plane*. Here, we come into contact with the purest part of our being: the ground of consciousness out of which the sense of soul originates—the *Pure Self*. In the Tibetan Bon tradition, the "ground of being" is depicted as an "emptiness that is clear light"—a pure state of consciousness that is empty of thoughts and luminous (Wangyal, 2012). This is the level of essence, or "seed state", in which we experience the fundamental qualities in us as lights, together with a sense of unity and cosmic consciousness (Harris, 1981; Wangyal, 1998).

The change of consciousness upon entering the Pure Self is quite radical; in the Sixth Plane we awaken to the experience of pure consciousness, pure vibration—free of impressions. The mystical experience of the Sixth Plane is called *Sat-Chit-Ananda* (pure being; pure consciousness; pure bliss) in Hinduism.

In this state of the Pure Self, we feel transparent, translucent, almost out of life, in an unreal place. In being barely conscious of our body, this sense of unreality is close to, but not the same as, psychological depersonalisation. The difference is that, rather than feeling disconnected from the body, our body feels like empty space and we are "connected" to light. We are free of thought and our emotions have a very different, fine, subtle quality. Up to the level of the Fourth Plane, we are aware of the full range of human emotions, but from Fifth Plane onwards, the emotions become less and less personal as the spiritual journey progresses. Fifth Plane emotions include awe, ecstasy, inner peace; in the Sixth Plane, the feelings become so fine they are only present "in potentia"—frozen, like unmelted ice.

The following excerpt from a Sixth Plane dream I had on retreat, is a literal illustration of this particular aspect of the Pure Self in the striking image of ice radiating warmth.

### Polar Bear

I came across a large fountain that was frozen. I marvelled at its orb-like structure as I scaled down the orb's frame. In the spaces where there would have been water, I looked through (the structure) and saw the whole cosmos! With brilliant blue sky as a backdrop, I saw huge, colourful planets in the sky space with bands of white snow and white clouds around, partly covering them. I knew each was a plane in itself, and that I was being given the privilege of seeing something of these subtle realms. It looked breathtakingly beautiful, but I didn't want to "fall through" the gaps in the structure into this inner space, so I carefully climbed across and down. I stopped on the way (in the fountain) to rest on an ice rock, and it spoke to me, saying, "Don't you mind the ice?" I said, "No, it's lovely," and some of the ice became water as I sat on it. It felt completely pure. Then I rested my head on the ice rock and realised I could see its "polar bear" nature within the rock … and there was a feeling of warmth coming from the ice rock! I felt completely innocent.

Upon waking, I am stunned by the dream's beauty and vastness. It seemed to take me to a place of boundless, universal perspective, which dwarfed the importance of my mind world.

At this level, there is a tremendous sense of clarity, spaciousness, and freedom, but also detachment, as we reach a place in us that is impersonal and remote. In Buddhism, the skeleton Buddha represents this stage as the death of the existential self, which brings total freedom. Or, we can think of the Hindu Rishis, sitting alone in the Himalayas with nothing to warm them. In terms of consciousness, this level is at the borderline between spirit and life. It is where the self dies in order that spirit can be born in us.

Sudden "road to Damascus" experiences aside, it is usually only through the exclusive attunement to light that we can become conscious of spirit (Bucke, 1923). Everything may become light in dreams and light appears in meditation—the white, luminous mind of Tibetan Buddhism. The nature of this light is feminine. The divine feminine is symbolised by Mary in Christianity, as the Skekinah in Judaism, and Fatimah in Islam and these may appear in Sixth Plane dreams.

Dreams at this level show landscapes of snow and ice, images of white birds flying, amazing clear blue skies, along with a feeling of clarity, purity, and freedom. They are often set in remote places, high up in the mountains, removed from life. These are places of stillness and unreal beauty where eagles soar. One retreatant recounts a Sixth Plane dream towards the end of her retreat: "I see my spiritual teacher on a huge snow-peaked mountain in the middle of a pure, blue sky". Creatures present in dreams show either the qualities of detachment or purity.

Perhaps the most important psychological block to the experience of the Pure Self and the inner light is our guilt and resentment. Whilst we may have set these issues aside at a mental level earlier in the journey, such negative impressions seem to penetrate even to the level of our essence. As a result, a sense of inner imperfection stands in the way of accessing divine perfection, causing resentment towards oneself, others, and God. The distortions of this plane can take the form of intolerance of our own, or others', imperfections; coldness; or as a constant striving to be perfect—the "addiction to perfection" described by Marion Woodman (1982). This can also present itself through the fear of discovering our imperfections by avoiding engagement with life. These themes will be present in our dreams.

Table 5.2. Themes and features of the Sixth Plane—The Pure Self.

- Purity, innocence
- Stillness, spaciousness, serenity
- White light, luminosity
- Ascending
- White birds, e.g. dove, swan, eagle
- Clarity e.g. crystal, diamonds
- The Virgin Mary, the Shekinah, Fatimah, Buddha, forms of the divine feminine
- Eternal, timeless, cosmic consciousness
- Non-attached, freedom, indifference, remoteness
- Immaculate landscapes of snow, ice, snowy mountainous regions, like the Alps, the Andes
- Colours—white and pale blue

The psychological blocks can be dissolved when we are able to develop compassion towards ourselves and others. Our perfection lies within our limitation; perfection (divine transcendence) and imperfection (divine immanence) sit alongside one another. From the detached space that we encounter in our dreams, we are able to see what lies behind our struggles and understand the inter-connectedness of life. This enables us to forgive.

Thus, in the gnostic and mystic visions, the divine perfection is sought within us; it is only in the act of surrendering our ego to this perfection within that we begin to experience its nature, which is pure spirit, pure energy, pure consciousness, pure bliss. So, in a way, this surrendering is an act of forgiveness—forgiving ourselves, others, and God. It is a kind of baptism that we experience, a true inner cleansing.

## The alchemical stage of Citrinitas

The ascent of consciousness through Albedo culminates in the level of Pure Self, followed by the mystical stage of *Citrinitas*—a transcendental stage, represented in alchemy by yellow (the colour of the sun), symbolising universal spirit (Evola, 1995). Typically, Citrinitas is not observable as a discrete event or process; usually, there is a direct transition from the Pure Self to the descent in Rubedo. It is difficult to describe Citrinitas because of its transcendental nature; it is a stage of "no self".

Citrinitas, in its most profound form, is a mystical stage—a state beyond the planes of consciousness, beyond existence. Although the experience of this stage is "out of life", so to speak, it should not be considered as a separate realm. Indeed, from the spiritual perspective, the manifested universe—this life—continually emerges out of, and depends on, the transcendental consciousness for its existence. Existential consciousness emerges out of the transcendental (nothingness).

In this stage, spirit absorbs the soul so that soul is completely merged with spirit. It is the *royal alchemical marriage* in which the individual consciousness of the soul disappears and duality ceases (Jung, 1983). No self is left; only a transcendental state of oneness. It is the state of union. This is the greatest spiritual challenge—the union with the Self, union with God, experiencing oneness as the only reality (Abt, 2004). That is what alchemy is essentially about—the journey to oneness (See Figure 3). In Buddhism, it is called *sunnyata* (emptiness, pure bliss); the Sufis call it union with God—*fanā*.

Figure 3. The royal alchemical marriage.
Copyright © Adam McLean 2009.

In order to proceed from Albedo to Citrinitas, our sense of selfhood has to be broken down. In such a radical phase of ego disintegration, a person can easily identify with the contents of the collective unconscious instead of transcending it to reach a truly non-dualistic state of being. Some mystics have described the experience as an abyss of terror. It can feel like a mental breakdown; the transition from the Pure Self to Citrinitas seems similar to a schizophrenic state, except that one is carried by a sense of purpose and destination. Not paying any attention to what one sees, hears or thinks prevents ego inflation, as well as disintegration on returning again to everyday life. This is where the traveller on the path is really tested. At this point, faith is crucial; it is what holds us together. It cannot be stressed too strongly that someone who has an unstable or fragile sense of self should not be allowed to attempt such a radical experience.

When approaching Citrinitas, confusion reigns; it is impossible to focus, thought processes come to a halt, and one enters an empty, trance-like state, which is beyond being and doing. Only through surrendering to the divine will, can the clarity of the transcendental state transpire. An incredible sense of peace, bliss, and lucidity accompanies this experience; it is beyond words. Suddenly, profound intuition speaks to us through sound, image, or realisation. "Spiritual intelligence" has become conscious in us.

Citrinitas does not manifest in dream images, but it can be inferred from the feeling tone of the dream—a sense of nothingness, timelessness, bliss. In profound spiritual experiences, the transcendental light appears, initially, as *black light*, but then reveals itself as an intensely luminous, colourful light at this high point of the spiritual awakening process. The spiritual *winds* may form part of dreams and visions and become very powerful, drawing consciousness inwards. Visions become revelatory, theophanic, ecstatic. There are no psychological issues to be considered in Citrinitas as it is the stage of "no self". Dreams at this stage will reflect this absence of psychological material; our minds become simply a mirror of our pure essence and oneness.

More commonly, Citrinitas is experienced in a less dramatic way. Usually, it comes as a flash of insight concerning our life or ourselves. Such an experience of our spirit makes a deep and lasting impression upon us—often resulting in a life-changing decision. Citrinitas is not easily recognised and is rare, but its presence is implicit in the PTP.

Table 5.3. Themes and features of Citrinitas.

- Disintegration of self, sense of dying
- Sense of no body
- A very subtle sense of body as light, expanding
- Transcendence, oneness, beyond time, ecstasy, bliss, peace
- Nothingness, emptiness
- Black light
- Spiritual winds
- Intense white light, tunnel of light
- Seeing light above crown of the head
- Sun
- Beings of light, orbs of light
- Regression to the source of everything (the alchemical *prima materia*)
- Seeing ancestral lineage (human or non-human)
- Fish
- Coniunctio of soul and spirit—marriage
- Flashes of many colours (particularly golden), emerald green, coloured and black dots, black

I encountered the black light of Citrinitas in the following dream.

### Black Light

I become lucid as I notice light radiating from within the landscape.
I surrender to the guidance of the dream and find myself being
swept upward and inwards with a tremendous inner force. The
landscape disappears and I am aware only of a luminous black
light all around me. All awareness of space and time disappears—
there is only oneness.

Towards the end of a long retreat, a man in his early sixties had the following dream where Citrinitas is a "low-key" experience.

### Empty

Indistinctly, I see the smiling face of my (retreat) guide. Also a space
that had been full is empty now. It needs filling. A voice says "This
is where Christ is held". The emptiness refers to my heart centre
being emptied of myself.

A second example shows a more radical experience of Citrinitas,
where the self actually disintegrates to become "no self". During her
Citrinitas transit towards the end of a fifteen day retreat, this retreatant went through a series of visionary experiences (in the waking state)
which are given in summary form.

### No Self

*Disintegrating self*
1. Untidy house, chaos, can't find anything, can't do anything.
2. Vision of being in the sea. Light appears/disappears. I am lost.
   Sea is on fire. Hands reaching up out of sea. Sea monsters try to
   grab me.
3. I see black dots in front of my eyes, appearing all over.
4. I see chaotic pictures of body parts and stone carvings all
   mixed up.
5. I experience myself rising into a dome of a cathedral of light.
   Beings of light appear.

*Virtually no self*

6. I see intense white light above the crown of my head. I am rising up to the light. Light starts to pour down from crown into centre of my chest.

*No self*

7. Light expands, filling my body and beyond. Body-ness disappears completely. Sense of light but no sense of self.

*Porous sense of self*

8. Sense of being amongst stars. Memory of past returns. I experience the essences of people.

*Porous sense of self/no self*

9. Black, white and coloured dots in front of my eyes. Visions of purgatory—destruction. Skeletons, skulls, hands reaching out from rubble and endless crumbling of stone. Whole cities collapsed, buildings, mountains, all collapsing. Felt devastated. Sense of "dark night of the soul".

This series of visions culminates in the experience of a dark night of the soul, indicating that the retreatant is on the cusp of a major spiritual transition (Corbin, 1994). After this experience of the disintegration of the self, this woman moved into the Rubedo stage, quickly and easily, where she integrated her experience, showing greater insight into her process. Some of her subsequent dreams, which expressed her readiness to go home and re-enter into life, are included in the Rubedo section of this chapter.

## The alchemical operations in Citrinitas

In Citrinitas, the mystical stage of the sun, there will be:

- purification principally by fire (*calcinatio*), which becomes extremely intense (rare);
- *sublimatio* experienced as insight and realisation (more common);
- the royal alchemical marriage (the *third coniunctio*);
- the *third mortificatio*—death of the state of "perfection".

For the mystic, the predominance of sun energy at this stage can manifest in calcinatio dreams of hot deserts, together with very dry throat and dehydration in the waking state. More typically in therapy, though, such transcendental experiences do not manifest since it is unusual for a client to become totally free of the mind, let alone have a transcendental, or even celestial, experience. Instead, clients experience great insights in sublimatio-type dreams showing the presence of the transcendental function—that which enables opposites in our psyche to unite (Edinger, 1991).

In ideal form, the *third coniunctio* of Citrinitas is symbolised in dreams by the king and queen of the royal alchemical marriage, representing soul and spirit united. In the PTP, we approach this state in gradual steps; first shown by dreams in which we unite with our inner contra-sexual figure. The coniunctio opposites of spirit verses matter might also be expressed in dreams in forms representing our higher self (the angel, for example) and our lower self (an instinctual animal, perhaps).

In the following series of dreams recorded by a woman approaching Citrinitas during her transformation process, the marriage of king and queen and then her own marriage mark coniunctio and the end of Albedo. The second dream shows Fifth Plane themes of ritual, singing, the presence of the transcendental in the number three and, finally, the Sixth Plane sense of isolation—a "very lonely place to be". The third dream indicates that purification has led to the experience of Citrinitas.

### Getting Married

There is a very young king and an older queen; they are getting married.

### A Very Lonely Place to Be

I am getting married; there is a Buddhist religious ceremony. It is Christmas and there are three young men, one especially ardent, who carry out a ceremony where they are receiving gifts. They are singing in wonderful tenor voices. The animals have been let in; they are gentle and well behaved. In the dream, I am aware of a wall or mask which I show to other people to hide my devotion and love of God; and how other people's forms of enjoyment and entertainment are not mine—and that feels a very lonely place to be.

Ananda

There was a dream of purification. Then I woke up with a bitter taste in my mouth and my body a little faint. Later, I woke up with the sound of the "Ananda" song in my mind and the feeling of nothingness and great peace.

Finally, there is the death of the perfect state through a *third mortificatio* dream in order to allow the re-entry to life through the passage of Rubedo.

## The alchemical stage of Rubedo

So far, we have witnessed the journey from Nigredo through to Citrinitas. Now, the most important part of the cycle follows—the return to the earth in the *Rubedo* stage. The lessons of the process must now be integrated into everyday life. It is the stage of coming into life.

In alchemy, the purpose of the Rubedo stage was to enable the alchemist to integrate the psychospiritual outcomes of the process into a coherent sense of self before re-entering the world. It was recognised that it could take quite some time, possibly even years, to fully synthesise and substantiate the insights and experiences. Likewise, in the context of our PTP, it is crucial that the treasure found in the dream images and insights gained through the experiences of the subtle self can be incorporated and bear fruit in daily life. It is a great challenge—perhaps the most difficult part of the journey. Once again, we must bring our will to bear upon our manifestation in life. Consciously working with the dreams can really facilitate here.

In this journey of descent through Rubedo, the planes are again revisited in reverse order, although they are not as clearly differentiated as in the ascent. Once again, worldly themes and concerns appear in the dream imagery; typically, in scenes of being back in the city, eating and drinking, and celebrating.

Rubedo is the red stage in alchemy, symbolising the descending spirit (white signifying spirit in ascent in Albedo). It is often clear that Rubedo has begun when the colour red (or red-brown, signifying spirit *in* body) becomes prominent in dreams at the stage of union of spirit, soul, mind, and body. The ultimate goal of Rubedo is described as the *spiritualisation of matter* and, simultaneously, *materialisation of spirit*

Table 5.4. Themes and features of Rubedo.

---

- Return to worldly life/work
- Personal issues return, but seen from a transpersonal perspective
- Instinctual forces return
- Balancing of opposites
- Coagulatio—food
- Celebration, e.g. drinking wine
- Rebirth, resurrection
- Androgynous figures
- Appearance of the crone, mother earth figure
- The number four, mandalas, symmetrical shapes
- Personal and worldly settings
- Profusion of colours, profusion of treasures, riches, colourful foods, flowers
- Gold, gold/silver, black, black light, emerald green
- Red, red-brown, red blood

---

(where the black of Nigredo has become white, then gold, emerald green and a multiplicity of colours) (Jung, 1983).

In the dream research, it was found that most people travelled through Rubedo quickly and experienced only a small number of the themes listed in the table above. The issues they had wrestled with in Albedo returned on the descent, but with less intensity and with the view, now, to incorporating and coagulating the experience in their personality. Those retreatants who had progressed to a point in their lives where few psychological issues arose in Albedo experienced fewer problems in Rubedo. By contrast, psychotherapy clients took much longer to complete the Rubedo stage in comparison to Albedo, and compared to retreatants. Seen in the context of a lifetime, there may be many cycles of ascent and descent before we reach the fruition of Rubedo.

The two dreams below (consecutive in the dreamer's process) show the transition from the "feeling of nothingness and great peace" back to worldly life.

Taxi

I get into a taxi and the woman driver is very pregnant. She takes me to where I want to go (home?) and I make all the preparations for the birth.

### Diamonds

I am preparing for a journey and I have flown into Heathrow Airport and am coming through customs. I have three very large diamonds with me and I wonder if I will be stopped, although … I have come by them legitimately … I get the phone number of a third person from a male cross-dresser (he is a secretary from a London newspaper) … he is going to polish up the diamonds for me … Eventually, the stones are ready and I put one in my crown, one in my third eye and one in my heart. I wake up suddenly in the night and a gold light is just hanging in the air.

Several of the themes listed in Table 5.4 are present in these dreams: return to worldly life (taxi, airport, customs), the city (London), rebirth (the pregnant woman driver), treasure of the transcendental (three diamonds), an androgynous figure (the male "cross-dresser") and finally the gold light "just hanging in the air". In alchemy, this carrying over of the gold into waking life is a very significant step on the path towards the materialisation of spirit (Evola, 1995). The three diamonds are placed inside the body, in the three upper chakras—a coagulatio, bringing the spiritual into the body.

The dream excerpts below follow on from the intense "no-self" experience of the retreatant given in the Citrinitas section.

### My Beloved

I was transported to a café with a dance floor in my home town and there I was dancing with my beloved, who was really my own self. I danced in and out of his/her enfoldment, never losing touch or the sense of the loving gaze.

### Switzerland

I was again on a mountain top with snow and light and I saw a tall figure of light—my spiritual teacher. He put his arm around me and I said: "Show me". He showed me the immense landscape from the mountain top—the stars, the villages and towns below, a French village with a round cathedral and greenery and water … We walked downhill and came to a green place with people and cows and milk. They were making cheese so I realised that this was Switzerland. We went to a shop and bought wine.

### The Party

> I cooked food and had a desire for good, healthy, home cooking,
> like soup and salad and baked things … I cooked lots of delicious
> dishes and prepared a party. The whole house was lit with candles;
> there was classical music and I had created cosy places to sit and
> talk.

This series begins with a coniunctio in which the dreamer realises that
she and the "beloved" are one. Then, she returns to the mountain top
(with "snow and light"), of the Sixth Plane and Pure Self, and meets
her spiritual teacher, who helps her to make the transition downwards.
Green appears repeatedly, together with signs of life—the cows, milk,
cheese and wine. Finally, there is a ritual celebration to honour successful re-entry into life.

A woman in psychotherapy has the following dream which seems to
encapsulate the development of ascent into the Rubedo stage.

### Family of Monkeys

> I am running up the stairs in a tall building with a family of mon-
> keys, all different ages … At the top, I have an ecstatic experience—
> reciting words from scripture. There is reference to a birthday. I am
> floating with ecstasy. Then, I need to unravel the rainbow-coloured
> muslin bandages on the monkeys (I am their mother?).

The ascent of the "tall building" is suggestive of the ascent of her psyche; the monkeys, representing the return of the instinctual, accompany
her. The ascent culminates in an "ecstatic experience" and "birthday".
But then there is a need for an unraveling of the "rainbow-coloured"
coverings; a reversal of the mummification process leads to an unveiling
of her reborn self.

## The alchemical operations in Rubedo

In Rubedo, there will be:

- *coagulatio* and *calcinatio*—the two most important operations for the
  incorporation of spirit and soul into body and mind;
- *solutio* follows; and, finally,
- *the fourth coniunctio*.

*The alchemical operations of coagulatio and calcinatio in Rubedo*

In Rubedo, spirit and soul must be helped to incarnate into life; the transcendental experience has to become concretised. Coagulatio of our subtle consciousness into physical reality occurs when our spirit begins to re-enter the physical world and our consciousness embraces the grosser, material aspect of reality. Dreams of cooking and eating are typical of this operation in Rubedo.

"The Party" dream quoted earlier typifies classical coagulatio imagery (cooking, celebration, and a profusion of delicious dishes) and hints at calcinatio—"the whole house was lit with candles".

In a second part of the same dream, calcinatio is developed further—a test tube is taken out of the flames and "gold" is discovered. The retreatant finds a way to retrieve it from the incubating receptacle (the retreat process, symbolised by the test tube) in order to materialise the "gold" of her process.

### Gold

I was back in the chemistry laboratory at my old university. I took a test tube out of the flames and looked at it. It had a black background and there were many patches of gold on this. It reminded me of a painting by Gustav Klimt of a Madonna. I was left with the problem of how to get the gold out of the test tube. There wasn't enough of it to be scraped out or filtered off. The only way to do this was to sublimate it onto a piece of glass.

The calcinatio at this stage of the PTP is, according to alchemists, the most intense; the strength of the fire having the power to change the structure of the psyche at a "cellular" level. In this way, calcinatio now prepares the mind and body to receive and manifest pure spirit in the alchemical "gold".

*The alchemical operation of solutio in Rubedo*

Solutio is necessary to ensure that soul and spirit can "flow" into the body and mind so to speak, allowing our awareness of our subtle body and the corresponding subtle levels of self to be "dissolved" into the gross self (which lives in the world). For this solutio, the heart has to open once again, and it does so with the loss of the high state of consciousness in Citrinitas and Albedo. This loss is felt as a sadness—a pain that breaks open the heart—whereupon the compassion of the heart begins to flow. It was Oscar Wilde who asked, rhetorically: "How else but through a broken heart may the Lord Christ enter in?" (Wilde, The Ballad of Reading Gaol (V), 1897, p. 122) Rubedo flows from the broken heart.

At the end of her retreat, a woman has a "broken-hearted" dream where she says goodbye to the innocence of the inner world she has been inhabiting on retreat and encounters the critical world (which is also within her). The number four indicates the completion of her process.

### Four Tickets

My young daughter is distraught. We are saying goodbye to young infants. I feel that a part of life is closing down. I comfort her. Later, I take the four tickets she has forgotten to school; the teacher treats me with unwarranted contempt.

### The alchemical operation of coniunctio in Rubedo

The final operation in Rubedo is the *fourth coniunctio*—marriage with the earth. We now conjoin completely with our earth nature, which has been transformed through the process from the gross to the subtle. Finally, the soul, the spirit and the body are together. (David's dream "Luminous Face", in "David Awakens" is a very good example of the fourth coniunctio).

This concludes our description of the journey through a complete alchemical cycle containing the ascent and descent through the planes of consciousness. Of course, Rubedo does not signal the end of the Psychospiritual Transformation Process. It's the end of a cycle (perhaps a retreat or a particularly intense period of personal growth), but not the end of transformation. The larger cycle can be observed again and again in the course of a lifetime, be it on retreat, in psychotherapy or in spontaneous transformational phases of our life.

The cyclical nature of the process is clearly seen when the dreams of the same person are compared from PTP to PTP. The dream research has documented the progression in the transformation process, year after year, with each PTP representing a cycle within a much larger process. In the beginning of the process, the stage of Nigredo is prolonged and intense. In subsequent cycles, it shortens each time whilst the Albedo stage becomes longer. Once Albedo is "fully developed", Nigredo and Albedo are "shortened", but Citrinitas and Rubedo grow in richness, profundity, and duration. It's rather like a wave or pulse of intense energy that moves from Nigredo through to Rubedo as the PTP is observed over time.

### The upper energy centres

The throat centre

The Yogis refer to this as *vishuddha*—the centre of vibration, communication, sound, and intuition. The Buddhists see ego pride and its opposite—envy—as a distortion of the true qualities of the throat centre. The Sufis see this centre as the entry point to our individual soul consciousness, which contains divine qualities. The implication is that, whatever our self-image, our true being is invested with spiritual richness. Vanity is a false attempt to identify with this true richness. Similarly, envy is the projection of the richness of our own soul. In David's "Radiant Happiness" dream (04/2009) in Chapter Five, the themes of music and light indicate the opening of the throat centre.

When working with the Waking Dream Process and tracking the dream through the body, sensations felt around the ears, the throat, shoulders, back of the neck, or the shoulder blades, are likely to be connected to the throat centre. Sometimes, blocked anger or tears can be experienced as a pain or constriction in the throat. Again, focusing on the felt experience provides a direct connection for the dreamer to whatever blocks there are and a way in to what is lying beneath.

Ava's dreams show the opening of the energy centres from base to throat in "Turning in Bliss" (06/2002) and the full activation of the throat centre in "Resurrection" (04/2006) in Chapter Five of the "Travellers' Tales". However, the throat centre was already open earlier in "Blinding Light" (05/2002) and "White Light" (02/2003).

The third eye centre

In the Vedantic tradition, this is the *ajna* chakra which, as in the Buddhist and Sufi traditions, holds the capacity for seeing the subtle light of the aura and the light of spirit. This energy centre is associated with the sense of inner sight. The Buddhists see it as an extension of the crown centre. The Sufis call it *latifa khafiya*—the centre that casts a revealing light on everything, carrying, as it does, the qualities of insight, light, and the capacity to intuit visually.

The appearance of intense light and colour in our dreams is the first sign of an awakening of the purified kundalini energy in the third eye centre. This can develop to the point where dream images radiate light. This is exemplified in David's "Star Exploding" dream (03/2010) in Chapter Five. In Ava's process, we see this in the dream "Lit from Inside" (12/2005).

Waking dream explorations that pinpoint sensations in the centre of the brow or left or right temple indicate a stimulation of the third eye. Ava experiences this on waking from "Very High Up" (06/2002). Focusing on these sensations as a portal to the third eye can facilitate its opening.

### The crown centre

In Vedanta, the crown centre is called *sahashrara*. The Sufis call this the truth centre—knowledge that is revealed to us. In Buddhism, pleasurable distraction is the shadow aspect of the crown consciousness. This is the result of samsara—remaining in a state of illusion or dualistic consciousness. When we overcome this dualistic consciousness and thought, we begin to experience the pure energies of the crown centre as the light of illumination and true self-realisation.

In meditation, this level is experienced in terms of feeling energised (by pure spirit) and sensing subtle vibrations in the body. Stimulation of this centre is experienced as a tingling sensation in the crown of the head. Heat in the crown is not a healthy sign and should be dealt with by grounding in the body (such as foot massage) and reconnecting with personal feelings. Both practices help to drain the untransformed raw kundalini energy from the crown back down into the body.

The crown centre is instrumental in the entire process of awakening. It is active from the start, activating the kundalini and working in tandem with the third eye and throat centres, in particular. When the crown centre opens, intensely bright light appears in our dreams (and we can experience it in the waking state too). We begin to have transcendental experiences in our dreams—experiences of ascending consciousness that lead to a sense of bliss. In the "Travellers' Tales", we see this in David's "Luminous Face" dream (08/2012). In Ava's process, the crown is stimulated in dreams such as "Very High Up" (06/2002), leading to the experience of intense bright light in a number of her dreams until light radiates from her whole being in "The Sun" (04/2006).

## Travellers' Tales

### David awakens

In February 2009, David had a dream that seemed to signify a significant shift in his consciousness, experienced in the dream as a "mysterious otherness".

> Numinous Fish
>
> I'm in a small dingy on a lake … I see the shapes of huge, multicoloured fish below … Suddenly, there arises a brightly coloured fish … It is numinous and shimmering in the light, like Excaliber held aloft above the water … Its body is silvery-orange, glistening and radiant, but most arresting is a huge eye that looks at me fixedly … Other fish are tugging my jacket edge, trying to entice me into the water … I don't feel threatened; I am apprehensive of the sheer mysterious otherness of the fish and I do not want to join them in the water. (David, 02/09)

The central image of the dream is the "numinous" fish—a powerful spiritual symbol in dreams in the approach to Citrinitas. We see the Fourth Plane colours of silver and orange, but the multicolours and radiant, sword-like light ("Excaliber") of the emerging Fifth Plane as David begins to awaken beyond the mind. We can see the progression from "Yellow Fish", early on in David's process, in that this fish tries to entice David into the water (though he is not quite ready). The guidance of the dream is encouraging David to enter the water—to participate in, and experience, its life force, which represents for David, perhaps, the emotional life as a gateway to the numinous.

Working with the dream using the Waking Dream Process (focussing on the "huge eye" of the fish), helps David to incorporate the potential held by the fish into his solar plexus and sacrum, where life force had been absent up to this point. The work on "Numinous Fish" was a significant developmental step and it felt good for David.

David had the following dream (quoted in summary) during a period of intense inner struggle.

## White Horse

I'm in a large Georgian mansion in the country. The house belongs to a famous artist ... His portraits ... have a rather distant, anaemic quality to them that doesn't particularly appeal to me ... These are the later works of the artist completed before he died [whilst horse riding] ... I seem to have become the artist, living out his final journey ... Standing there, waiting, is a large, strong and beautiful white horse ... harnessed to a small, but very grand-looking open carriage ... I step up into the carriage and take hold of the reins ... I feel very secure and safe in this carriage with this wonderfully responsive horse leading the way ... I see in the distance another big country house that is, perhaps, our destination ... I then find myself walking down a passageway in the house I had seen ... The atmosphere and energy of this place is that of death ... I look for the white horse and see lying on the ground a dying horse the colour of reddish copper ... its face has an expression of such anguish and suffering, it is unbearable to gaze upon it.

As I stand there, the horse begins to metamorphose into the shape of a human being ... a large bronze statue of a heroic warrior. The face is noble and proud beyond measure and is full of dignity, carrying in its expression the suffering of man upon the battlefield of life ... I know he is still dying ... and help him up. He stands and I see that he is dressed in finest military uniform with medals on his chest. I look down and see the white horse is lying there, harnessed in fine ceremonial garb. The statue ... has now become fully human—an old general, the embodiment of virtue and strength ... He sits down upon a throne-like chair ... and begins to sing. His voice is strong, deep, and full of heart-breaking resonance. It is a song to end time and to celebrate all that is noble and heroic in the heart of man. It is the most beautiful thing I have ever heard and I ... weep uncontrollably ... He is no longer dying ... I take his hand in mine. (David, 02/2009)

The qualities of the Fifth Plane are now evident: in the Georgian mansion, "ceremonial" garb, "throne-like" chair, singing, nobility and dignity. Fourth Plane qualities and metaphors are also present in the military themes: "uniform with medals", "heroic warrior", "battlefield of life", "virtue and strength". Here we see the overlap between the planes, which is quite common (except between the Gross Mental and Subtle Mental Planes, and between the Third and Fourth Planes, where the qualitative shift taking place sets them apart from one another).

This powerfully affecting dream represented a turning point for David in terms of his inner masculine. His profoundly moving encounter with the noble, heroic, male archetype opened David's heart. The mortificatio operation (accompanied by the "reddish copper" colour of the Wise Self) was necessary to kill off the "distant, anaemic" (lifeless) aspect of David and leads to his resurrection in a new, more soul conscious, form. All his life, David had been unable to access the qualities personified in the heroic warrior because of the lack of a strong and present father, though these qualities were within him. The climax of the dream ("the song to end time and to celebrate all that is noble and heroic in the heart of man") has a "heart-breaking resonance"—the heart quality that often comes through in the Fifth Plane.

In March 2009, David dreams of being in a "remote, mountain region" (his dream hideout) where his spiritual teacher forewarns him that "something very frightening is about to come". The sky darkens and a huge tidal wave surges towards him, carrying with it hundreds of African elephants with "long carved tusks" and "big flapping ears". David lies down and is not harmed by the wave as it washes over him. He is undergoing a momentous purification (solutio) as deeply buried emotions of fear emerge from his unconscious.

These emotions, it transpired through the therapy, were connected with the elephant theme of his dream. It is not the first time that this motif will appear. A few months later, David dreams of a noodle soup containing pieces of chicken in the shape of elephants! However, it was only in intuiting something of the elephant in a painting that David showed me that the origin of the elephant dream motif was recovered from David's memory. His mother had experienced the terror of a rampaging African bull elephant whilst alone in a safari camp and heavily pregnant with David. Her husband (David's father) was away at the time, leaving her alone in an unprotected area. Clearly, her terror was also felt by her unborn child. David's mother did not touch or speak to David for the first year of his life. What Winnicott described as "the maternal holding environment" (Freshwater & Robertson, 2002, p. 26) was completely absent, so it was not surprising that such feelings (the terror was also the lack of love) remained buried in his unconscious for so many years.

There is a further significance in the "elephant wounding". It seemed to represent for David his split-off earth nature which needed reconciling with the spiritual aspect in him. The seventeenth century alchemist, Maier, has shown that, throughout the alchemical process, there will be "locked-in" instincts that present themselves for transformation (de Jong, 2002). In David's process, it took a long time for these "earthy" parts of himself to come through for purification and healing.

As part of the integration of the remaining split-off instinctual energies, David has a frightening dream set "in some subterranean place that has the atmosphere of a sewer" of a white rat with a tail that is "long and thick like a snake". In working with the dream, using the Waking Dream Process David overcomes his fear of the rat and is able to incorporate its energy in his solar plexus, where it felt comfortable. In this way, some of the earthy, instinctual qualities emerge consciously, giving David some inner strength. On a later occasion, he dreams of a woman whose arms turn into snakes; the heads of the snakes are anaconda-like—huge, pink, and fleshy. David's initial fear in touching the mouths of these snakes becomes amusement, even pleasure. The monstrous feminine is transformed into something that David can experience and enjoy. In these instances, the snake symbolises the instinctual in David's process, but also a progression of the awakening kundalini energy.

In April 2009, David dreams of a complete emotional separation from his brother with whom he had been enmeshed since childhood, perhaps as a consequence of having a physically absent father and an emotionally absent mother. As part of this dream, he is hiding from a marauding dragon and then has this realisation: "It is the purifying fire of the dragon breath that is upon me … I visualise this purifying process going on within me". This calcinatio is connecting David with his powerful fire nature so as to help him separate out from his enmeshment with his brother. In alchemy, the psychic forces involved in such a complex enmeshment first have to be separated out. Unlike the dragon of his "Green Dragon" dream (in Chapter Four), which was "alien", this dragon is "within". The dragon is also a sign of the awakening kundalini energy and transformation of fire.

In a further dream, following a long sequence with an angry, frustrated energy, David finds a special place epitomising the Fifth Plane qualities of radiance, light, and heartfelt music that is boundaryless.

### Radiant Happiness

There is an entrance way through into a delightful area with grass, flowers, elegant walkways and archways … the quality of light is wonderful—both energising and invigorating … I realise that this is a place that everyone would like to come to, but somehow are too busy or distracted to find. As I stand there, some beautiful music starts playing. It doesn't seem to have a location but is everywhere. The sound goes straight to my heart and I am instantly filled with a radiant happiness—light and wonderful. I walk around looking at everything, intoxicated by the experience. (David, 04/2009)

Then came a dream of a painting in the style of Kandinsky—very colourful and vibrant.

### Kandinsky Painting

As I get closer and closer, the quality and details of the colours become sharper. This has an inner effect within me, like impending revelation or the resonance of deeper and deeper meaning. Finally, I am right up close to the picture with a final light revealing radiant reds. As I look closely, the colour seems to have a dynamic life, with movement and luminescence. (David, 06/2009)

The central significance of the Kandinsky painting is its "luminescence" (the "radiant red" of fire transformed into the light of the Fifth Plane) and the reference to "impending revelation". Very soon after, David has a companion dream of a cube which, like the Kandinsky painting he notes, "stirs me deeply and draws me in". One face of the cube shows an African village; another shows purple and brown colours. The cube is a symmetrical symbol, holding opposite sides in balance. Purple (a sacred, Fifth Plane colour) and brown (an earthy colour) are opposites held in the same image. David's cube holds different psychic aspects, but now they seem to be in balance. In this way, the cube was a landmark symbol of the self for David and initiates a series of important dreams primarily concerned with balance.

Shortly after, in a dream he calls "Bliss", he dreams of being half way up a mountain. He looks up towards the peak and sees elephants and rhinos running across the slope; looking down into the valley, he sees "a magical land—mystical and luminescent in the sunshine". He feels blissful and, as he arches his back lying down, a deep held-in stress is released. He wakes up "with a strong, blissful resonance" emanating from his solar plexus centre. Using the Waking Dream Process to focus on this, David experienced a soft, warm energy in his sacrum, and light and joy in his solar plexus. It seemed that something of his "lower" (instinctual, sexual) aspects was being integrated. The references to "luminescence", the "mystical" and bliss in the dream, on the other hand, suggested the approach to the Sixth Plane and Citrinitas. It seemed that the process was active in both directions—upwards and downwards—as reflected in the symmetrical images of the dream (of the mountain peak and the valley), showing a counterbalancing of heaven (on earth) and earth (in heaven).

At around the same time, David dreams that his brother tells him presciently that: "A transformation of astounding proportions is about to take place ... Huge tectonic movements begin and great plates or stratas of rock start to slide and shift. Mountains collapse and rise up again in a new place so that, where the mountains were, new valleys form, and vice versa". In another imaginal form, we see the balancing of "heaven and earth"—an expression of the idea "as above; so below" found in hermetic texts (Jung, 1983). In Nigredo, the basic connection between heaven and earth was made culminating in the "Road to Heaven" dream, but these dreams seem to indicate that a new, inner, psychic balance had been achieved.

Significantly, David has his first fully lucid dream shortly after, where he realises the illusory nature of his mind trap. His spirit is overcoming his mind or, to put it another way, his mind is giving way to the power of his spirit. Again, in September 2009, David has a lucid realisation in a dream and changes the operating dynamic of his mind. At first he is driving through a dense forest and being pursued. Suddenly, he emerges out of the forest into bright sunlight. The road leads up a cliff face; down below is a valley (the theme of above and below again). He decides to drive his car off the edge and plummets into space ...

Heather

I fall into a deep rock pool, entering the water gracefully. The crystal clear water is ice cold and is both vitalising and invigorating. All my senses are sharp and there is a wonderful lightness of feeling ... My hand falls on some vegetation and, looking down,

I see all around the pool a carpet of heather. The colour of the heather is the most beautiful, deep, emerald green ... I gaze at it for a long time, then run my hand through it, marvelling at its feel and texture ... It is so real in its presence ... I wake up and can still feel the texture of the heather as if it were still there in my hand. (David, 09/2009)

The reluctance to be immersed in water of "Numinous Fish" is now gone as David breaks through a mental barrier in this lucid dream. His journeying in the preceding dreams has enabled him to participate in spirit (water). The "crystal clear" water that is invigorating and "lightness of feeling" is suggestive of the presence of Sixth Plane consciousness and the "emerald green" heather a sign of the transcendental. Most significantly, this dream seems to signify that David has reached a place of embodied "realness" in himself and his experience. Note how he brings the sensuousness of the dream experience into his conscious awareness as he wakes up.

A dream the next month confirms the passage through the Sixth Plane.

### Beautiful Snow

I'm with a group of people and we are on a very high mountain pass on our way to a temple retreat. As we proceed along, we come to a section of the pass that has had a fresh fall of snow. It is several feet thick and very powder-like in nature ... I gaze at it and marvel at its pure, pristine quality. It is so white and pure and quite beautiful. I continue looking deeper and can see very subtle, translucent colours of green and blue, like those icebergs that float in arctic waters reflecting the sharp, clear marine environment about them. I am enjoying the experience so much I want to lie down deep in the snow and to remain there, but the leader of our party urges us on so we all continue to trudge up the mountain path. (David, 10/2009)

The mountain pass on the way to the "temple retreat" is "very high"; the snow is "white and pure", "pristine", very fine in consistency and with a "very subtle" translucence. The dream speaks of a very subtle level of consciousness. David wants to stay there but the journey must continue!

The following month, David has a landmark lucid dream—a healing coniunctio.

## Compassionate Woman

I'm in a large elegant town house ... I hear a knock at the door and open it to see a beautiful young woman standing there ... She comes forward into my arms and we embrace—a very sweet and intimate embrace ... She has come to help me ... She tells me that I am too isolated and that she has come IN to take me OUT ... She starts to describe to me in precise detail the condition of my innermost diffi-culty and suffering. Suddenly, we are outside, walking down a path between avenues of beautiful trees with parkland on either side. It is sunny, but bracing and fresh. At this point, I become lucid ... The young woman continues to articulate and mirror back to me my existential predicament with a veracity that renders invalid any contradiction or challenge ... After a while, I say to her with careful deliberation that, in all these years of struggle and practice, I had always felt and experienced that I was making progress, but that, at the core, I had always suffered from the deepest schizoid split—a devastating lifelong inner pain ... As we are walking back, I feel that I have, for the first time in my life, revealed to another being the truth that I have always kept hidden. It is a momentous feeling ... I am overwhelmed with tender heart feelings ... The woman's eyes are full of compassion. (David, 11/2009)

David's anima guide figure has come "IN" to his isolation to draw him "OUT" (his capitals) into life. In the dream, David feels that he has revealed the deepest level of his pain and has been witnessed in it. There is a deep connection with the heart. It seemed that David was at another turning point in his process which could allow a new sense of identity to emerge.

Several positive and lucid dreams followed, including the dream below, heralding the passage through Citrinitas and Rubedo. In his gar-den, some children tell David that there is a wondrous bird next door. On his way to see it, he sees his neighbour wallpapering the outside of the house with "beautiful, brightly coloured" wallpaper.

## Red-plumed Bird

I see a large cage and inside, on a perch, is a big, beautiful bird with lots of flowing plumage. The bird is totally red in colour—a deep, rich crimson hue ... The door to the cage is open ... This bird is very old and wise and reminds me of Rinpoche. (David, 03/2010)

The bird's red plumage, its "wise" old eyes, together with the new, "brightly coloured wallpaper" on the outside of the house (representing, perhaps, the manifesting or bringing out of the inner riches) indicate the beginnings of Rubedo. We note the outside, inside theme again—a balancing of the two—in the same way that the earlier phase of dreams had balanced upper and lower. We worked together, using the Waking Dream Process, to look at, touch and then incorporate the energy of the red bird into his being.

Shortly after, David experienced an extraordinary lucid dream.

### Star Exploding

I am lying on the floor in a strange, otherworldly state. Suddenly, I become lucid and conscious I am dreaming. I look up at the bedroom wall and see it dissolving away into black open space. As I lie there, staring into the space, a face appears. It is a female face with strange, white, ivory appearance and beautiful eyes. It is suspended in front of me, shimmering and radiating with an inner light. It magnetises and captivates my whole being. I gaze at it with an extraordinary intensity, not content until I can realise its very essence. The intensity increases and I suddenly become aware that this face is me—that I am one with it. At the moment this realisation dawns, the face explodes into white light (like a star exploding) before empty, open space ... I stay like this for a long time ... E walks in—her dress is red and her face a curious, but beautiful, orange mahogany colour ... We kiss very sweetly. (David, 03/2010)

This dream exemplifies the way in which Citrinitas and Rubedo often overlap and why the two are often seen as one stage in the process. The face (of his feminine soul nature) is "white", "shimmering and radiating with an inner light" and David is intensely drawn by it until, suddenly, he is "one with it" (coniunctio), and has transcended any bodily or psychological sense of self. This oneness culminates in the face exploding into white light, followed by empty, open space. This is an experience of Citrinitas—no self, neither masculine nor feminine. The experience of oneness with the female face of light marks the apex of his ascent. The red dress of his friend (E) at this point seems to confirm the presence of the red descending spirit in alchemy (Rubedo) that is becoming personalised in David. The coniunctio with the woman with orange, mahogany-coloured skin appears to indicate that the return to earth of the new self is underway.

Several dreams involving "coming down to earth" were recorded by David over the next two years. However, one dream, in 2012, stands out.

## Centaur

I am undertaking an epic journey. There is a group of us travelling together. At some stage in this odyssey, we travel deep inside a mountain through secret tunnels and dark passageways to reach a sacred space right in the centre of the mountain. The space is large and has both a mythic and mystical atmosphere about it ... Then, some cataclysmic or disastrous event befalls this place and we all have to flee to save our lives ... Several of my travelling companions die and there is great sorrow and suffering as a result ... Then, some kind of a miraculous event takes place and the dead members of our group are resurrected and brought back to life.

At this point, when joy and hope returns to us all, I become aware of a centaur (half horse/half human figure) standing in front of a sheer rock wall ... It reaches out and touches the rock with its hand. The rock appears to dissolve; it is still there, but has somehow no form or substantiality to it. I walk straight into and through the rock, followed by the centaur. As we proceed, we encounter different strata or layers of rock. To begin with, the centaur continues to dissolve the rock by touching it, but after a while I find that I can do it myself. I and my companions then carry on for some time, ploughing on through the rock, going ever deeper.

Finally, we break through into the inner space at the centre of the mountain ... Suddenly, we round a corner and enter the magnificent, cathedral-like cave ... I look up and see flying creatures and recognise one as a phoenix ... I walk over towards some large stone stairs that sweep up towards a central altar space. Overcome with intense emotion and happiness, I fall upon the stairs and cry deep into my heart. (David, 02/2012)

This dream narrative describes a journey to a "mythic and mystical" space in the centre of a mountain (the sacred centre of the self (Jung, 1983))—a journey to the "earth's core" first encountered in the "Heaven and Hell" dream some twenty years before, where David was "born" into his process. This time, the journey ends with death (mortificatio) and resurrection (Rubedo) to a new self. It seems to be the story of David's "epic" journey.

The guide figure comes in the form of a centaur. It is a form of what Jung calls the "Spirit Mercurius" (1983), which he defines broadly. *Mercurius* is our guiding spirit—sometimes a trickster, sometimes a hermetic guide figure with the wisdom to steer us through the inner, psychic realms. David's centaur has the ability to penetrate and pass through the layers of rock in the mountain (David's rock-like defences). At first, it is only the centaur that has the power over matter, but after a while, David finds that "I can do it myself". In this way, the centaur might represent the therapist upon whom David projected his own power at first, before realising that the power was within himself. In Greek mythology, the centaur Chiron was known as the "wounded healer"—an archetype which is really to do with the suffering within that empowers healing.

The centaur itself is an Orphic figure (a mediator of spirit and instinct) and represents the integration of the sacred, human, and instinctual aspects in David—earth and spirit, or body and mind as Wilbur suggests (1999). At the core of the mountain, lies the sacred, cathedral-like, inner space, which had appeared in dreams many times over the years (the cathedral-like barn on fire and the cathedral-like space "black with smoke and dirt" of "Dark India" in Chapter Four). If we look back at the prophetic dream of "Heaven and Hell", we can see its origin in the "small chapel with a simple altar and cross upon it". The image of the phoenix speaks of rebirth and awakening to the spirit within the earth (Roob, 2005). Finally, David is led to the central altar space—his sacred essence—and is overcome with heart-centred soul feelings.

In August 2012, David once more encounters his spiritualised anima (his soul nature), which was consciously experienced in "Star Exploding" over two years earlier.

### Luminous Face

Out of nowhere, there manifests a face filling my vision and my consciousness. As soon as the face arises out of nothing, I become fully lucid within the dream. The face is black and oval in shape ... female, with almond shaped eyes. The face has a definition and luminosity to it that is mesmerising—more real somehow than objects we can see through our own eyes. I am captivated by the shimmering intensity of the face—awestruck—but I am also startled by the eyes in this face. They are fierce and unyielding, shining with clarity—strong, feminine and ever so present. As suddenly as the face appears, it dissolves away into nothingness. (David, 08/2012)

The beautiful, feminine face is a luminous black, showing the strength, clarity, and richness of spirit in the earth body—Rubedo. The archetype of the sacred earth feminine has been constellated in David. This completes his journey of the healing of the inner feminine archetype, previously shown in the dream images in many forms.

In a counterpart dream a couple of months later, David records a significant healing of the inner masculine. He dreams of meeting a woman to whom he is strongly attracted. They embrace before a succession of "A-list Hollywood stars (all male)" enter the room, one by one, to pay respects to the woman.

### Gene Hackman

Lastly enters Gene Hackman, who also approaches the woman and greets her. Up until this point, I have been an observer only of this ritual taking place, but instead of leaving, Gene Hackman turns towards me. I am impressed with his aura of health and wellbeing. Although I am a little overawed, I exchange some words with him. He looks me directly in the eyes and says: "We really nailed it didn't we?" As Gene turns to leave, I stand and look at the woman. My sense of myself and my world is in harmony and balance. (David, 12/2012)

When we explored what Gene Hackman meant to David, he seemed to embody masculine qualities of heroic strength in the face of tremendous inner sensitivity and battling with external obstacles. This dream completes his integration of the positive male archetype, leaving David with a sense of himself "in harmony and balance". It represents a counterbalance to the feminine archetype that is, perhaps, the "tall, elegant" woman in the dream to whom the masculine figures pay respects (and who first appeared in his "Heaven and Hell" dream). From here on, more positive masculine figures appear in the dreams and the shadow aspects (such as aggression, ruthlessness, coldness) gradually disappear.

David's process continues to unfold, but a dream in 2013 seems to bring to a close a long and painful chapter that begin whilst still in his mother's womb.

Elephant

I'm in the bush, maybe on safari … I am standing out in the hot sun watching animals coming and going … After a short while, a large elephant also lumbers into view … Then the elephant comes to a complete stop and rests back on its hind legs almost as if it is squatting, whereupon it proceeds to produce an enormous turd. It is a huge turd, almost the size of a small car. It seems impossible for an animal, even an elephant, to push such a thing out of itself. The turd lands on the ground with a heavy thump. The elephant happily lumbers off, relieved it seems, of a great burden! (David, 02/2013)

During his journey through Rubedo, David encounters the more earthy, animal forces and learns, through multidimensional dreamwork, to embrace them. The "Elephant" dream seems to signify the integration of this earth archetype. He is finally at peace with the earth. The split between spirit and matter, thought and feeling, feminine and masculine has been healed at last. On analysing David's dreams, it was clear to see the evidence of this balancing in the activation of higher and lower energy centres in Rubedo. Through a process of alternation of higher and lower centre activation which culminated in upper and lower centres acting *in tandem* with each other, in the same dream, harmony had been created—like a musical chord or harmony of voices.

David had come out of his deep depression and he was functioning well at work and socially. His meditations, which had always been very important to him, but with which he struggled at the start of the process, were deeper and stronger.

A dream shortly after "Elephant" seems to confirm, in its clarity and unworldly power, the beginnings of a new ascent, a new cycle of awakening; one that might contain far less trauma and psychic healing, but show a greater awareness of the inner landscape of his being.

Magical Object

I turn and suddenly find I am now in a completely different place … a valley surrounded by high mountains … There are streams and waterfalls and the place has a magical feel to it, like a hidden or secret land. I am wondering what I am doing there when a very native-looking man approaches me. He looks like a medicine man and a tracker of some sorts; maybe he has been tracking me

... He comes up to me and opens his hand ... In it, is this object which has the shape of a sphere-like disc (like an ice puck). Its appearance is beguiling. At first glance, it looks smooth and very solid, marble-like, heavy and hard, but at the next moment it seems far less substantial ... very light and impermanent. It has a white, translucent colour or quality to it ... As I look more closely, I see alphabet letters are carved into the surface all over it. The man explains to me that to commune with the spirits that inhabit this place, to communicate with this hidden world, to know this world, I have to learn how to use this object, learn how to read the secret language carved into the object. I feel close to this world and want to stay. I wake up. (David, 04/2013)

In the dream, he meets "the tracker" (of his journey, he wonders), who gives him an object reminiscent of the alchemical philosopher's stone, urging him to learn to read this treasure in order to understand, and communicate with, the spirit of the hidden world. David feels close to this world and wants to stay.

The strong transference that characterised the therapeutic relationship for many years, which enabled David, not only to feel held in his process, but also reparatively held, was reflected in the large number of dreams in which I appeared. Now, I no longer appear in David's dreams. Now he knows that the "tracker", the "centaur"—the one who has the power and knowledge—is him.

*Ava awakens*

Early in 2002, Ava has a remarkable dream (while alone in the mountains), which seemed to prefigure the awakening to come. As such, it is an example of a ladder dream (referred to in Chapter One) that not only moved her from one level of consciousness to the next, but was transforming in itself. She encounters her beloved (animus) dream figure in a new form of the "Master".

### Spheres of Consciousness

My husband and I are at an exhibition. I am introduced to a man— the Master Benshen. We are in a large room, like a temple. The Master approaches me and says: "Why don't you come to me: how long would it take?" ... I abdicate my will to him and find myself alone in his presence ... I sit facing him, close my eyes, and, immediately, all my senses disappear and also the feeling of time. I see golden light flickering up—first like lightning, then it stabilises. I am very excited: I can see the light! Ecstasy. Timelessness ... Where he was sitting, there is a light brown fog in his shape. I stretch out my hand and, sure enough, nothing is there; he is gone, but now I see the light even with open eyes. It is changing as I move my head, and there are strange sculptures appearing—abstract forms, which flare up in strong colours (blue, red, yellow, and so on). I move my head back and forth; the lights come and go ... How long have I been sitting here? ... My husband left around noon, so I must have been there for over three hours ... I must go now and say goodbye, but the Master is not there. I return to the garage to meet my husband. What he says brings me back to earth again. I wake up to feel a strong movement in my solar plexus. The dream was more real than my reality in bed! (Ava, 02/2002)

Ava reported experiencing a defined shift in consciousness as she moved from place to place in the dream. Her diary records the experience of moving in and out of the different states.

*Level 1: Outer reality*: Me in bed, alone in a cold house, standing on a mountain slope. That felt quite unreal when I woke up.

*Level 2: "Usual" dream level*: Feels not much different from outer reality. Beginning with my husband in an exhibition; ending with my husband in the garage.

*Level 3: Deeper level*: Feels like a dream compared to level 2. From the moment I leave my husband on the doorstep and follow the Master, until the moment of my "Aha" at the end.

*Level 4: Outside of time and space*: I lose my senses, experiences of colours and light. Maybe there is a fifth level, when I open my eyes and half wake up in that state, and the light continues.

In a further dream account at this time, Ava records that the "colours won't leave me alone" (referring to the archetypal colours appearing in her dreams) suggesting that her consciousness is now imbued with these colours.

Soon after, Ava's awakening began to show itself in earnest in a series of dreams.

## Blinding Light

I go to a musical show. Although I have a ticket for row 21, I find myself in the first row. The star calls me on stage three times to sing and dance with her. I am blinded by the stage lights. I wake up unable to open my eyes at first. (Ava, 05/2002)

Here we see the Fifth Plane musical concert motif (which is also Ava's personal theme) and the appearance of intense light accompanied by the number three, indicating the emergence of the transcendental. We might well wonder about the number "21" (the language of the unconscious is always meaningful) and whether, as a multiple of three, it might refer to the seven chakras which were an ongoing theme of Ava's dreams. We are reminded of the "Circle of Love" dream in Chapter Four where she thinks of singing to the audience, but decides against it. Here, she is repeatedly invited to sing, but does not yet do so.

But there is a dying that must occur for Ava to move forward. In a mortificatio dream the following month, Ava dreams that her son has died and is distraught. She finds herself in an unfamiliar place.

## Emptiness

The land is somehow marshy, very fine; white, swamp flowers grow there. They are blowing in the wind, almost transparent. I have no feelings, only crying; no understanding or explaining; only crying. Peace, emptiness. I wake up in this place of peace and emptiness ... and stay there for a while, as if I were on the other side of death myself. Then the contents of the dream hit me: my child is dead. Pain penetrates my lower body. (Ava, 06/2002)

The landscape she finds herself in here is "very fine", "white", "transparent"—a higher level of consciousness than she has encountered before. This is reminiscent of the alchemical dictum: "sow your gold in white, foliated earth"—the fine, white ground from which the gold of the process is harvested (de Jong, 2002). Paradoxically, the death and her crying (solutio) lead to peace and emptiness—the peace of the Fifth Plane, but also the beginnings of no self. Her psyche has been shattered and the mind emptied out (fanā in Sufism), making way for something deeper to emerge. Just prior to this dream, Ava had woken up from a dream with an unbearable pain in the crown centre.

Following *this* dream, however, Ava wakes with pain in her lower body. It would seem from this that the awakened spirit is no longer trapped in the crown, but has descended to the lower energy centres, which are increasingly activated as the process goes on.

Then, the same night, Ava dreams that: "I am in a place where cheerfulness and strength reign. I can feel how strength is emanating from me, dissolving all the problems". Ava comments in her dream journal: "death and resurrection in the same night". In these companion dreams, the death of the mind has led to the awakening of the soul feelings. "Something has changed" she notes.

Shortly after, Ava has a lucid, sublimatio dream where she and her husband are "in the same dream … high up".

### Very High Up

We are in a wide, open landscape, high up. We go up a free floating staircase, as if we were flying on clouds—whitish-yellow … I eat an orange but it is not juicy. I take the dry stuff out of my mouth … I feel sick, pain in the stomach. Is it fear or sickness? On waking, I come down to earth, as if coming from very high up. I feel sick, with pain in the crown and third eye. (Ava, 06/2002)

From the colours of the dream, we can have a sense that Ava is experiencing something of the sun energy of spirit now that the crown centre is opening. At this point, the energy is too strong, drying her out (the orange "is not juicy")—calcinatio—and making her feel sick, but this will change as she moves through her process. In a further dream, Ava meets a man who is "like a part of me".

### Turning in Bliss

He holds me around the waist with his right hand; I hold him with my left hand and we start to dance, turning clockwise. A large room opens up, with shining parquet floor. We can take big steps, turning, turning. I am in bliss … I am dancing with a god. Five times we receive a cup of tea … Everything is light green. Then it is like a vision, with a feeling of utter meaningfulness. I see the five teacups one above the other; they are five chakras, which are turning. I have now reached the fifth chakra. We continue to turn on and on in bliss. (Ava, 06/2002)

In this coniunctio dream Ava meets her beloved again in the new form of a "god" with whom she dances. The five cups of tea symbolise, she realises, the five chakras, from base to throat, which are all turning (energy centres turn in a clockwise direction as they open). She "reaches" the throat chakra and turns "on and on in bliss". The peace of the "Emptiness" dream, the height of "Very High Up" and the "bliss", "meaningfulness", "shining" floor and "light green" colour of this dream would seem to confirm the presence of Fifth Plane consciousness, which is related to the throat centre. The crown centre energy descending into her body following the "Emptiness" dream opened the way for Ava to enter the Fifth Plane (the crown, third eye, and throat centres are interlinked at this stage). This time, she does not wake up feeling sick.

A few months later, Ava dreams of a huge, square castle. This is followed on the same night by a dream of very intense, blinding light—"too much light" for her to open her eyes. It is likely, in the context of Ava's process, that this is the light of the soul—the white light that has the intensity of the sun within it. The square is a symmetrical symbol of the self (see Chapter Six) (Jung, 1983). This pairing of dreams show that Ava's psyche is developing the capacity to be in relationship with this powerful light.

Attunement to the Fifth Plane continues and deepens in the dreams that followed, and there is a further symmetrical image in a dream of a cube-like house containing a "secret". She is able to "communicate with the secret" and her "whole body is covered with a light green powder". The sun energy of the transcendental is evolving from orange and yellow to green (albeit pale green at this stage). Early the following year, this phase of dreams comes to fruition.

### White Light

The white light appears. It is a light source like a star, coming from the right, moving very slowly towards the middle of my head, then standing still there. Everything becomes white and light around me … I think: "Aha, this is now the white light—just lie still". But maybe I'm not even dreaming … I'm not sure which is dream and which is not. I just remember the light and the peace it brought me. (Ava, 02/2003)

The light of the soul is much more conscious now for Ava; it is all around her and merges into the waking state, showing the continuity and stability of the Fifth Plane consciousness within her. Again, a feeling of "peace" accompanies the light. We can see the shift in Ava's dream consciousness compared to her dreams of the lower planes. Although the soul light was starting to be present in the "Spheres of Consciousness" dream that bridged the Fourth and Fifth Planes, it was a projected light (albeit creating a sense of timelessness). Now, however, the white light is part of the sense of self.

Ava's entry into the Sixth Plane was established a month later in a series of dreams. As is often the case, however, there was some overlap at the end of the Fifth Plane in a dream of snow high up in the mountains and "glittering, cold, white light" and, in another, "deep, powdery snow, up to my neck" which is "dry and light like feathers". In these dreams, Ava begins to experience the emotional "coolness" and "dryness" of the Sixth Plane, its fineness and the quality of the light.

Ava's story of awakening continues to unfold through musical imagery and analogy in a dream of a choir singing "Immaculata Vergine". Music and singing in Ava's process is an example of a personal motif that is interwoven with the process and reflects the transformation of the dreamer in its evolution. In Ava's case, the metaphor of singing seems to represent her state of realisation and the expression of her soul. It is at this point in Ava's process that the call to sing (of "Circle of Love" and "Blinding Light") is finally answered—she joins in with the choir and participates in the immaculate divine feminine of this level of consciousness. On waking, she has white light around her head and kundalini heat moving up her spine. The positioning of the light around her head is an early heralding of Citrinitas.

The same night she is "shown a picture, narrow and high, of angels in pastel colours, going up and down". Shortly after, she dreams of New York and Mont Blanc together. In this dream, Ava is reconciling the opposites of the mind world (symbolised by New York) and spirit (the "white mountain").

Two years pass by, during which Ava undergoes many purifications and deaths in dreams in preparation for the opening to the transcendental. In September 2005, Ava has dreams of a "golden deer" and of "golden inlays" in her teeth, which need replacing. As we have seen before, gold is an alchemical symbol of the eternal, untarnishable spirit. In the Sixth Plane, this spirit was experienced as an intense, white light. Now, in Citrinitas, it becomes gold. At this stage, Ava was beginning to "see things others don't see, like light around mountains, trees, people (usually white)".

In the "Gold Teeth" dream, there was "a large square of fertile dark-brown earth" on the dentist's waiting room floor. Ava notes that: "this is the first time ever that I actually put my hands into the earth; it felt very good". The square is, as before, an indication that the gold is now part of the self. The earth is a sign, perhaps, of the materialisation of spirit—the union of spirit (gold) and matter (the earth)—to be established in Rubedo in the journey ahead. In a similar vein, around the same time, she dreams of "sparkling light from above *and* from below" and that her therapist "is sometimes a man; sometimes a woman". Ava is undergoing a balancing process of above and below, masculine and feminine, akin to David's dreams of reconciling heaven and earth.

Before Ava can proceed in the journey, there must be further purification—by death once more. She is with a "tall man" (another form of the beloved) on the top of a hill.

### Death by Poison

I know that I will soon die ... I would like to kiss the tall man and say goodbye to him ... I go away from the people with the beloved ... We start going down until we reach a wooden wagon on which we put all the empty flower pots we are carrying—round, clay pots, reddish-brown ... and a bucket with a white liquid in it. This is the poison I will drink and then die ... I wake up with a big pain in the heart chakra; it is like a big, open hole. My breath is heavy and fast, almost panting. (Ava, 10/2005)

We note that the poison is "white" (purifying spirit) and that the pots (empty, as yet) are "round" and "reddish-brown" (the colour of spirit in matter and the shape of symmetry and wholeness). The pain in her heart is part of the further opening of the heart centre needed at this stage in order to reach Citrinitas. That same night, she has a second dream about a new, but dangerous, project in China and wakes with pain around the throat. In alchemy, death precedes birth—the self must die in order that the spirit may live. This dream opens the way for a momentous shift in Ava's PTP. A lucid dream two months later marks the point of awakening with a realisation typical of Citrinitas (together with the presence of "black" in the dream, along with light).

### Lit from Inside

I am standing on a hill, looking down on a shining lake which forms a curve around the hill. There are mountains in the background—very beautiful. On the lake, I see a little boat with two men in black; it is racing very fast to the right. I zoom closer and see that the two men are carrying black lances in their hands, pointing them towards the water (probably, they want to kill large fish). They should put away their lances, I think, and immediately they point the lances upwards ... I look into the landscape and admire the intense light. There is no sun, but everything is lit from inside, shining in very intense colours—red, blue, green in front; at the back, the white snowy mountains ... Gradually the colours lose their intensity; I notice that I am waking up. (Ava, 12/2005)

Not only does Ava become lucid, but she has an important realisation in the dream. She sees the intense light, but without the presence of the sun. The light of spirit is no longer held in the sun, external to her. Ava is experiencing a conscious perception of the inner light, the light of her soul, in the form of a landscape infused with the "intense" colours of spirit (the inner sun). Soul and spirit are together now; not in a mystical union, but in a symbolical union. This is an experience of clear light— the omnipresent light. No explicit dreamwork was done on this dream and was not necessary, because the deep impression of peace, light and beauty carried over into the dreamer's meditations and, eventually, into her life.

Six weeks later, Ava finds herself in a new, "strange" landscape.

### Sulphur in the Centre

I go to an island ... Then comes a path, in circles or spirals, always to the right ... The landscape is strange, a feeling of danger, also strange light. It seems to me the curves are getting narrower. I am inside a building now; a woman is coming towards me and says: "Have you drunk the water with sulphur?" I continue in circles which get narrower and narrower and reach a room containing several brick-red hoses with clamps on them. One of them says SO2 (sulphur). (Ava, 01/2006)

Here, we see the alchemical formula for the spirit of the sun in the earth—sulphur (Evola, 1995). The female guide in the dream seems to be prompting Ava to drink the sulphur solution to which she has been led by the process of "spiralling inwards to the centre" (Ava's words). Notice the appearance of the "brick-red" colour, symbolising the presence of the descending spirit.

Rubedo beckons in the form of an initiation in a full church.

### Initiation in Red

All of a sudden, lots of young people get up and walk up front, all dressed in red costumes. Some sort of initiation or confirmation is taking place. In the choir, they all lie flat on the ground. (Ava, 02/2006)

In this dream, the choir symbolises the return to earth in Rubedo in lying "flat on the ground". In another dream at this time, Ava is given gold and silver watches, representing the alchemical union of sun and moon, soul and spirit (Roob, 2005). Gold and silver had been motifs through Ava's process, but had never appeared together until now.

Shortly after, her dream brings an invitation to sing with a famous opera star; she accepts and takes centre stage to sing the lead role in "La Traviata". This is the culmination of the expression of her soul through the metaphor of music and singing. It also marks the emergence of a spiritual quality from a psychological block which first took the form of the artistic animus figure who was inauthentic and suicidal (in "The Famous Writer"). Through the music-themed dreams, the block in Ava has been transformed and she has overcome the alienation expressed by this original animus figure. The animus has been incorporated as the confident "sun force" in conjunction with her feminine "soul feeling".

Once again, a death is necessary before Ava can proceed to Rubedo. She sings as she dies in her dream and wakes with a pain in the heart. When she gets up to meditate, she experiences a "white and very hot kundalini rising". The opening of the crown centre in Citrinitas has triggered a further opening of the heart and more kundalini energy; the whole energy system is now active and interlinked. Then, a few days before Easter, Ava dreams again.

### Resurrection

I walk through a foreign country with a little boy ... We pass a big house; he is curious and wants to go in ... Inside, there are many doors made of old wood. We open one after the other, look into the rooms—everything is beautiful, but no trace of people ... The boy drinks from the faucet, drinks and drinks until he falls to the ground and falls asleep. I have an impression that he is dark red from head to toe. I fill a green bottle with water. Then I am alone, high up in the mountains—huge rocks, no vegetation, strong winds ... Then I see a child being blown towards me by the wind. Immediately I realise, this is something very important. The child is wearing a blue jacket. It is saying something quite unfriendly to me. I pay no attention and say: "You have such beautiful blue eyes". Now the child softens a little and says: "You have blue eyes too, but your hair is dirty". "Yes", I say, "but I do have blue eyes like you". Now comes a strong gust of wind which blows the child away. I shout very loudly: "My child, my child, will you come back?" I hear the answer: "Yes—resurrection" ... There is bright light, roaring songs of praise and I wake deeply impressed with burning fire between heart and throat. (Ava, 04/2006)

The little boy, who is her guide in this dream, is the "philosophical child"—the product of the union of soul and spirit (de Jong, 2002). Together, they enjoy the newfound spaciousness and beauty of Ava's psyche—the house, which has yet to be reinhabited. In the redness of the boy, we know that the red, fiery spirit is descending (hence the "green bottle with water"), awakening Ava's consciousness to life again. Yet her mind needs further purification now that the descent has begun. She must not pick up the old scripts again: "the child is unfriendly"; "your hair is dirty". By emphasising the clarity of the blue of their eyes, Ava is affirming her own intrinsic, spiritual nature. There is a sense of loss in her when the child is blown away, but the invitation to rebirth brings the waking experience of fiery spirit entering the heart and throat centres in a calcinatio purification (the energy has penetrated from the crown now).

Shortly after, Ava finds herself travelling to and fro between Southern Italy and Africa on a ferry in a dream. The descent has brought Ava down towards Africa—the earthy continent. Yet, "it is a very short ride" between the two and, on the Italian side, she finds "a green meadow with artworks" where she can "climb up a very steep ladder". In this way, she keeps the connection with the pathway of ascent.

This long cycle of dreams reaches the stage of materialisation of spirit in one, short dream.

### The Sun

I have no awareness of the outer world and, inside, everything is black, dark. All of a sudden, at the lower left side, the sun appears, shining up at me—extremely bright, white, light yellow. I look directly into it. I am quite shocked; it is such a surprise. After a while, the energy rises up through me and out through the hands. I can feel it streaming out of every finger for a long, long time. It is as if I had long, luminous green fingers. (Ava, 04/2006)

The light of spirit is radiating through her body and she is conscious of it. The sun is embodied; she *is* the light. The transcendental shows itself in the colour green—healing and life-giving for Ava, perhaps; in alchemy, it is the light of Hermes, the light of the Holy Spirit (Jung, 1983).

Finally, music is once again the metaphor for her journey of awakening.

### Continue by Singing

In the other land ... I am supposed to find the way. I recognise it has the structure of the opera; I sing a melody and, by singing, I move everything in the right direction. I know how it will continue. (Ava, 05/2006)

She recognises the "structure" of the landscape of the "other land"; in becoming whole, she has connected with her deeper self and knows how to find her way and what lies ahead.

We can see in the dream cycle presented above that Ava has undergone a profound spiritual awakening. She has at last brought together a degree of unity of body, soul, and spirit, which changed her whole perspective of life and of herself. The process of awakening did not stop at this point for Ava. Indeed, it progressed further, through three additional lengthy cycles of dreams to 2009; culminating, finally, in a series of profound mystical experiences (states of unity consciousness).

The transformation process had an impact on her body, which became rejuvenated (particularly the physical heart). Her meditations reflected the same profound experiences encountered in the dream state. She began to have more and more lucid dreams. Today, Ava has become an extremely proficient dream guide, combining the spiritual and psychological aspects in her work of helping people to pursue the path of psychospiritual transformation and awakening through dreams.

## Summary

Clearly, in David and Ava's journeys of awakening, dreams have been central and so much more than just by-products of what they were going through. Their dreams have mirrored back to them the landscape of their consciousness, which changed as their consciousness changed. We have been able to see a broad, but undeniable, similarity in the qualities of their experiences as they progressed through the landscape of awakening.

The dreams of David and Ava have brought them hidden treasures, new powers, and sent them guides to help them on their way. We have been able to watch some of these motifs (David's "cathedral space", Ava's music and "beloved") evolve over time as a unique expression of the dreamer's inner world. In these ways, the consciousness of the dreamer expressed itself through the imaginal world, which acted as a bridge between matter and spirit.

In each case, the emergence of spirit and psychic healing have gone hand in hand. We have seen the interrelationship between the psychological and the spiritual and the way in which overcoming psychological blocks has cleared the path for the dreamer, allowing them to take the next steps. Furthermore, we can see how it is spirit, in itself, that heals. In David's case, in particular, we saw how spirit enabled David to access and overcome the psychological wounds within him. We saw, too, that the psychological issues became more and more refined as the process continued. In addition, a progressive rebalancing was taking place via the polar opposites of the masculine and feminine energies, and the more subtle, spiritual and earthly energies.

Furthermore, we have seen the way in which consciousness was expressed through the subtle dream body at each stage; the energy centres reflecting and activating the consciousness of the dreamer in the dream and waking state. In this way, the spiritual experiences in the dreams were *embodied*, not just imagined.

Through this symbiotic process, the dreamers, in their different ways, arrived at a completely new perspective of themselves and their lives—a transformed sense of self and reality which is fundamental and permanent. This is the true meaning of spiritual realisation.

Ava and David not only observed their inner world, but were deeply committed to engaging with it (mind, body, heart, and soul) and, in doing so, found the key to the unfoldment of consciousness—to awakening through dreams.

## CHAPTER SIX

# Special features of the landscape of awakening

We are near waking when we dream we are dreaming.

—*Novalis*, 1997

In our travels through the landscape of awakening, we have encountered its many unique features and forms. In this chapter, we will look at four characterising features in more detail.

## *Light and colour*

As we have seen in our travellers' journeys, a primary sign that the awakening process is underway is the increased appearance of light and colour in dreams. In David's initiation dream ("Heaven and Hell") he has a glimpse into the awakening ahead and finds that: "lights and colours of every hue are all manifest in this vast heavenly space". On the journey, the light and colour develops "a dynamic life with movement and luminescence" (David's experience of this light in his "Kandinsky Painting" dream). This leads to intense, white light (Ava's "Blinding Light" and "White Light" dreams, for example), luminous black light (David's "Luminous Face"), and green light (Ava's "The Sun") at the height of awakening. Throughout this process, the light phenomena in the dreams impacts the dreamer to the extent that a very different and more profound sense of self, and of reality, is experienced (Hamilton, 2009). In David's words, it has an "inner effect within me, like impending revelation, or the resonance of deeper and deeper meaning".

The current literature on the role of colour and light in dreams represents two different perspectives. On the one hand, our knowledge of colour and light is based on the modern understanding of light (and colour) as being externally perceived. Our brain registers colour and light according to the laws of optics. A variety of tests on the psychological effects of colour has been developed (Luscher, 1969) resulting in generalised descriptions of the influence each colour has on us. Further, Robert Hoss has suggested that these influences can be translated into our responses to colours in dreams (Hoss, 2005). It does seem that we ascribe particular meanings to colours based on universal and personal associations (rooted in life experiences). In our subjective experience of the world, our response to colour reflects these layers of meaning and also our mood. This, as Hoss suggests, is the same in dreams: colour has personal meanings and associations, but it also reflects our mood in the dream—the feeling behind the dream. Colours, as such, can be seen to function as symbols in most people's dreams. This is the psychological perspective, which works perfectly well within a personal, developmental context.

However, the meaning of colour and light in dreams, when experienced in the context of spiritual awakening, needs to be understood totally differently. Here, we are speaking of qualitatively different colours that appear in the dreams—colours that are infused with the light of pure spirit and defy accurate description or comparison. This is colour and light of which the dreamer says, "I can't describe it". These colours are not to do with physical light or associated with any life experiences; they are a *direct apprehension* of the light vibration that is coming from a much deeper, subtler source of consciousness—spirit. It is the presence of this transfigured light in dreams that is the mark of awakening.

Once we go beyond the conditioning of the mind, then light and colour is experienced far more vividly and clearly. Colours are seen in their pure essence, their "original state". Although no significant research has been undertaken to compare the colours in these various subjective mystical experiences with those of "ordinary state" colours, there is enough evidence to suggest that we are touching on a level of light and colour that is archetypal and transcendental.

At the start of the PTP, there is a great deal of darkness as we descend into the unconscious—much of it the darkness of distortion. But there is another kind of darkness that features later on in the process: a naturally occurring darkness which acts as a veil to protect us from too much light. Veiling is an essentially feminine expression (Jung, 1983). The dark and nourishing womb is like a veil protecting the baby from the light and other experiences for which it is not yet prepared. The same protective function is needed with children; we try not to expose them to things they are not ready for, we protect them. Similarly, veiling has an important spiritual function. When Hazrat Inayat Khan, a Sufi mystic, had the experience of enlightenment, he declared: "I thanked the darkness that brought me to the light, and I valued the veil which prepared me for the vision in which I saw myself reflected, the vision produced in the mirror of my soul" (Khan, 1962, p. 137). Only then did he speak about light.[1]

In our dreams, this kind of darkness acts as a temporary protection until we are ready for the hidden light to be revealed. This is called *dark light* or *black light* in the sense that the light is present but veiled from the eyes of the dreamer (Corbin, 1994). Darkness is acting as a veil protecting us from premature exposure to the hidden, psychic forces of our inner world. Much of our spiritual journey involves casting a light into the deep, inner darkness—becoming conscious.

The following dream illustrates with striking clarity that, when the depths of darkness in our psyche are plumbed in our dreams, we may find light in it.

### The Black Lake

I am friends with a boy who has an otherworldliness about him. I watch him dive into a lake that does not appear to reflect light as it is a pitch-black colour ... I find myself naked and diving into the black surface of the water ... and am surprised to note that I can see shafts of golden light penetrating to the depths where the bottom of the lake is covered with squares of copper in abstract designs, much like those of Islamic prints. It seems to me that the open spaces in the design where more blackness resides suggest that the lake is even deeper.

As the PTP progresses, the vibratory nature of our consciousness changes and, as it does so, we observe an increase in the variety and intensity of colour. Recent phenomenological studies of light in lucid and non-lucid dreams show that both the quantity and quality of light experienced in the dreams increase as we probe deeper into our inner world. We perceive progressive levels of light of incredible brilliance, disclosing subtler realities that are held within our psyche. This parallels the writings of the well-known physicist Dr David Bohm, a protégé of Albert Einstein, who spoke of the "implicate state of light" and matter whereby creation is conceived as levels of light, energy and matter that are "enfolded" within each other, with each level giving birth to the next successive level in an unfolding succession of light, non-physical to physical (Bohm, 1980).

The progression of the experience of light can develop to the point where dream images glow with, or radiate, light (as in Ava's "Lit from Inside" dream where the light was intense and omnipresent). Ultimately, one can experience a dream of pure light, without any images, known as the experience of *clear light* in Tibetan dream yoga.

Figure 4 shows how the levels of self were identified in Ava's process through the appearance of light and colour during her first two cycles of dreams. The number of times that light and colour appeared explicitly

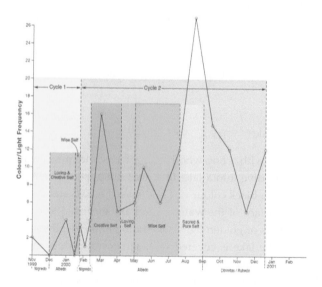

Figure 4. Cycles of light and colour in Ava's PTP.

in the dreams for each month (Colour/Light frequency) was added up. The totals are shown by the graph points. These points coincided exactly with the appearance of each level of self in the thematic analysis of her process. The graph shows the appearance of each plane of consciousness as she transited through her process from November 1999 to December 2000. As time progressed, more light emerged in the dreams, peaking in the Fifth and Sixth Planes. This pattern of increase of light continued in subsequent dream cycles (Hamilton, 2006).

Mystical experiences of colour and light have in common the sense of attention and consciousness being totally captivated and uplifted. Many describe the experience as transcendental. Inevitably, consciousness descends and returns to the mind level where colours are perceived, once again, through the "overlaid" faculties of human mind and body. The colours and light take on the same quality and intensity as before yet, in spite of the dimmed, "veiling" effect, a residual sense of the unadulterated light and colour is retained through the descent of consciousness, from the transcendental to the personal, dualistic state. It is our imagination that acts as a bridge between the two states, enabling some kind of continuity of experience to be carried from level to level—from the very subtle, inner worlds to the gross, externally-perceived, physical light.

The experience of encountering these colours, particularly when using the Waking Dream Process to explore the dream consciously, transforms our consciousness and acts as a gateway to a much subtler state (Botha, 2011). We are transported to the pure essence, the original source of the colour; ultimately, in the case of pure light, to a state of oneness (Norbu, 1992). In this way, many of the experiences of colour and light in the PTP can realise their transformative potential.

To try to restrict the dreamer's experience of colour in the PTP to their worldly, mental association is to confine their process to the personal, subject-object dichotomy and risk denying the opportunity for transforming and transcending their personal perspective.

In summary, we experience our inner light in dreams as subdued, veiled, or even completely blocked, by our psychological issues in the earlier stages of the PTP; later, as the blocks are cleared, light appears in our dreams as a metaphysical phenomenon. For this reason, both the psychological and the metaphysical perspectives are needed when understanding, and working with, colour and light in dreams in all their fullness.

## Lucid dreaming

Lucid dreaming is a catalyst for the exploration and transformation of the human psyche—transforming our perceptions, our consciousness and, ultimately, awakening us to a greater reality beyond dreaming. Once we are lucid, we have the power to interact with the dream and go deeper and deeper. Starting to dream lucidly is an important element in spiritual awakening.

For David and Ava, lucid dreaming began and became more frequent as the PTP progressed. Lucid dreams were a natural component of the awakening experience in its later stages. Furthermore, their lucid experiences were crucial in facilitating and *accelerating* that process. Lucidity enabled them to enter into their state of consciousness more fully in the dream and, crucially, to bring that experience "out" into waking consciousness as an embodied reality (see David's "Heather" and Ava's "White Light" dreams in Chapter Five). In this sense, lucidity acts as a bridge into life for the emerging consciousness.

In a lucid dream, we are asleep, but we become aware that we are dreaming. At this point, a higher or more subtle consciousness is in charge of the dream and can redirect or change it as desired. When we re-engage in conscious (concrete) thought in a lucid dream, however, we slip out of the lucid state (in which we have awakened beyond the mind) back into the more objective, dualistic state of mind of everyday life. Maintaining lucidity in a dream is a delicate balancing act.

There is a changed sense of time and space in lucid dreams. The spaces and the images in the dream open up, time dilates, and the dreamscapes become progressively more colourful and more beautiful. Some lucid dreamers recount experiences of timelessness and a sense of the numinous. Simultaneously, there can be profound feelings in lucid dreams that can even develop into ecstatic states.

Documented experiences of lucid dreaming suggest (so far) that the idea of space and time as constant is illusory (Waggoner, Hamilton, Middendorf, 2013). Indeed, lucid dream experiences can lead to what the Tibetan dream yogis call the *dreamless state*—a transcendental experience in which there are no images, no sense of time or space; only a *clear light* (Wangyal, 1998). This marks the beginnings of illumination, where we have transcended images and gone beyond duality to a non-dreaming, awakened state of unity.

The phenomenon of lucid dreaming allows us to observe the contents of the mind and to sense, or even experience, that which is beyond mind. Furthermore, it leads us to wonder who or what is the observer, the "I" in the dream? It would seem that the "I" that is participating and observing lucidly in the dream is a higher dimension of awareness beyond the mind world.

As we lucidly observe our inner reality in the dream, we discover that the mind world is merely a construct, evidenced by the fact that the dream can be altered at will. The alterable aspects of dreams are those which are psychological—mind creations originating from past impressions, old ways of interpreting our worldly experiences, and our own conscious and unconscious sense of self. But, there are aspects of lucid dreams that cannot be changed. As we go further on the path of awakening, we start to open to beings in our inner world that are not our own creations and which represent neither our mental constructs, nor aspects of our deeper self. Many lucid dreamers all over the world have encountered these beings in their lucid dreams. Robert Waggoner, in his book *Lucid Dreaming*, says of these entities:

> Though they may represent a minority, a certain set of dream figures once again show us that the expectation effect only goes so far. By acting unexpectedly, they do much to express their own validity, semi-autonomy, and viewpoint. Consider this lucid dreamer's surprise when her expectation is unmet:
>
> "I was lucid and saw this man. I asked for his name and he replied, "Otto". As planned, I asked, "Can you warn me the next time I'm dreaming?" He immediately replied, "No!" I was really surprised and asked him, "Why not?" Then Otto said, "Because this is real … " (Waggoner, 2009, p. 58)

In *Lucid Dreaming*, Robert Waggoner sets out with the common assumption that there are no "other worlds" and dreams can only be a form of our projections. In order to test the reality of his lucid dream characters, he asked all "thought forms" to disappear from the lucid dream. To his surprise, "one group [of dream figures] suddenly disappeared, while the other group looked at me with something close to utter disdain as if to say: Can't you tell the difference?" He goes on to have experiences in his lucid dreams in which the contents of his dreams are substantiated and has encounters with what he calls "spiritual realities". These experiences change his view and lead him to conclude that there are many levels of dream reality.

The implication that there are inner realities other than the mind and its dream world represents a clear departure from the modern scientific perspective. Lucid dreams show us, on the one hand, that our mind world is constructed and, on the other, that there are subtle worlds beyond the mind, in which our psyche participates, that transcend it. This resonates with the views of many modern physicists—that, beyond our 3D world, lies a series of inner spaces or dimensions (six in all) (Yau & Nadis, 2010). In experiencing the objective reality of these subtle dimensions through lucid dreams, we are returning to the ultimate origins of existence. In this way, they broaden our sense of what is "real" and change us profoundly.

In taking us beyond the personal dimension, lucid dreams can lead us to a greater sense of who we are and our relationship to the universe. In awakening to this deeper reality, we actualise the potential for manifesting the essence that lies within. Ultimately, this is an awakening to transcendental consciousness when, behind every dream, we find the divine light; not more dreams, just pure light.

Ava's dream "Lit from Inside" (see "Ava Awakens", Chapter Five) illustrates how lucidity can lead to an awakening of consciousness in the dream. As she becomes more conscious, she goes deeper and touches on the hidden treasure behind the dream. The dream begins with a scene of extreme rush and stress. Ava realises, almost immediately, that there is no point in rushing around. This insight results in a breakthrough and changes the dream (and the dreamer's consciousness), leading to a conscious perception of the inner light.

Lit from Inside (preamble)

Somehow I realise that it doesn't make sense to be rushing like that; it will bring no success … and, at that moment, I realise: I am in a dream! Finally, I am lucid! I don't have to hurry any more; I can look around quietly, being careful not to wake up. I am standing on a hill … (the dream continues).

No explicit dreamwork followed this dream, and was not necessary, because the deep impression of peace, light and beauty carried over into Ava's meditations and, eventually, into her life. One particular aspect of the dream is very important to mention. In it, Ava remembers: "that I should not be changing things in a dream, but rather watch them unfold". This was of crucial importance at this point in her process because, had she continued using her powers to change things to her liking, she would not have reached the sunless landscape radiating an omnipresent, all-pervading, intense light. This kind of place cannot be reached by our will or by our constructive imagination. The way of transcendence is indifference—just being with the dream and letting the opening come. It is not desirable to bring our own limited desires and understanding into our lucid dreams.

It is true that lucid dreaming gives us instant access to enormous resources, to "everything you need", as experienced lucid dreamers would say, but only if we are aware enough to *know* what we need. There are many levels of lucid dreaming; only the most highly evolved lucid dreamers can keep the overview of the process *in* the dream and enough conscious awareness to use the opportunity afforded by lucid dreaming responsibly as guidance on the spiritual path. In allowing the reality beyond our psychological constructs to emerge naturally and freely, we ensure that the path to awakening is unobstructed.

There are similarities between the experience of lucid dreams and the awakening of our consciousness experienced in the Waking Dream Process as we will go on to see in Chapter Seven. There is also similarity with what Jungians call *active imagination*, as Waggoner points out: "Various of the Jungian-oriented psychotherapists told me that lucid dreaming reminded them of what Jung called 'active imagination', except that I was doing it in the dream state, not, as Jung described it, in the meditative state" (Waggoner, 2009, p. 285). There is even a similar sense of "strangeness", accompanied by a kind of tingling of spirit energy and excitement. There is no doubt that lucid dreams and multidimensional dreamwork share enormous potential for creative and spiritual unfoldment, for awakening through dreams.

## Visionary geography

For Jung, the goal of individuation is balance (1968). In the pursuit of wholeness and realisation, one of the most important elements is the balancing and reconciliation of opposites, and we have seen this throughout the processes of our travellers. For Ava, there was a significant reconciliation of the loving (more heart-centred) and critical (more mind-centred) parts of herself early on in her PTP. In "Shining Gold", we saw the coming together of masculine and feminine aspects and, later, in a dream where Mont Blanc and New York are side by side, the mind and spirit worlds meet. She dreams of "sparkling light from above *and* from below" and that her therapist "is sometimes a man, sometimes a woman" in further balancing dreams. For David, there is a long road to balancing upper and lower, spirit and body, in dreams where the higher and lower worlds mirror each other, culminating in "Gene Hackman" where he declares: "my world is in harmony and balance". It is clear from their stories that balancing these fundamental aspects of the psyche through their dreams was integral to the awakening process.

David and Ava's dreams and all the dream research showed that direction (as in, north, south, east, west; up, down; above, below; left, right; in, out—explicit or implicit) has an extremely important role in dreams in terms of the balancing of the psyche. It has been found that the directions indicated in dreams are not arbitrary; rather, they represent significant signposts for the dreamer as to where they are and where they need to go in terms of their development and unfoldment. For this reason, directions in dreams must be observed very carefully as important clues as to how to balance the psyche. Henry Corbin's used the term "visionary geography" to describe the inner world and its landscapes to the mystic as a "spiritual body—celestial earth". The journey through this "celestial earth" gave the mystic a geographical sense of travelling through an inner landscape that is similar in appearance to the earth, but which, in fact, is a subtle earth experienced in the subtle body. The origin of the term dates back to the ancient Mazdean tradition (Corbin, 1990). Here, it is used with specific application to the understanding of the dream journey through the inner landscape (Hamilton, 2009).

If we apply the metaphor of *visionary geography* to dreams, then going north in a dream means that the dreamer is heading out of life, their consciousness moving upwards towards the head (which may feature prominently in the dream) and crown centre. Or, to put it another way, the dreamer is becoming more aware of spirit and less worldly in their consciousness. Similarly, if the dreamer is going up in the dream (going uphill, flying, climbing a ladder, and so forth) or is in a high place or "above", it would indicate that the energy and consciousness of the dreamer is ascending in the body to a higher centre. Or, if the dreamer is stuck in their worldly mindset, then images of ascending might appear in the dreams by way of balance. Ascending can be a positive development or a pathological escape into fantasy as we have seen in the "Travellers' Tales". Dreams of dangerous ascent could warn of a need for groundedness. In David's "Perfect Landing" dream (in Chapter Four), his first plane crashes before the second makes a safe descent.

Going south in dreams could indicate that the dreamer is coming more into life and worldly concerns, their consciousness descending and incorporating a more grounded aspect of the psyche, particularly if they have been in an elevated state of consciousness. So it is that Ava travels to Africa from Southern Italy at the end of her PTP. The guidance of the dream could be indicating that the dreamer needs to come out of their head and into their feelings and their body. Or, it could indicate that they are going into their buried "stuff", their unconscious material. Likewise, if the dreamer descends in the dream (down stairs, climbing down ladders, downhill and so on) or is in a low place or "below", then the dreamer's consciousness is moving downwards in the body with the focus in the lower energy centres and on the more instinctual forces within. This downward movement of the psyche may show itself in the dream in images relating to the legs or feet, underground places, basements, the bottom of things, and so forth.

Going west (or going to the right) points more to the mind world, the man-made world, represented by the Occident. If the direction in the dream is to the right, or if something appears to the right, a more active and expressive aspect of consciousness is emerging in the dreamer. So, if the dreamer is too passive in life, then the balancing (or compensating) image (going west or right) may be an invitation to develop the expressive aspect. Or, the reference to the right may show an imbalance in the dreamer where mind is predominating over feeling. "The Cleaver" was an example of this in Chapter Four where the critical mind of the dreamer is symbolised by the ruthless man wielding the cleaver in his right hand.

Travelling eastwards (or to the left), on the other hand, is the direction of the Orient, the East—the home of the soul. It is the journey towards spirituality and the finer feelings of the inner world. A reference to the East in a dream signifies a longing in the dreamer to make this journey. At the end of the Fourth Plane, David sees a huge storm coming from the East; his journey to spirit will not be easy. Similarly, if the direction of the dream is to the left or if something appears on the left, a more receptive aspect of consciousness is wanting to be known in the dreamer. In "Boat Journey" in Chapter Four, the dreamer leaves her worldly life (the land on the right) and journeys by sea to the island (where her soul feelings are to be found) on the left.

The left in dreams is also very often connected with the feminine aspect, just as the right is associated with the masculine. In Ava's "Turning in Bliss", the beloved takes her in the dance with his right hand while she reciprocates with her left. In "Yellow Fish", David turns to the left to find the woman he desires (his feminine aspect) in the dream.

There are also the directions of "in" and "out" which signify the movement in the psyche of the dreamer inwards towards the inner world, or outwards towards life. These directions may have spiritual or psychological significance, or both, as was the case in David's "Compassionate Woman" dream where she came "in" to his isolation to take him "out" into relationship and life, but was also taking him further in his spiritual journey.

Ava provides an example of visionary geography in two dreams she had about six months apart, showing a development in the balancing of her psyche through visionary geography. In the first dream, "Huge Ship", she is alone in struggling to steer the ship, which has veered "too far to the *left*". When the motor of the ship fails, she loses control of it and is in danger. She seeks advice from a *man* by telephone about how to "get down to the propeller" to fix it. On re-entering the dream, Ava was clear that she needed to "dive *down* and see what's wrong" and that her mistake had been to turn the ship around, rather than continue in "the *direction of the stars*". The second dream is almost like a sequel to the first.

### The Cruise

I have just run over the water to reach the boat which was already waiting there. The female boat captain has seen me and is waiting, so I can jump in. Then, she leaves up the river into the harbour of New York. The people on the boat are Swiss; they have taken a week-long cruise on that river, from the left … I am wearing a shining, white T-shirt and a blue and white silk scarf, the colours forming two triangles. In the harbour, I meet my husband who is a guide. He wants to show me things I have not yet seen. We drive to the right, to the ocean; it is not far. There, we walk on a wall with a railing out into the water, up to the waist, looking towards the East. There are cliffs in the sea, something like a huge cardboard box. We are deeply touched and find that infinitely beautiful.

In the first dream, the emphasis is on the left, danger, and going down. In the second dream, there is a female boat captain who has successfully taken the Swiss party on a week-long cruise. She brings balance to the remote masculine of the previous dream, and there is a balance between masculine and feminine within the dream in the form of the partnership between Ava and her husband. Furthermore, left and right, east and west are equally present in the dream. Ava can run *over* water this time, now that her need to "dive down" has been met, and she wears a scarf with colours in two triangles which make a symmetrical square—a very important sign of balance in her psyche. In the final balancing image, man and woman stand in water up to the waist looking towards the East, deeply touched by the infinite beauty. In this pair of dreams, we can see the way in which the directions are there as guidance for Ava—a map of her psyche—showing her where she is in her journey and where she needs to go.

Chapter Seven will look at how visionary geography in dreams can be "tracked" in the body of the dreamer in facilitating the creation of balance in the psyche. In the section that follows, we will explore further the presence of symmetry as a measure of the transformed psyche.

## Symmetry

In nature, where there is beauty and wholeness, we will find symmetry. Yet, (as cosmologists now know) the whole of creation was born out of asymmetry, without which nothing would have existed (*New Scientist*, 2012). Likewise, the matured, awakened self is born from the imbalances of the psyche, triggered by the tension of opposites. The wholeness resulting from the balancing process manifests in dreams as beauty and *symmetry*.

Symmetry appears through beautiful images in our dreams, through harmony in forms and colours, and in the balance between the aspects of the dream. Symmetrical images in dreams are a reflection of the balancing of psychic polarities taking place in the personality and are often a sign of awakening. Furthermore, the emergence of symmetry often heralds lucidity. Symmetry can occur in a one-off, significant dream, or in short dream sequences, but it is only when we look at the presence and development of symmetrical images over an extended period (several months, a year, or several years), that it becomes evident that symmetry is a very important hallmark of transformational dreams.

Furthermore, it is apparent from the Psychospiritual Transformation Process that there is an evolution of symmetry. It is clear to see that something is happening in the psyche of the dreamer; it is as if *something is actually being constructed*, not only in the mind, but in the whole being of the dreamer. The newly awakened, conscious self is taking shape—made from the building blocks of the subtler, archetypal levels of consciousness (just as the physical body is made up of the building blocks of DNA). These building blocks—vibratory patterns—were always there in us, but they are being unveiled in the transformation process, stage by stage, level by level, until the "construction" is complete and the "inner architecture" of the psyche is revealed. This unveiling of the psyche's structure can be observed in our dreams through the language of numbers and shapes and, ultimately, archetypal forms.

It has been discovered that one of the ways in which symmetry evolves in dreams is in a progression (but not necessarily linear) in dream images of numbers and their corresponding geometrical shapes, culminating, ultimately, in a perfectly symmetrical image (Hamilton, 2011). In mathematics, all numbers are the products of prime numbers. All geometric shapes are the product of prime-sided shapes (du Sautoy, 2008). It is suggested, therefore, that when symmetrical geometrical shapes appear in our dreams, they are a reflection of something fundamental—they are the basic forms emerging from our essence, our oneness.

In dreams, the "something fundamental" is the emerging archetype, manifested as a quality. Where an archetype is incarnating, or being born, into the psyche, the archetypal form first appears in the dreams disguised in separate, seemingly unrelated, insignificant images. The overall picture at this stage would be rather like a child's "dot-to-dot" puzzle. However, on closer examination, there will be an underlying quality or theme that connects the points (the dream images) to each other. What links the symbols is their purpose in revealing a particular archetypal quality emerging into consciousness. In time, the dream sequence will reveal the archetypal quality in the form of a rich or beautiful symbol that shows symmetry. Daily meditation on this symbol in the waking state further catalyses awakening in the dreamer. This is the point at which the dreamer becomes conscious that something significant has occurred in their dreams and in their psyche, and the quality begins to come through in their personality.

The archetype reveals itself incrementally in images containing numbers and shapes (explicitly—one, two, three, a circle, a square and so on; or implicitly—a circular pool, a two-sided wall, three men, a cube-shaped room etc.). Numbers are implicit in the symmetrical shapes, which, in turn, are related to the emerging archetypal aspect. Jung, of course, was the first psychologist to talk about symmetry occurring in the process of individuation (von Franz, 1975). For Jung, mandalas were the symmetrical form that signified the developing individuation process.[2] Jung wrote about the role of numbers in dreams and his observations led to insights into what each number meant in the dream, or how the number behaved in the dream. Further, he said that numbers emerge from a numinous continuum; in other words, there is an essence or essence of spirit that actually contains all numbers (von Franz, 1974).

In a sequence of dreams, the numbers that appear in the dreams are secretly revealing the emergence of a new, developing, inner order within the psyche. Eventually, that order manifests as a symmetrical image. Even numbers that appear in dreams tend to be associated with balance and indicate the balancing of opposites in the psyche. Odd numbers, particularly prime numbers (three, five, seven, eleven, thirteen, seventeen, and so on), indicate increasing order—a hierarchical order of consciousness. They show a development of sophistication in the "inner architecture" of the dreamer (von Franz, 1974).

In terms of the "core" numbers one to five, there is, broadly speaking, a progression of these numbers into their corresponding shapes through the PTP, reflecting the dreamer's degree of development. The number one (or the numerically equivalent ten, 100, 1,000 etc.) is a symbol of unity. One does not always appear as a number in dreams at the outset as it is the unconscious source from which the sequence of numbers (and shapes) will emerge. Later, however, the appearance of a circle or sphere signifies the conscious union of the personal self with the emerging archetypal quality (Edinger, 1991). Where there is a sphere in the dream (which is three-dimensional), or someone standing in the middle of a circle or the middle of a sphere in the dream, this indicates that the dreamer has actually integrated the particular archetypal theme that has been emerging throughout the dream sequence. Ava's

"Circle of Love" dream in which she stands in the centre of the circle of loving students, is a good example of this.

The appearance of the number two is the first step towards the development of the geometrical image of the square which, later, may develop into the cube (the three-dimensional square). The cube is the foundation structure in the "building of the psyche". Two can also develop into a rectangle and cuboid. The number two is the most common number at the start of a dream sequence, often in association with activation and balancing in the lower energy centres. According to Jung, it symbolises the conscious emergence of an unconscious aspect of a polarity in the psyche, which implies that a balancing is taking place. In a dream, there may be something on the left and something on the right (two aspects), or the dreamer goes from upstairs to downstairs (two places), or there is a male and female present (two people). In each case, two opposite elements in the psyche are balancing each other out. When the number two occurs, it is usually followed by the appearance of a symmetrical geometrical figure—a square or a rectangle. In the earlier part of his PTP, David encounters two fish in "Yellow Fish" as he faces an unconscious aspect of himself. Later, he has a dream where he and his brother sit on opposite sides of a table, arguing at first, but then embracing. This was an indication that David was reconciling two warring aspects of his psyche.

Mathematically, the number three relates to the triangle, which Jung believed symbolises the rediscovery of the original unity, indicating the presence of spirit. When two opposite parts or points in the psyche appear alongside each other in balance (forming the base of the triangle), a third point appears, making a triangle—indicating the integrating presence of the transcendent function[3] (the apex of the triangle). Typically, this would be represented in a dream by three people forming a triangle, or the movement between three physical locations, thereby tracing out a triangle. In "The Cruise" dream in the previous section of this chapter, the colours of Ava's scarf form two triangles which make a square, like the upper and lower triangles in the Kabala (Halevi, 1986). This seems to reflect the conjoining of opposites which has occurred in the two dreams to create symmetry and balance.

Four is a further psychospiritual development of three. Jung talked about the number four as a symbol of completion of a stage in the process of individuation, an indicator of balance in opposing forces in the psyche (Jung ref). Geometrically speaking, it will appear as a square or a rectangle. The cube or cuboid represent a more complete stage of development. So, when a stage or aspect of the process is completed, the number four appears, symbolised by the four sides of a square, or *quaternio* (four aspects) signifying that the opposing forces in the Self have reached a new state of balance (Jung, 1983). So, as David goes further in his process, he dreams of a beautiful square wooden box in "The Pedicurist" and of the cube which holds the opposites of his psyche in balance and "stirs me deeply and draws me in". As Ava's PTP progresses, the square appears as a huge, square castle, a cube-like house (which contains a "secret") and the "large square of fertile dark-brown earth", heralding Rubedo and the completion of her process.

The combination of numbers three and four in Jung's alchemy, where three different actions must be performed four times over, bring about completion of a process (Jung, 1983). When the numbers three and four appear together (either as three and four, or thirty and forty and so on), it is hypothesised that they refer to the existence of an invisible matrix containing twelve pieces of information, each piece being an aspect of the archetype. This matrix acts as a net within which the incarnating archetype is contained and nurtured. From within this matrix, a new symmetrical shape (image) will emerge, embodying the essential quality of the incarnated archetype. Once it is present in the dream state, it is already, or will soon become, a conscious part of the dreamer's personality. In terms of a geometric shape, if three and four (or the triangle and the square) are combined, a pyramid shape or tetrahedron (two pyramids, base to base) is constructed, which, when it appears in the dream, indicates a further development of the archetype that is establishing in the psyche. In David's dreams, this is shown in the cathedral motif—a combination of tetrahedron and cuboid.

Finally, the number five will often appear as a centre point within a square, cube, circle or sphere. The centre point represents the fifth point within the shape—the "master" point, through which the dreamer actually begins to relate to the other four balanced aspects of the psyche that have been constellated. Jung does not speak of the number five, but von Franz suggests that the number five is associated with the presence of the individuated Self (von Franz, 1974). When it appears, the self is becoming conscious and beginning to hold together the tension of the opposites. This is the apex of the transformation process. Ava dreams of five teacups—the five chakras—in "Turning in Bliss" (where she and her beloved are joined in a symmetrical embrace) as she approaches the highest point in her PTP.

The final image in the evolution of symmetry in the dreamer's PTP will be the symmetrical and beautiful image; most often, a cube-shaped or sphere-shaped image (the latter being the most perfectly symmetrical shape). In David's case, this was the luminescent "sphere-like disc" of the "Magical Object" dream, which was the key to all understanding. For Ava, a mandala appears in a dream (at the end of a cycle of dreams involving the balancing of upper and lower energy centres) which opens the way to the awakening described in "Travellers' Tales". The image appears as a drawing of: "A square on top, two lines down to a circle with an oval inside, then two flesh-coloured spirals, like umbilical cords, spiralling around each other three times. From above, it can be seen that the circle has a cross in it".

The square holds the balance of the four elements. It connects, via two lines, to a circle, which is a symbol of self. This circle has an oval within, which might indicate a new heart centre capacity (she senses the heart centre turning upon waking). The "flesh-coloured" spirals, like "umbilical cords", or a double helix, are suggestive of the ascending and descending spirit (red and white spirit) in balance and physically embodied—*born* into consciousness. The circle with a cross on it seems to show the inverse perspective; that is, instead of the square containing the circle, the circle contains the square. Like David's mountains appearing where valleys had been and vice versa, they are interchangeable in the balance of Ava's psyche (echoing the quantum physics idea of entanglement (Kumar, 2009)).

This symmetrical dream image seems to encapsulate, wordlessly, what has happened in her process—that spirit is interwoven into the very fabric of her inner world. Spirit has become conscious; a profound psychospiritual transformation has taken place.

*Three examples of the evolution of symmetry*

Example one

We saw in Ava's journey to awakening, the significance of the theme of music in her unfoldment. The theme evolves over the whole course of her PTP and its cycles of dreams. It first appears in a dream where a piano tuner has come to tune her "brown" piano, the *lower* octaves of which are "badly out of tune". Part of the work ahead was the tuning and balancing of upper and lower. Ava herself observed that the piano seemed to be the metaphor for her dreamwork and the "tuning" of the soul, with the seven octaves of the piano corresponding to the seven subtle energy centres.

In a further dream, there are "two female leading parts" in an opera and the tenor has asked Ava if she would be willing to "sing the title role next year". The appearance of the number two suggests that the expressive aspect of Ava is emerging into consciousness. The singing theme continued to evolve over time in the balancing of masculine and feminine (right and left) and upper and lower in dreams of a little *girl* (who wears *four* different dresses, the *third* being white with gold and the *fourth* sky blue) and a little *boy* (both singing stars) travelling with Ava to sing *four* concerts together in *four* different European cities; Ava singing the "Gloria" with her husband (masculine and feminine are together in adult form); until, a year later, Ava sings soprano reaching all the *high* notes with a famous prima donna (having developed the ability to reach the highest and most subtle level of conscious attunement within her being).

Then, she has a dream where she has to accomplish *three* things: write about a play, perform music on a piano, and perform a concert— all in *four* hours as part of a "cooking course". Here we have the three-four matrix birthing the emerging soul quality. The reference to cooking symbolises coagulation of that quality. Finally, Ava sings "La Traviata", as the prima donna wearing a beautiful pink silk gown (the colours have evolved over time from the brown of the piano towards beauty and light).

In the process occurring within these dreams, music and, in particular, singing in operas, was the symbolic image representing this attunement of her consciousness in the dreams. For her, these were the instruments of the soul. A further dream in a subsequent series seems to echo the earlier "Four Concerts" dream where the main characters were the little girl and boy singers.

## Red and White Roses

Cecilia Bartoli is giving a series of concerts, at the end of which an admirer comes on stage, kneels before her and hands her a red rose. She takes it; then he comes again and showers her with white roses. She likes it, so she talks to him and tells him that she is going to tour through the US, with eight stops, and he could join her and bring her roses at the end of every concert. First, she will be in the mountains, in a beautiful hotel … Then close to a lake or on an island in the East … Then, in the middle of summer, she will go south (North Carolina I think), a resort with a golf course, all green meadows … The trip will take them all across America to the West coast.

The little girl and boy have grown up now. She is a diva with the beautiful first name of Cecilia (patron saint of music), who will perform at *eight* concerts (double quaternity) where her admirer will give her *red and white* roses *eight* times. Whilst the four European cities in the "Four Concerts" dream are not identified, we now have geographical indications of the *four directions*: north (mountains), east (lake or island), south (golf course), west (West coast). This is completely balanced in terms of visionary geography. Balancing is also present in the red and white roses, which are the symbols of ascending and descending spirit and reappear eight times in the coniunctio between the young man and the young diva. Through the dreams, balance and symmetry are being expressed through colour, number, direction, and the music motif.

### Example two

More recently, in 2008, Ava's dreams show the further evolution of spherical symmetry and the emergence of the quality of radiant light in a process lasting about seven months. She dreams of a magical baby, who grows miraculously fast, and a female teacher whose face is radiant with light. A few months later, she has a vision (a waking experience) of her sleeping grandchild surrounded by a "sphere" of golden light (here the light and the infant of the first dream are found together). Then, she has the following dream.

#### The Lamp

I am with mother in her bedroom … I have brought her a present, a lamp. round as a ball, whitish transparent, with silver. The lamp is made of two half-spheres which can be pushed into each other so that the lamp looks like a half-sphere. I mount this lamp on the ceiling in the middle of the room.

The lamp is *round* as a ball and it is placed in the *middle* of the room, which is important—not to the side or the edge. The middle of the room (as with the number five) signifies the centring of the dream psyche. The lamp is made up of two hemispheres; the two components of this ball of light are two symmetrical shapes, two opposites.

In the next dream, a child is "shining from *inside*" (now, the child and the light are one) and wants to eat (to coagulate) a blue star fruit (the star, in this case, was a symmetrical, eight-pointed star). A further, concluding symmetrical image emerged in a subsequent dream.

### Candle Inside

There is a little white candle inside of me, in a round glass container, radiating a soft light around me.

Now the light is "inside" Ava; the whole archetype—light—has been incorporated into her consciousness. In Ava, this manifested as the ability to see colours and lights in people's auras. She began to see the non-physical lights at night and she began to see her own light. In other words, the archetype of radiance was actually manifesting in her personality; the inner reality mirrors the outer reality.

### Example three

For this dreamer, the appearance of the numbers three and four is part of an evolution that will lead to spiritual awakening in the dream "Good Friday Snake".

### Snake Bite

Back at my parents' house … My parents are sitting on the couch. They are forty years old and I am three, hiding behind the big green chair opposite the couch (a place I often hid). I see myself bump into a coiled snake that is sleeping behind this chair … The snake is terribly beautiful … It is also very large—about three to four inches round and over eight feet long. Slowly, the snake moves around the

chair and then suddenly rears back and lunges forward to bite my
father between his brows. My father dies. And I wake up.

The dreamer's parents were forty years old when she was three years
of age. Then, three and four (inches) and eight (feet) describe the size
of the snake. But this is not just a cognitive estimate; it is also, perhaps, a metaphor for something fundamental that is manifesting in the
dreamer's psyche. Here, the numbers three and four act as the matrix
containing the image of the emerging archetype—the kundalini energy
of spirit. The number eight in this particular dream, provides the third
dimension of depth—the length of the snake. Being a multiple of four,
it consolidates the form of the image of the snake (which began as a
worm in a much earlier dream) in her unconscious.

Some time later, the three-four matrix appears again and yields its
treasure.

### Good Friday Snake

At about three or four in the morning of Good Friday, I have the
following dream: I wake up in the bed of the "ideal" bedroom I
created for myself when I was a teenager ... I am lying down in
my antique, four-poster bed with my husband on my right. He is
sleeping peacefully. Suddenly, my eyes are drawn to the moonlight
caught in the immense three-part mirror on my dresser opposite
the bed. The mirror has a strong, wood frame that curves along the
top and is straight on the sides. There is a large central portion and
two smaller side mirrors. It's like a large triptych behind an altar.
The mirrors radiate moonlight. Curled up three or four times at the
base of the mirror is a large, very earthy, powerful rattlesnake ...
[the dream continues].

In *this* dream, the snake has come to bite the dreamer (not her father,
as before), transforming her consciousness and opening her to an experience of inner light and energetic power that changed her sense of
herself and her life (see Chapter Seven). As in "Snake Bite", the snake
image manifests in a three by four matrix (it is three or four in the morning; the three-part mirror; the four-poster bed; the snake coiled three or
four times). The snake image has evolved now to a three-dimensional

coil, indicating that the essential quality is establishing itself in the dreamer.

The dreamer of "Snake Bite" above went on to have two further dreams which exemplify the significance of the number five beautifully.

### Fifth Beam

There's a temple I saw once before in a dream ... The outside is all done in blue lapis stone. As I stand at the open door, I can only see a deep, velvety blackness ... There is a large stone slab under the central dome and, here, light streams down onto the slab through the soft darkness ... I approach the slab and stretch out on it with my feet towards the temple's door. Four women come out and stand at my shoulders and ankles. The light from the dome separates into beams that come in at four angles and cross at my centre. Another fifth beam comes down vertically from the dome. A figure walks towards me ... He takes my head in his hands and leans over to kiss me between my brows ... It is hard for me to accept this kiss, but I realise it's time to do so.

In this spiritual dream, the four women and the four beams of light contained within the circular dome suggests the archetypal, alchemical image of the mandala (a square within a circle). The dreamer now situates herself (consciously) at the centre of the matrix. The fifth beam of light is the "master point" of the dream and triggers the appearance of the healing figure. Here, she is kissed, rather than bitten, in the third eye, suggesting a further evolution of consciousness from the snake dreams. The same dreamer has the following dream at the height of her awakening process.

### Five-pointed Star

As I look up at him, it's as if a metal band about four inches wide snaps open across my chest. Suddenly, I feel myself go out of my body. My self expands and lifts out of my chest and hovers in the air over my bed ... A clear five-pointed star appears in each of my eyes and expands to fill me with a powerful light. I think my eyes must be open as bright, white sun enters the window and fills the room.

The metal band "about four inches wide" snaps (as her heart centre opens) and she begins to experience a freedom from the body and mind and to see the "celestial" light—the light of her own being. Now the five points of light, which appeared in "Fifth Beam", transform into the five-pointed star, filling her with light—the transformed symbol is integrated as light.

## CHAPTER SEVEN

# Working with dreams

My smallest work in the inner plane is worth more than all I do in
the outer world.

—*Hazrat Inayat Khan*, 2010

## Applying multidimensional dreamwork

The multidimensional dreamwork approach applied in the therapeutic
setting combines creative imagination, psychological understanding,
bodywork, and healing. Exploring the dreamer's experience on all levels, using the body as a guide, the deeper reality of the dream and the
dreamer's being, can be accessed. Through the image of the dream we
enter the mind world and the subtle worlds beyond; through the feelings of the dream we are connected with our soul; through the physical
body we find our subtle body; in the energetic intensity of the dream,
we find spirit.

The dream is worked with in a dynamic, but sensitive and supportive
way in order to activate the potential for transformation held within it.
During the dream exploration, the meaning and intention of the dream
become clearer to both the dreamer and the dream guide. In making the

meaning of the dream more conscious, the dreamer can begin to benefit from the guidance which the dream has offered in its deeper wisdom. The approach is particularly valuable when used with someone undergoing a radical shift in the sense of self and the emergence of something new in the psyche.

The method I call the Waking Dream Process is a powerful method of waking dreamwork, developed over many years. By tracking the dream through the body and, simultaneously, engaging the realm of imagination consciously, the psychological, as well as the transpersonal aspects hidden within the dream are revealed and encountered. Using the Waking Dream Process, the dreamer re-enters the dream in order to experience consciously what is held in it; *the consciousness of the dreamer is awakened to the inner world in the waking state*. In this state, we are not only remembering the dream, but also participating once again in our dream world with the creative imagination. The dream comes alive.

The realisation that we are back in the dream is similar to the experience of becoming lucid within a dream. It is a kind of "waking up" within our dream world. We have the same sense of freedom to experiment or discover new dimensions of our being. The main difference between the exploration of a dream in the waking state and in a lucid dream experience is the degree of involvement in the experience. In lucid dreaming, the dreamer is intensely and exclusively focused in the dream, whereas the Waking Dream Process could be called "partial" dreaming. In spite of this, in the Waking Dream Process, one can re-enter the dream and be sufficiently engrossed to do the necessary psychospiritual work consciously and effectively, whilst maintaining a degree of objectivity and freedom.

Furthermore, experiences in the Waking Dream Process can be further actualised and integrated in the follow-up work that dreamers undertake after a session. Astounding progress in the transformation process can be observed when the dreamer takes this seriously, going back to the key waking dream experience in a daily meditation until this specific aspect of the work feels complete.

## Working with images

The Waking Dream Process provides us with an opportunity to mine the riches of our dream imagery. In the Waking Dream Process, we are invited, not only to explore the conscious meaning and associations of a dream image, but also to re-enter, to re-experience the dream image. By using the imagination consciously as a creative tool, as well as exploring the image energetically (through the body), we enter into its consciousness, and connect with the feeling and accompanying sensations it holds. "When we experience the images, we also directly experience the inner parts of ourselves that are clothed in the images" (Johnson, 1986, p. 25).

Exploring the images in this way frees up the "stuckness", or it may give us an insight into the nature of a psychological complex that is acting as a block to growth. In directly experiencing these parts of ourselves, we are able to transform them, integrate them, to realise their power and potential by releasing the spirit within. If the images open onto the subtle worlds (or there are no images, just light), in connecting with them more consciously, we are transforming our consciousness. In either case, we are engaged in a process of enlargement of our psyche, of ourselves.

In working with a dream symbol in the Waking Dream Process, we work with it actively, using creative imagination, to build a bridge to the source of the symbol—the origin of the dream's wisdom. The symbol is a gateway; it opens the door to the inner self. Particular images tend to hold the main feeling and charge of the dream, particularly the central image of the dream, which holds the transformational potential (Hartmann, 2011). This is recognised by the energy it evokes in the body of the dreamer during waking dreamwork. Key dream symbols often have something magical about them, or they have a magical context; for example, a baby speaking like an adult, a fish that flies, walking through walls, and so on. In staying with the image, the feelings and sensations, the consciousness of the dream transforms, opening up the gateway to a deeper realm of the self. This is the purpose and guidance of the dream.

The symbology of the colours in dreams of awakening can be considered to be archetypal; that is, coming from a deeper level than the personal. When tracking a person's dreams, the guide will notice a shift in their consciousness when they start dreaming in colour, rather than black and white. When contact is made with the inner life, colour (natural colour, rather than synthetic) starts to appear. The way the dreamer experiences the colours in the dream and in the waking state is the primary determinant for the meaning and value of the colour to the dreamer.

Research has shown that there are a number of symbols that commonly occur in the PTP (Hamilton, 2006). Many of these have been illustrated through the "Travellers' Tales". A simple, quick-reference guide to some of the main symbols is given in the appendix to this book ("Symbols of transformation"). The symbols listed in this appendix do not represent a comprehensive compendium of transformative symbols; nor are they explained in depth. The list is given as an aide-memoire to be used in conjunction with the book and should not be applied to dreams in a simplistic way without a full understanding of the dreamer's process and unique context.

It is important to note too, that in a non-transformative context, some of the symbols included will have a different meaning. For example, dreaming of a celebration following someone's birthday party in waking life is simply a reflection of the impression of the party. Similarly, a psychic dream foretelling the birth of a child has a very different meaning from such a dream occurring during a PTP. Also, each symbol allows for innumerable variations (in colour, in context, in magnitude and so on) in its capacity to symbolise the changing inner state of the dreamer. For instance, houses that grow bigger and lighter from dream to dream seem to indicate a growing, clearer, more positive sense of self. Similarly, the colours of symbols that go from darker to lighter hues seem to be indicating a growing sense of spirit.

Chapter Six looked at the idea of visionary geography in the relation to the landscape of awakening. One of the key aspects of multidimensional dreamwork in practice involves tracking the directions taken by the dreamer and/or dream characters, as well as the direction suggested by the key images. It is important to note the presence or absence of balance in the dream images in the process of tracking the dream in terms of upper and lower, left and right and so on, and "mapping" the directions of the dream onto the body. When the geographical directions in the dream and the movements of the energy in the body of the dreamer are linked, the dreamer can be guided to a more balanced state.

The Waking Dream Process can help the dreamer to follow the guidance of the dream imagery (whether that be to follow the direction indicated because it is desirable, or to pursue the opposite direction in order to create balance in the psyche). In the latter scenario, the dreamer is invited to be with the felt experience of the presenting image first and then explore its counterpart or opposite; or the dreamer may find that, in staying with the initial image, being with it, that it transforms itself naturally into something more balanced. The principle can be applied to Jung's four psychological functions,[1] if that is the therapist's modality, allowing for a greater balance to be created between thinking and feeling, sensation and intuition.

The same process is relevant to the elemental balance in the dream. For example, where there is an expanse of water in a dream, the dreamer could be invited to enter the water (if their need is to be more in touch with their feeling nature or to undergo a purification, for example); or they may need to find the solid ground in the dream in order to "anchor" themselves. By feeling their feet on the ground in the Waking Dream Process, the dreamer is taking the first steps towards achieving a new, inner balance. The work begun on the inner plane must, necessarily, find its counterpart in the outer world; the one is a mirror of the other. So, by encouraging the opposites to appear in waking dreamwork and bringing them together, the dreamer grows towards balance and wholeness in life.

In terms of numbers and symmetry in dream images, what is important is not to get bogged down in the detail, but to look out for some kind of development or evolution in dream images over time in terms of numbers, shapes, and symmetry as a sign that something is emerging and constellating in the dreamer. As we saw in our travellers' journeys, there is an evolution of light, symmetry, and dream symbols through the Psychospiritual Transformation Process. One of the most important tasks of multidimensional dreamwork and the dream guide is to track the presence, progress, and development of these things through the PTP and, in doing so, hold the bigger picture for the dreamer. It is only by tracking the dreams and interacting with them in the context of the dreamer's process that we can really begin to understand.

In the case of frightening images, the dreamer can re-enter the dream in a waking state, with the support of a dream guide, and face the nightmare scenario. The grip of the feeling of the dream may be broken if they can overcome their conscious attitude (fear) and face the unconscious aspect that is present in the dream (which they have, until then, been avoiding consciously). The energy that was locked up in this unconscious, regressed form becomes a conscious part of the dreamer. For instance, the spider may change into a small, frightened boy or girl who simply needs holding and reassuring. In focusing on and embodying what we encounter, we may discover a more subtle feeling and awareness that was waiting to emerge consciously. This, in turn, may lead to a deeper understanding of ourselves. This new awareness is the "guiding spirit" behind the dream.

## Working with the subtle body

Chapter One defined the subtle dream body and its importance in psychospiritual transformation in enabling us to perceive the world of dreams and the subtle realms beyond. In "tracking" the dreamer's experience in the physical body in the dreamwork, we are actually working also with the subtle body (the subtle energy level) to unlock psychic "charge" held there. "Tracking" the sensations and feelings in the body accesses the emotion held in the dream images, as well as the subtle dimensions behind the dream. In this way, we enter into the subtle world through the subtle body.

In fact, our subtle body is not located within us; we are *contained* by our subtle body—we live within it. So, when we invite the dreamer to "turn within" at the start of the Waking Dream Process, what we are actually asking them to do is to enlarge their consciousness beyond the body, to expand their awareness to the subtle worlds. When we do this, we can "see" on another level (physical seeing is the counterpart of subtle seeing). In working with the body, we go beyond the mind; we are working with the interface between light (subtle body) and heat (gross body).

So, as with any psychotherapeutic work, working with dreams through the body will unlock memories held in it, traumas perhaps. Time and great care must be given to these things arising in the therapy as a result of dreamwork. Sensations arising in the body during the work will also connect the dreamer to the subtle body and its energy centres. Furthermore, the energy centres activated by the dreams will, in turn, act as portals or gateways to the different levels of consciousness. In working with dreams through the body, we are working with the whole person—body, mind, soul, and spirit.

Each image that is explored through the Waking Dream Process in the body will connect with a particular energy centre: for example, an image held in the arms and hands links to the heart; images in the legs and feet link to the base centre; images in the thighs link to the sacrum centre; shoulders, shoulder blades, and ears link to the throat centre; eyes to the third eye centre; mouth to the sacrum; nose to the base centre. Images held in other parts of the body are easier to link to the energy centres. Chest and lungs link to the heart centre; solar plexus to the solar plexus centre; lower abdomen to the sacrum centre; throat to the throat centre; brow and back of the head to the third eye centre; and top of the head to the crown centre.

The accessing of a particular level of consciousness via the subtle body often results in the dreamer experiencing sensations around the associated energy centre upon awaking or during the waking dream-work. Dreamers experience subtle sensations that appear to be physical whereas, in fact, they have nothing to do with the physical body. Experiences typically include sensations of heat or cold in the body; the perception of energy moving in the body from one part to another; hearing sounds that have no physical cause; seeing colours, auras, and light that do not appear to have a physical source; sensing smells and having unusual tastes in the mouth without any apparent cause. The awaking of an energy centre is subjectively experienced as being discharged into the physical body in these ways. When an energy centre opens, our consciousness has access to the inner plane or inner level of consciousness the energy centre is linked to. This is experienced as a "charge" in the consciousness of the dreamer.

Sensing the movement of energy in the body is a very important part of the Waking Dream Process. During the process, the guide explores and tracks the dream story through the dreamer's body. In this way, the dream is experienced as a journey through the body. Maintaining the connection between the dream and the dreamer's body promotes the authenticity of the dreamwork, as well as helping to "ground" the dreamer. In this way, the process of balancing is embodied, the journey is embodied. As Robert Johnson emphasises: "Ideas and images from your dream should enter into your emotions, your muscle fibres, the cells of your body. It takes a physical act. When it registers physically, it also registers at the deepest levels of the psyche" (Johnson, 1986, p. 101).

## The Waking Dream Process

The description of the Waking Dream Process given below can only be a basic guide and not a full description of a process which is, essentially, intuitive and creative, and also complex. Every dream session is unique in the sense that the dreamer and dream guide are engaged in an organic process with no predetermined outcome. It is important to emphasise here, that the description for the role of the guide and the Waking Dream Process procedure are not sufficient in themselves as training in multidimensional dreamwork and the Waking Dream Process. The skills and understanding required are learned over time under the supervision of an experienced dream worker. The importance of guidance and supervision, personal and spiritual development, and personal experience of multidimensional dreamwork, cannot be over-estimated. That said, it is hoped that this chapter will serve as an introduction to the multidimensional approach to dreams for the reader as dreamer and potential "dream worker" in the therapeutic context.

## The role of the dream guide

Waking dreamwork is a joint endeavour—the dreamer's exploration of their inner world, with the support of the dream guide (the therapist). Both the guide and the dreamer go deeper into the psyche; it is a shared journey where both play a part and make a contribution.

The dream offers guidance to the dreamer; the dream guide, in turn, facilitates insight into and amplification of the guidance inherent in the dream. The guide combines insight into the dreamer's psychology with their perception of the spiritual quality that is coming through (or trying to come through) in the dream. Much will depend on the clarity and insight the guide is capable of, as well as their attunement to the dreamer, their sensitivity and their responsiveness; that is, the ability to feel what the client is feeling. A skilled dream guide has the capacity to enter into the consciousness of the dreamer and their dream. Intuition plays a big part in knowing where the "hot spots" of the dream lie, what to handle carefully and what to focus on.

The guide needs to be supportive of, and sensitive to, the client's thoughts and feelings, and to judge the readiness of the dreamer for the dreamwork in the context of the therapy as a whole, and session by session. The guide has to make an assessment as to how deep the dreamwork should go and, of course, be guided by the dreamer. The dream guide must always take great care with a person's dream world. As with any therapeutic work, being clear, sensitive, supportive and responsive helps to build trust with the dreamer and to build a relationship with them that provides a safe container for the material emerging from the dreamwork. It is vital that the dreamer trusts and feels safe with the dream guide.

The dream guide is rarely directive. Until the therapist is experienced in dreamwork, it is better to be guided by the dreamer's feelings and instincts, which are paramount. It takes many years of experience in working with people's dreams successfully to be able to sense what is needed, moment by moment.

Holding the overview of the process is a crucial part of the role of the dream guide in the Waking Dream Process. The guide acts as a conscious resource in helping to orientate the dreamer, who may be lost in territory without a map. Keeping the dream connected to the body, the dream guide has a compass for navigation.

## Procedure

1. The guide explains the purpose of the Waking Dream Process and outlines the process for the dreamer.
2. The dreamer is invited to retell the dream as they remember it, including as much detail as possible (with their eyes open). The dream guide listens, and watches the dreamer telling the dream (noticing the points of hesitancy or emphasis, the presence or lack of affect and so on), whilst simultaneously paying attention to what he or she inwardly senses, feels, and intuits.
3. The dream guide then gathers more information about the context of the dream. This includes the time of night of the dream (dreams in the early hours of sleep after midnight tend to come from a deeper place than those near waking); the feelings the dreamer woke with; and what was happening in the dreamer's life around the time they had the dream (the life context). These factors may help with understanding the dream and what is behind it.
4. The dream guide might, if appropriate, ask the dreamer about their associations with the more significant dream images—the symbols and symbolic actions (this is more important for symbolic dreams at the personal, rather than archetypal, level). How might these be connected with their present life or past? What do they mean to the dreamer?
5. It may be, at this early stage, that one particular image stands out. This is the energy "hot spot"; everything in the dream will centre around, or lead up to it. It will also be experienced by the dreamer as holding most of the energy, focus, and message of the dream. This symbol evokes far more energetic sensation (and feeling) than the

other images when it is located in the body. If there is a central image (and there may not be), this is noted by the dream guide.

6. The dream guide will then ask the dreamer if they feel comfortable enough to explore the dream by retelling it as they re-imagine it (in the first person)—like replaying a film (this time, with eyes closed). It is explained that the imagery of the dream will be explored as part of this retelling. Once consent is given, the dream guide proceeds to the next stage.

7. The dream guide now asks the dreamer to close their eyes (and keep them closed until the end of the process), find a comfortable breathing pattern (breathing in through the nose and out through the mouth) and to use the breathing to turn their focus inside. Then, the dreamer is asked to go to the beginning of the dream and describe the opening scene—its setting and atmosphere; for example, night or day, city or countryside, peaceful or busy, gloomy or upbeat etc.

8. The dream guide then explores with the dreamer the imagery at the beginning of the dream and the dreamer is invited to make imaginary physical contact with it—to touch it or an aspect of it, go into it; for example, touch the green grass, enter the water, go through the door. The dream guide enquires as to what the dreamer is experiencing whilst touching this inner, imaginary world. Once a feeling has been named, the dream guide asks where the dreamer might be holding this feeling *in their body* (it can be anywhere in the physical body). It might be helpful to ask the dreamer to place their own hand on this area in order to help with focusing on it, and to ask the dreamer to move to the right (or left) if the image or dream event is located on the right (or left). Imaginary physical contact engages the sensation function, which links, naturally, with the feeling function.

9. Further images and associations might well arise from this connection with the body and can be explored, as appropriate. Once the experiencing of this opening scene seems complete to the guide and the dreamer, the dreamwork can then proceed again to the next part of the dream. This is the beginning of the inner exploration of the dream world through the use of visionary geography. In tracking the dream in this way, the pathways of the waking dream journey through the body become apparent (and may follow the traditional meridian lines of acupuncture).

10. The dream guide's knowledge of the dreamer and their intuitive grasp of the dream will inform their sense of where the dreamer needs to be and where they need to go in the dream. Highly charged images and those which seem to represent signs of life (e.g., green in nature, water, new life), openings or images of connection (e.g., mirrors, doorways, archways, bridges, pathways and so on) are particularly important. If there is a colour in the dream which has energy, the dreamer can access the feeling held in it by meditating on the colour in the session. As they move through the dream together, the guide will ask the dreamer, at key points, what they are experiencing and where they feel that experience in the body, and to focus on, and stay with these feelings or sensations held in the body until a shift is sensed in the latter. Through this process, the dreamer is beginning to make this relatively unconscious image conscious; insights or a shift in perspective may follow.

11. Particular time will need to be given to the "central" image of the dream—the one with the most "charge". This is the part that holds the underlying emotion of the dream and the transformational potential. Indeed, if there was limited time, this would be the image to work with exclusively. It might be that the dreamer needs to touch the image, to go into it, or to look into its eyes and dialogue with it (if it is an animal or a person). Once they have made a deep connection with it, it may be that the image undergoes a natural transformation, or the guide may have a sense that the dreamer needs to incorporate it into their being consciously. This can be facilitated by asking the dreamer to take the image "into" their body, locate it, meditate on that area and, by using the breath, absorb the energy held there into their whole being. In this way, the gift of the dream is received and integrated.

12. While the work is taking place, the guide carefully notices the dreamer's body language, voice, breath, as well as the dreamer's associations, bodily sensations, and feelings. Meanwhile, the dream guide pays attention to their own personal feelings, sensations, and thoughts, and uses this *countertransference* (the therapist's internal responses to the client) to inform the session.

13. The dream guide also notes energy *block*s in the body (something feels blocked, stuck, or uncomfortable, with accompanying anxiety) and invites the dreamer to stay with them consciously until such time that they experience a clearing.

14. If a dream contains an aspect that is experienced as dangerous or harmful, the dreamer might feel able to try to encounter the negative images in the waking dreamwork. If the dreamer can make contact with this negative image by simply staying with it, touching it (no thoughts) until it feels comfortable, then it can be transformed. By allowing the presence of the "shadow" aspect, its energy changes; that is, in sitting with the image, we bring our conscious awareness and our light to the shadow, thereby changing its distorted form into its essence—a pure quality. In doing so, we make it possible to integrate this aspect into the conscious personality and achieve a greater sense of balance. However, this must only be attempted if the dreamer is in a stable mental state and is willing to re-enter the dream in the waking state and encounter this "shadow" aspect of the dream.

15. Above all, the dream guide must *always* respect the wishes of the dreamer during the exploration, particularly with regard to sensitive material that is emerging and as to whether the dreamer wishes to proceed or stop. It might be that the dreamer needs to pause and receive support from the dream guide before continuing; or they may wish to stop the dreamwork. In the latter case, it is the dream guide's responsibility to help the dreamer to hold the experience and see it as part of the process of opening up the inner psychic pathways that are blocked. They may feel more able to explore their inner world further, at a later time.

16. The *experienced* dream guide might suggest fresh or new ways of looking at the images that arise in the exploration. They may suggest appropriate changes to the negative images, if this is helpful or necessary. It is important to balance, on the one hand, respect for the client's need to stay with an experience and develop the necessary capacity to handle it, with, on the other hand, gently opening new vistas or ways of seeing themselves.

17. Once the message of the dream has emerged from the exploration of the imagery, the dream guide will ask the dreamer if they feel ready to conclude the dreamwork. It is very important that the process feels complete to the dreamer and, in ascertaining this, it can be helpful to ask if anything else needs to happen. When the dreamer is ready, they are asked to slowly bring their awareness back to the room and open their eyes.

18. The dream guide first asks the dreamer to reflect on, and share, their experience and its applicability to their life. The dream guide then

offers their perspective and insights with regard to the emerging message of the dream in the context of the therapy and the PTP, perhaps pointing out its significance in terms of the alchemical operations or stages, levels of consciousness or some other aspect of the Multidimensional Dreamwork Model (or, of course, anything else that seems helpful). It is extremely important that this takes the form of a dialogue with the dreamer leading, ideally, to a shared understanding of the dream.

19. A very important aspect of the role of the dream guide is to help the dreamer to bring their experience into their everyday life consciously. This can be done by inviting the dreamer to meditate upon the central image (its colours, light, or symmetry) as a daily practice and to externalise the dream images and "gifts" in creative ways; for example, painting or sculpting the image, creating an "altar" containing the key elements in symbolic form and so on. These external expressions of the dream help to "breathe" life into it and ground it in conscious life (Garfield, 1995).

20. This process becomes easier and more productive if dreams are explored over a significant period of time. This can lead to considerable growth and change in the dreamer. However, it is emphasised that the process must be allowed to unfold naturally, as opposed to pushing changes through in repeated intensive dreamwork. The psychic changes that take place are considerable and, as with a physical operation, the dreamer needs time to recover and assimilate these changes and insights. Too much change too quickly can be overwhelming.

## The Waking Dream Process in action

Using the multidimensional approach to dreams, we can sub-divide dreams into the three basic categories set out below.

### 1. Personal dreams reflecting everyday life

These dreams are the most common. Some of these dreams are called "day-residue" dreams, simply reflecting the impressions of the day. As such, they need no interpretation.

### 2. Personal dreams with symbolic elements

These dreams are a mixture of the personal and the transpersonal dimensions. The multidimensional dreamwork approach works with this type of dream to bring psychological healing, but also pays attention to worldly symbols acting as a gateway to the spiritual. Working with the symbols in the dream uncovers what the dream is hiding and opens the dreamer to the inner world of the spiritual realm.

### 3. Impersonal dreams

These dreams seem very unreal and unrelated to personal experience. They can be either psychic (precognitive) or purely spiritual dreams. In the latter, the spiritual realm makes an impression on us; when we awake, we are still conscious of the spiritual energy. Sometimes, the message of these dreams is so direct there is no symbolisation at all, but the message can also come through a spiritual or archetypal symbol that has no personal meaning. The dream can still be explored through the Waking Dream Process (and in meditation) to reveal deeper insights and realisation.

Whilst there are clear differences, there is no strict boundary line between personal and impersonal dreams. It is more useful to think of a continuum with the day-residue dream on one side and a purely spiritual dream on the other. Examples one and two below illustrate how the personal or psychological aspect veils the transpersonal. Both dream examples are drawn from a long dream sequence. In the first example, Ava is the dreamer (we had worked together many times when this session took place). The second case demonstrates, in a more dramatic way, how effective this approach can be.

### Example one

The account of the dreamwork is based on part of a recorded waking dream session. Since this dreamwork was carried out during a dream workshop attended by approximately twenty people, the guidance incorporated some teachings of interest to the whole group. The session lasted about thirty minutes, so there was a slow, spacious rhythm to the session which it is not possible to convey in a written account of it.

#### Meeting the Bull

I am going up in a little gondola. I first thought it was a ski-lift, but I get into the gondola because there are children in there, and my husband is in the gondola in front. At the top, there is a huge fair—surprising. I thought there would be nothing up there. Many stores, vendors. To the left, there is a ski race, slalom—wonderful, the small curves they can make.

I want to continue up to the right, on a small path. Not far up, there are animals in the way, including a bull. He attacks me. I am frightened and jump over a wooden fence to the left. I am safe and go back down. I can't find my husband any more.

(The guide initiates the Waking Dream Process—the dreamer turns within and describes the scene, setting and atmosphere before revisiting the first part of the dream.)

DREAMER: I'm going up towards the right—no snow on the right, just rocks. I decide to go through all this crowd of people and then out and continue ascending, and that's where the bull is.

GUIDE: Ok, so now, tell me about the bull. What does it look like?

DREAMER: Well, at first there were many animals there (I didn't differentiate them), also strange animals.

GUIDE: But it's the bull that you notice?

DREAMER: It's the one that charged me.

GUIDE: He is the one that's after you. It sounds like you need to meet the bull.

DREAMER: (pause) It's a stupid bull!

GUIDE: Ok, maybe, but perhaps there is another side to him too; none of us are all just one thing.

DREAMER: He is red.

GUIDE: He is red? That's quite a bull.

DREAMER: He has horns.

GUIDE: Well, how would it be if you just stand still? (pause) Don't run. (pause) Come up to him and look him in the eyes (pause), pat him on the head, get to know him; perhaps he is a part of you. Maybe, the reason why he is chasing you is that you keep forgetting him, running away. I wonder if you need this bull to help you in everyday life. See if you can make a connection with the bull. (pause)

DREAMER: He kind of wants to look down if I want to look in his eyes. He's got to lift his head.

GUIDE: Mhm …

DREAMER:  He's kind of sad. He has large black eyes.

GUIDE:  So, look into his eyes and, as you do, reach out to him. Now, as you touch him, where do you feel that in your body?

DREAMER:  All the feeling is in the solar plexus right now.

GUIDE:  Place your hand there and focus on it.

DREAMER:  (tears) He looks so strong, but he is not so strong.

GUIDE:  Mhm, you see, perhaps he feels ashamed because you think he's stupid all the time. He's like a bull without horns—a very sorry bull. Can you give him a chance to prove himself!

DREAMER:  How can I do that?

GUIDE:  Well, by befriending the bull, making him your friend, and letting him help you with his strength and power. When there are things that you can't move, he'll willingly push them for you. When there's a load that's too heavy to carry, he'll willingly pull it for you. And he'll be very proud, because he's working for you—he feels that he has a use on earth. So if you think of power, it is not necessarily something dangerous, or stupid, or bad; when it's harnessed, it can be put to good use.

DREAMER:  (long pause) He's got a golden crown now.

GUIDE:  Now just allow that feeling of power to emerge from your solar plexus and permeate your whole being. (long pause) How does that feel now?

DREAMER:  Great.

GUIDE:  (pause) Ok. Here is a new meditation practice for you—meditate on the bull. You could think of the bull as the power in you. Don't deny that power. It is simply a quality, an energy that is more "earthy", that is there to help you. If it's in the service of the divine in you, it's perfectly good. It may help you in your next step. Does this resonate with you?

(Ava responds positively and the individual dreamwork is concluded).

GUIDE:  (to the group) In many of the major spiritual traditions, the foundations of creation emanate from a quaternity—a throne of four figures (Ezekiel Chapters One and Two). For example, the Bible (the Old Testament) refers to the four beings in the vision of Ezekiel: one is divine man, one is the divine courage (the lion), one is the divine insight (the eagle), and the fourth pillar of the "throne of God" is the divine power, which is the bull. Now, if you remove one of these pillars or principles, you cannot build anything. They are the fundamental building blocks of life and of the self. When you recognise the spiritual significance of power, which even your "stupid" bull can carry, then you have begun to tap into a secret. Perhaps that's what is symbolised by the golden crown on the bull.

The dreamwork reveals what is hidden behind the fear of the bull and what it is that the bull is holding for Ava. It facilitates a deep experience of a, hitherto unknown, kind of power. This experience happens in the imagination, but at the same time, it is very real. Imagination has served as the bridge between outer and inner reality. A key point in the dreamwork was locating the bull within the dreamer's body (her solar plexus) in order to access the quality of power. Doing the meditation practices which followed logically from this work, served to "embed" the experience for Ava and integrate it into her life.

The most important aspect of this dreamwork is that the guide encourages the dreamer to stay with the energy of the image once they have contacted it. If they patiently stay with it and wait, they will develop a capacity to hold its energy, to feel its presence. As a consequence, the form and the quality of the energy of the image will change. In the above case, the bull developed a golden crown. This is what we call the *transformation of energy*. The frightening animal above was a split-off part of the personality. When Ava meditated on it in the dreamwork, it could not remain in such a repressed and alienated, split-off state and integration followed. What happens psychologically is that we transform the energy from its primitive, regressed state to a more consciously functioning, humanised state.

### Example two

Some dreams, such as the example below, are a mixture of the personal and the transpersonal, containing both imagery that is coming from a deeper level within us, and references to our life events or known aspects of our personality. Dreams can use imagery from our outer world, our life experiences, to symbolise something that is going on within us at a deeper level than we are conscious of. Most therapeutic dreamwork is based on this understanding. In this example, the dreamer had only worked on a few dreams prior to this session.

### The Healer

I see a plate with rice and green worms. I pick out and separate the worms from the rice. Later, I enter a room with no corners. A man, a healer, comes in. I rest my head on the man's lap (to the left side). The healer sees that I need healing in relation to an old wound. The healer says that this wound occurred in Piedmont forty-five years ago.

She summarised her experience of the Waking Dream Process as follows.

My guide asks me about my life forty-five years ago. I was very unhappy at home because my parents ran a business there. The phone was ringing constantly. I felt unsettled—almost "homeless". This memory connects me with another memory twenty years ago when I was pregnant and living with friends in Piedmont. At that time, too, I felt unsettled and a lack of a sense of being at home.

My guide asks me to pick up one of the green grubs and hold it. It becomes an entwining, cocoon-like thread enclosing me in an oval shape (which my guide later pointed out was like a womb, but also symbolised my aura perhaps). I notice that there is a sense of no energy in my left shoulder. My guide asks me to focus on it. I do so and, suddenly, there is a massive explosion of energy there and around my left ear. Immediately following this, I am aware of being enveloped in a sense of peace. My guide also experiences this. Since the work, I have felt a new sense of being in life and at peace. (Later, my guide suggests that this might be the energy of spirit descending into life—incarnation—which comes down from top left to bottom right in the body).

By enquiring about the reference to "Piedmont forty-five years ago", the guide helps the dreamer to make the connection with the past and the old wound that needs healing. The dreamer is invited to engage with this separatio dream (she separates the worms from the rice) in a dynamic way—interacting with the dream images by picking up one of the green grubs. Their green colour seemed to be a clue to the life force of spirit they were holding and this was verified by the dreamer's experience in the dreamwork. "Tracking" the dreamer's experience in the body (on the left side, as indicated by the dream) was also key to unlocking what was held in the dream. In this case, the sensation (or lack of) around the shoulder was the opening point to the energy held there. In embodying the dream, a difficult early childhood memory is accessed and the blockage removed to reveal the subtle energy behind the dream.

## Example three

The following dream of a woman in psychotherapy training is a dramatic example of a spiritual experience which was initiated by the dream and realised in the dreamwork.

### Good Friday Snake

At about three or four in the morning of Good Friday, I have the following dream: I wake up in the bed of the "ideal" bedroom I created for myself when I was a teenager. It is my room but different. The room is peaceful and lovely, full of moonlight. The white shutters are partially drawn to the sides of the window, slats open. The air is soft and fluid like water. I am lying down in my antique, four-poster bed with my husband on my right. He is sleeping peacefully. Suddenly, my eyes are drawn to the moonlight caught in the immense three-part mirror on my dresser opposite the bed. The mirror has a strong, wood frame that curves along the top and is straight on the sides. There is a large central portion and two smaller side mirrors. It's like a large triptych behind an altar. The mirrors radiate moonlight.

Curled up three or four times at the base of the mirror is a large, very earthy, powerful rattlesnake. It seems to have been waiting for me and lifts its head slightly when I look at it. In spite of my fear, I notice how gracefully and purposefully the snake slides down the dresser onto the floor. The snake is beautiful and luminous with moonlight. I pray it will leave the room if I stay very still, but it slithers along the left side of my bed towards me. I desperately want my husband to wake up, but he doesn't. Then the snake is on my nightstand and moves onto my bed next to me. It raises its head towards me. I am full of fear. I know I'll die as the snake lunges and bites me on the forehead (the third eye). At the same time, I think that my husband will wake up as I am bitten and fear he will be bitten too. I wake up sure I/we have been "killed" in the dream.

Afterwards, the dream haunted me. I felt as if those fangs had lodged in between my eyes and I couldn't get them out. I rubbed that space often. I found myself wondering what would have happened if I hadn't been so frightened and hadn't woken up when the snake lunged at me. Later my dream guide took me through this dream again. It was a very moving experience; in fact, I would say that it took place on a very different level of consciousness, beyond the physical body and the conscious mind.

She described her experience of the Waking Dream Process as follows.

My guide invited me to re-enter the dream and focus on the snake. Initially, I was full of fear of encountering the snake again. However, my guide played a supportive role in taking me through the dream. First, he asked if I was experiencing any difficulties in my life, and I told him I was having problems in my marriage. When I explained that the room represented my ideals about marriage, he said, "Life has a way of testing our ideals." I said, "Yep" to that. He asked what the snake meant to me and I said I thought something had to die. He reminded me that when something dies, something else is born.

Then he had me describe the room and, when I described how comfortable it felt, he asked me to locate that feeling in my body. When I gestured to my solar plexus, he asked me to keep my right hand there throughout the visualisation to ground the image in the body. As I looked at the snake and saw it move towards me, I felt an immense rush of power fill my chest, throat and back of my head. I lurched back in my chair. This power frightened me more than the snake. I was sweating and cold at the same time. I could feel myself shaking and thought this power would destroy me as it felt like it was splitting me open. My guide reassured me and helped me to feel safe with, and accept, this experience, to see it as a natural part of my spiritual enfoldment. That comforted me. He said I didn't need to fight it; the snake was an aspect of my own innermost self.

When I told him I couldn't get my husband to wake up in the dream he said, "Maybe he needs to be asleep because this is about you". That felt right so I turned back towards the snake. The snake came up the nightstand and my guide invited me to look at it and meet it. I did so and realised it was almost waiting for me to invite it onto the bed. When the snake came onto the bed, my guide suggested I let the snake do what it had to do. I waited, but the snake stayed curled up on the bed. I was about to let go of the experience when suddenly it leapt up towards my third eye, but this time it slipped into my third eye space, curled up in my head and dropped its tail down my spine, forming a column with its body. A wave of light and energy rushed up my spine. In a flash, it "shed" its skin and light through my whole body. It felt as if a large fountain of light and energy had suddenly sprung up from my feet. It became a timeless space. I stayed with it for some minutes. My guide then helped me to "ground" myself in my physical body and we reflected on the experience and its implications for me. When I said of the snake, "It didn't destroy me", my guide said, "Of course not; now it's part of you". I felt quietly content and at ease. I came out of the visualisation feeling a different person or, rather, more fully me. I felt the real possibility of a significant change happening in my life. I had awakened on a soul level and needed to be aware of that.

This dream was a development of an earlier dream ("Snake Bite"— quoted in Chapter Six to illustrate symmetry), which had signified the death of the ego perspective and marked the cusp of Nigredo and Albedo in the dreamer's process. As I worked with this later dream, I noted the progression from the previous dream—the development into Albedo in the images of moonlight, luminosity, whiteness, peacefulness, and beauty, together with the Creative Self motifs of mirrors, the snake and the evolution of the numbers three and four (as described in Chapter Six).

Little intervention was needed in guiding this dream, which had a huge power and momentum of its own and marked a significant point in this dreamer's awakening process and the activation of the kundalini energy as part of that. It was an affecting experience to witness its power sweeping through her body during the dreamwork. What was important was to reassure the dreamer during the process and to locate the comforting feeling of the room in the dreamer's body, using it as an anchor during the work.

We can see the marked difference here between the dream and the Waking Dream Process experience, though the one develops from the other. The dream occurs in the mind, but the waking dream helps to release the powerful, subtle energy that is waiting to emerge from a much deeper level of the psyche.

It is important also to note the difference between this dreamer's experience and that of psychosis (Sanella, 1987). This woman continued to be stable in her personality and was able to integrate the experience into her everyday life through active meditation and by working with her dreams. In psychosis, the person is not ready to integrate the experience, which will have no lasting positive effect on the personality.

## Conclusion

Working with dreams using the Multidimensional Dreamwork Model and the Waking Dream Process offers a powerful approach to the healing and transformation of the psyche. It has been used very successfully with clients for a number of years by psychotherapists trained at the Centre for Counselling and Psychotherapy Education. It enables the therapist and dreamer, not only to understand dreams in the context of unfoldment (its stages and associated levels of consciousness), but to unlock their true power.

Furthermore, the approach can be a used as a guide for anyone undergoing an experience of spiritual awakening or engaged in a process of inner exploration, personal growth, and transformation. Indeed, in comparing the inner landscapes and journeys of David and Ava with those of the dreamers of the dream research (Hamilton, 2006), there is a striking structural and experiential similarity between them, despite the different contexts (therapeutic setting, spontaneous unfolding of the awakening process and retreat, respectively).

It is hoped that following the journey of transformation through the inner landscape in all its fascinating complexity and richness will help dreamers to recognise and support the unfolding process that is taking place within, to see dreams in the broader context of a lifetime of transformation and, in doing so, value them as the treasure that they are.

> The man explains to me that to commune with the spirits that inhabit this place, to communicate with this hidden world, to know this world, I have to learn how to use this object, learn how to read the secret language carved into the object. I feel close to this world and want to stay. I wake up. (David, 04/2013)

"Magical Object" is the treasure of David's journey through the land-scape of awakening; it is a treasure for us all.

# Symbols of transformation

**Accommodation** *(e.g., house, palace, office block, hut, room)*

The buildings or rooms in which we find ourselves in dreams reflect the state of our psyche and unconscious sense of self. Size, shape, colour, and light are all significant. Size and shape might be significant in terms of evolving symmetry. The degree of colour and light, or lack of it, reflect the consciousness of the dreamer; a dark prison or a decrepit house speak of the prison of the mind and depression perhaps, whereas a golden palace, a grand building, reflect the magnificence of the inner self. In the course of the dreamer's process, as they become clearer in themselves, so their dream accommodation becomes bigger, lighter, more colourful, more comfortable and more interesting (e.g., the house of David's "New Family" dream). Images of temples, churches and holy places have the obvious spiritual meaning and characterise the Fifth Plane.

If building work is underway, the sense of self is changing; painting the walls might denote superficial change, but radical work; for example, new foundations, new roof, indicates that major changes in the sense of self are taking place. If the house is devastated (by fire or earthquake), it might be that there is a disintegration of the ego taking place as part of a PTP or life crisis.

## Animals *(invertebrates, reptiles, mammals)*

Animals and creatures reflect the level of consciousness of the dreamer and act as guides in dreams. Animals such as dogs or frogs (with their reptilian associations) symbolise the instinctual aspect or energies. Reptiles often seem to symbolise the untransformed or unconscious spirit that has fallen into abeyance. If animals are aggressive in the dream, they are trying to attract our attention because they have been ignored or neglected, or show the dreamer that the aggressive impulses are out of control. In the PTP, animals reflect the emerging spiritual quality in the dreamer; for example, David's red-plumed bird (the richness of his wisdom) and Ava's bull (her power). Sick animals show us where we are unhealthy. By paying attention to the animal, we discover what needs attending to in the body. At a higher level of consciousness, we might expect to see animals with finer qualities; for example, a gentle deer in the Third Plane, a pure white dove in the Sixth Plane.

## Babies, children, giving birth, rebirth

Birth and rebirth are metaphors for the emergence of a new aspect in the psyche as the dreamer moves through each stage of the PTP. Something new is being born, which comes from a more subtle (and innocent) level of the self. Birth or babies in our dreams are a sign that something subtle has coagulated in our consciousness. They are also a feature of Albedo, particularly the Third and Fifth Planes of consciousness.

## Birds, flying

Birds and flying represent ascent and are to be found in the Subtle Mental Plane and Sixth Plane, and as part of sublimatio purifications, where the dreamer rises in their consciousness.

## Black

There are two main kinds of blackness in dreams. The first has to do with what is unconscious or distorted and most often occurs in the Nigredo stage. Dark colours (black, brown) can also be associated with the earth element. The second occurs much later in the PTP and is a kind of veiling of the hidden light. This veiling becomes luminous blackness (the black light) before the light is revealed in all its glory.

## Blue

Blue is the colour of the air element. In the light spectrum, blue is the opposite of red; its temperature is cool. Whilst dark blue is often associated with sadness or melancholy, blue tends to show the subtle, spiritual side of our psyche, a higher consciousness. Sky blue, for instance, can refer to the imagination, creativity, the unlimited mind, which can fly like a bird. Dark blue is associated with the more intuitive aspect of mind. Deep blue is to do with our religious nature; for example, the Virgin Mary wearing the blue cloak—the "Blue Mary".

## Celebration

This is a sign of completion of a stage of the process, often appearing alongside the number four and food or eating. It marks the end of a particular struggle or something important that has been accomplished and incorporated (coagulatio).

## Clothing

The clothing that we or others wear in the dream, the colours of the clothing, like the accommodation symbol, seems to be related to the conscious sense of self at the time, for example, drab clothes represent a poor sense of self. Fresh and colourful clothing represents the taking on of a new sense of self; for example, in feeling more beautiful, we wear beautiful clothing, symbolising the emerging awareness of the quality of beauty in us.

## Death

Something must die in order that something can be born. Death is usually about transformation of the old self; resurrection and a new sense of self will follow. In such a process, a baby is often born in a dream soon after a dream of death. Death (mortificatio) is regarded as one of the main alchemical operations.

## Direction

Direction of travel in dreams is significant (see the section on "Visionary Geography"). Going north, or going up in the dream (going uphill, flying, climbing a ladder and so forth) would indicate that the energy and consciousness of the dreamer is ascending. Similarly, if we are travelling from the city to the countryside, we are moving to a more natural place in ourselves. Going south or going down stairs, climbing down ladders, downhill in dreams could indicate that the dreamer's consciousness is descending, becoming more "grounded" (as in Rubedo) or, it could indicate that they are going into their unconscious material. Going west (or going to the right) points to the mind world, the man-made world and a more active and expressive aspect of consciousness. Or, the reference to the right may show an imbalance in the dreamer, where mind is predominating over feeling. Travelling eastwards (or to the left) is the journey towards spirituality and the finer feelings of the inner world and indicates a more receptive aspect of consciousness in the dreamer. The left in dreams is connected with the feminine aspect, and the right is associated with the masculine. The directions of "in" and "out" signify the movement in the psyche of the dreamer inwards towards the inner world, or outwards towards life.

## Dragon

The dragon can be found in Subtle Mental Plane dreams as a mythical, magical creature and it can also signify the awakening of the kundalini energy in the dreamer (as we saw in David's dragon dreams). The dragon, as an archetypal symbol, symbolises the untransformed fire aspect of spirit.

## Elements *(air, fire, water, earth)*

The elements appear in PTP dreams as indicators of the "soul nature" of the dreamer or aspects of the dreamer that are emerging; that is, if the dreamer has a strong water nature, then this element will often appear in some form in their dreams or if the earth element is strengthening in the dreamer, then earthy images will start to appear. Or, it might be that a repressed fire aspect appears in the dream to show the dreamer of its existence in them. The elements also feature as alchemical purifications: solutio (water); calcinatio (fire); sublimatio (air); coagulatio (earth).

## Family *(e.g., parents, children, siblings)*

In alchemy, close relatives and people who are personally close or meaningful to us, symbolise those parts of our inner world that are coming very close to our conscious awareness. Close relations, close relationships, mirror the interaction between the different aspects of the dreamer's psyche as the transformation process evolves.

## Fish

The fish symbol is often associated with spirit (e.g., *ichthys*, the fish, was the first Christian religious symbol) and we have seen it in several dreams of transformation, notably in David's journey, where the symbol evolved through his process.

## Food

Food is used in the process as a metaphor for coagulating or assimilating something of the nature of the level of consciousness or the level of self being encountered. Often food is being shared as part of a celebration; through eating this food, an aspect of spirit is incorporated and embodied. The type and colour of the food (sweet, sour, heavy, light) might give further clues as to the meaning of the symbol.

## Gold and silver

Gold is associated with the sun and spirit in alchemy; silver is regarded as more feminine or receptive in its nature and, in alchemy, it is associated with the moon and with the soul. When two conflicting opposites in our psyche have been balanced or resolved, the colour or metal gold frequently appears, symbolising the eternal, precious treasure that has been discovered; it indicates that an aspect of our eternal or true nature (soul consciousness) is manifesting consciously. When gold and silver appear together in the same dream, a degree of balance between the masculine and feminine forces has been achieved in the process. Gold and silver often appear together in Citrinitas and Rubedo, symbolising the alchemical union of soul and spirit—the royal alchemical marriage in alchemy. In Ava's descent in Rubedo (in an earlier cycle of dreams), she dreams that her computer (symbolising the concrete mind) is "full of small silver and golden stars—very beautiful". This shows the presence of an archetypal soul-spirit consciousness having been coagulated in her conscious mind.

## Green

Green is the colour that shows the presence of the water element; it reminds us that something is greening, growing. Green is also in the middle of the colour spectrum; it is, thus, at a balance point. It is often associated with the heart and the higher energy centres. Generally, the appearance of green in PTP dreams symbolises the life force and spirit in the psyche. It is a healthy sign. As we saw in the "Travellers' Tales", green appears in Albedo and then throughout the PTP until it becomes emerald green at its height, showing the presence of the life force or spirit even more strongly.

## Guide figure

Jung refers to the guide figure in the transformation process as "The Spirit Mercurius". Mercurius is our guiding spirit. In the PTP, the guide figure appears to have an inner wisdom that knows, in advance, what the next step in the transformational journey needs to be, mirroring this back to the dreamer; for example, David's "Compassionate Woman" and "The Centaur".

## Healing

Images of hospitals, having surgery, taking medicine, doctors, nurses, dentists, are symbols of healing taking place during the transformation process. Of course, more subtle images such as healing rituals or the healing effect of a dream image can also be included in this category of images.

## Hermaphrodite

The hermaphrodite seems to symbolise the balancing of the masculine and feminine aspects in the dreamer—a physical embodiment of the conjunction of masculine and feminine. This is a first step towards the ultimate alchemical goal of the union of soul and spirit.

## Mandala

Mandala is the classical alchemical symbol of the circle encompassing the square. It signifies the balance of the four elements (earth, fire, water, and air) as well as the masculine and feminine energies. Further, it represents the coagulation of spirit (the circle as a symbol of self) within the psyche (the four elements balanced in a square).

## Masculine and feminine

A frequently occurring theme in the PTP is the interplay between the masculine and feminine figures, seen as a metaphor for balancing the active and receptive qualities in the dreamer. Psychologically speaking, this refers to the masculine and feminine sides of our nature. In alchemy, however, this can also refer to the so-called "sun and moon" forces in us, which are regarded as "spirit" and "soul" respectively. The union of masculine and feminine becomes, ultimately, the union of the great opposites of spirit and soul, (the former representing the impersonal, eternal, divine aspect in us, and the latter, soul, our individual nature). This is the royal alchemical marriage referred to in alchemy.

## Money exchange

During the PTP, exchange of money might suggest the exchanging of energy in the dreamer's psyche for a higher and more subtle energy.

## Multicolours

When many colours appear in one dream, often referred to by the dreamer as "all colours", this can point to an intensification of the process where many different energies or vibrations are present at once. This was called the *Cauda Pavonis* (the peacock's tail) by the alchemists and symbolised the awakened spiritual state of the alchemist. The full apparition of the Cauda Pavonis usually announces an imminent death and rebirth in consecutive dreams and indicates the presence of spirit.

## Nakedness

In the PTP, nakedness and being stripped of clothing is less likely to be a sexual reference than a metaphor for the deconstruction of the psyche's defences and ego identity. It is also a motif for the natural quality of the Third Plane.

## Nature, natural landscapes

As the PTP progresses, images of man-made environments will give way to images of nature and natural landscapes (often in the Third Plane), which become increasingly light and beautiful. Jung regarded trees as particularly important, the Tree of Life symbolising the living spirit in us.

## Numbers and geometrical shapes

The importance of numbers in dreams and their relationship to the development of symmetrical dream images is described in the section on symmetry. In summary, the number one (or the numerically equivalent ten, 100, 1,000 etc.) is a symbol of unity. The appearance of a circle or sphere symbolises the conscious union of the personal self with the emerging archetypal quality. The number two signifies the conscious emergence of an unconscious aspect of a polarity in the psyche, which implies that a balancing is taking place. The appearance of the number two is the first step towards the development of the geometrical image of the square which, later, may develop into the cube or a rectangle and cuboid. The number three relates to the triangle, which Jung believed symbolises the rediscovery of the original unity, an indicator of the presence of spirit. Jung talked about the number four as a symbol of completion of a stage in the process of individuation, an indicator of the completion of a balance of opposing forces in the psyche. Geometrically speaking, it will appear as a square or a rectangle. The cube or cuboid represent a more complete stage of development. The combination of numbers three and four bring about completion of a process. When the numbers three and four appear together, they refer to the existence of an invisible matrix containing twelve pieces of information, each piece being an aspect of the archetype. From within this matrix, a new symmetrical shape (image) will emerge, embodying the essential quality of the incarnated archetype. The number five is associated with the presence of the individuated self. The final image in the evolution of symmetry in the dreamer's PTP will be a symmetrical and beautiful image—most often, a cube-shaped or sphere-shaped image.

## Orange

Orange, like red, is associated with fire and sun energy; it expresses life force and spirit. It is often found in the Fourth Plane, but can also appear later in the PTP as a sign of spirit as we saw in Ava's process. It can also be found in Rubedo as an earthier colour.

## Organic images

As the PTP progresses, images of artificial objects made from concrete, plastic, fabricated metals are replaced by organic images of plants, trees, flowers, and objects made from natural materials, indicating the dreamer's connection to their inner nature.

## Purple

Purple is a sacred colour and is connected to the Fifth and Sixth Planes of consciousness.

## Red

Red is associated with the fire element, anger, blood, life force and spirit so the context of the dream is very important. In the ascent, red can be the rising kundalini energy, whereas in Rubedo, red is associated with the descending energy.

## Snake

The snake symbol can symbolise the instinctual, the reptilian aspect of our animal nature, or sometimes evil. In the PTP, it can also represent the kundalini energy of spirit as "Snake Bite" and "Good Friday Snake" illustrate. The snake often makes its first appearance in the Subtle Mental Plane as it did for David in "Green Dragon".

## Sound, music

Singing and music are particular themes of the Fifth Plane, but we also saw in Ava's journey how music can be a theme throughout the process as an expression of an individual dreamer's particular attunement.

## Sovereign, king and queen

The archetypal king and queen (or cultural equivalent) appear in the Fifth Plane and speak of the inner sovereignty of the dreamer. In alchemy, the king and queen symbolise spirit and soul; in the third coniunctio of Citrinitas, the king and queen of the royal alchemical marriage represent soul and spirit united.

## Sun and Moon

Sun and moon are very important symbols in alchemy, expressing the complementarity of masculine and feminine, the sun and moon forces in us, which are regarded as spirit and soul respectively.

## Transport *(e.g., car, bus, train, ship, plane)*

The motif of travel and the travelling vehicle (e.g., car, bus, train, ship, plane) appears in our dreams each time we move along in our inward journey to initiate or complete another stage of the PTP. Vehicles in a state of disrepair or broken seem to indicate the dreamer is having trouble transiting a particular stage.

## Treasure

Dreams of finding money, gold, jewellery, an abundance of treasure, are metaphors for the treasure of the heart, the hidden treasure of the soul.

## White

White (appearing in the Sixth Plane in the form of snow or ice) symbolises purity, immaculateness. White is a characterising feature of the ascent in Albedo, but paradoxically, is also associated with the Holy Spirit which comes down into us.

## Yellow

Yellow is often a colour of the earth element, but different shades of yellow can show very different qualities and the context of the dream and process is all important. Yellow can be associated with the sun energy, especially when it turns into gold. In alchemy, the sun is the symbol of the divine intelligence.

# NOTES

## Preface

1. These are the energy centres of the subtle body referred to in Sufi and Vedantic mysticism (see Chapter One, The subtle dream body).
2. Sufism, traditionally, has been associated with Islam. However, the Sufi perspective that I endorse acknowledges this great tradition in its roots and yet transcends it in recognising and embracing the equal importance and value of many other spiritual traditions. I am inspired by this universal spiritual outlook which was espoused by the great Sufi mystic, Pir-o-Murshid Hazrat Inayat Khan, when he came to the West from India in 1910.
3. During these solo retreats, I am silent, fasting, and engaged in spiritual practices from the early hours of the morning to after sunset, a period of approximately sixteen hours a day. I record my dreams at night.
4. Hamilton, N. (2006). *The Role of Dreams in the Study of Human Transformation*. References to "research" or "dream study" throughout this book always refer to this PhD thesis unless otherwise stated.

## Introduction

1. "The field of the finite is all that we can see, hear, touch, remember, and describe. This field is basically that which is manifest, or tangible.

The essential quality of the infinite, by contrast, is its subtlety, its intangibility. This quality is conveyed in the word spirit, whose root meaning is 'breath' from the Latin 'spiritus'. This suggests an invisible but pervasive energy, to which the manifest world of the finite responds. This energy, or spirit, infuses all living beings, and without it any organism must fall apart into its constituent elements. That which is truly alive in the living being is this energy of spirit, and this is never born and never dies." (Baring, 2013, quoting David Bohm, p. 345).

## Chapter One

1. Psyche, from the Greek word meaning breath, is used in this text to denote a totality of conscious and unconscious, mind and soul.
2. Archetype (from the Greek words meaning "first patterns") in Jungian psychology refers to an image or thought pattern that is universally present in the psyche and emanates from a collective unconscious that is shared by all people across time and cultures (Jung, 1983). Extending Jung's definition, the term archetype in this text refers to a fundamental vibration or quality that comes from a subtle level beyond the mind.
3. Black light is a transcendental light that appears to be black, initially, but later reveals itself as an intensely luminous, colourful light at the height of the spiritual awakening process (Corbin, 1994).
4. Oneness is an experience of union or non-duality where we are stripped of every vestige of our being, of every level of self—animal, human and even angelic (Khan, 2003).

## Chapter Two

1. Tibetan Buddhism refers to the phenomenon of the transcendental energy of the void being drawn in through the awakened subtle energy centres as "winds". These winds are experienced physically as a movement of cool air on and around the body (Gyatso Geshe, 1992).
2. Jung described the inner feminine and masculine figures as the archetypes of anima and animus. The inner feminine figure in the dream of a man is his anima, interacting with the dreamer to make him more "soul" conscious, that is, more receptive and aware of his inner, deeper feelings. Similarly, the inner masculine figure in the dream of a woman, called the animus by Jung, interacts with the dreamer to make her more conscious of her spirit in the process of transformation. In this way, the anima/animus figure is a spiritual guide acting as a bridge to the unconscious (Jung, 1979).

## Chapter Three

1. See Bion's notions of how the ego used the instinctual (e.g., anger, rage, fear) and mental defences (projection, denial, splitting etc.) to defend itself against the threat of loss, of emptiness, of "no self" (Grotstein, 2007).

## Chapter Four

1. Jung understood the quaternity system of orientation (e.g., four seasons, four elements) as an archetypal expression of the totality, and applied it to the totality of consciousness in terms of four aspect of consciousness (thinking, feeling, sensation and intuition [Jung, 1983].

## Chapter Six

1. Sufism is particularly helpful with regard to light phenomena in dreams related to awakening because the Sufi perspective links light and energy with consciousness (Khan, 1982).
2. In the analysis of a long series of dreams, Jung specifically identifies the mandalas as expressions of symmetry (Jung, 1968).
3. The transcendent function unites the opposites in a third position which "arises from the union of conscious and unconscious contents" (Jung, 1960, p. 131).

## Chapter Seven

1. Jung put forward the relationship between four functions, in two pairs of opposites: thinking—feeling/sensation—intuition (Jung, 1923).

# REFERENCES

Abt, T. (2004). *The Great Vision of Muhammed Ib'n Umail*. C. G. Jung Institute of Los Angeles.

American Psychological Association. (1991). *A.P.A Journal of The Association for the Study of Dreams. Dreaming Volumes 1–23*. Articles by Cartwright, Globus, Hartman & Kramer. Volume 1, no's 1 & 2; Volume 4, no 4. Educational Publishing Foundation.

Bakhtiar, L. (1991). *Sufi Expressions of the Mystic Quest*. London: Thames and Hudson.

Baring, A. (2013). *The Dream of the Cosmos: A Quest for the Soul*. Dorset: Archive Publishing.

Bohm, D. (1980). *Wholeness and the Implicate Order*. London: Routledge & Kegan Paul.

Botha, M. (2011). MA thesis, Northampton University.

Brennan, B. (1990). *Hands of Light*. New York: Bantam.

Bucke, R. (1923). *Cosmic Consciousness*. New York: Dutton.

Cartwright, R., Globus, G., Hartman, E. & Kramer, M. (1991). Articles in: *APA Journal of The Association for the Study of Dreams*, 1: 1, 2 & 4.

Chittick, W. (1994). *Imaginal Worlds of Ibn 'Arabi and the Problem of Religious Diversity*. New York: State University of New York.

Corbin, H. (1969). *Creative Imagination in the Sufism of Ibn 'Arabi*. Princeton, NJ: Princeton University Press.

Corbin, H. (1990). *Spiritual Body and Celestial Earth. From Mazdean Iran to Shiite Iran*. Princeton, NJ: Princeton University Press.

Corbin, H. (1994). *The Man of Light in Iranian Sufism*. New Lebanon, NY: Omega Publishing.

de Jong, H. M. E. (2002). *Consciousness: A physical perspective*. University foundation lectures. King's College, University of London.

de Nicolas, A. (1996). *St. John of the Cross: Alchemist of the Soul*. York Beach, Maine: Samuel Weiser, Inc.

du Sautoy, M. (2008). *A Mathematician's Journey through Symmetry*. London: Fourth Estate Publishers.

Edinger, E. F. (1991). *Anatomy of the Psyche: Alchemical Symbolism in Psychotherapy*. Chicago: Open Court Publishing.

Etevenon, P. (2004). *Dreams and inner consciousness—Following Sr. Aurobindo's vision of evolution*. Proceedings of twenty-first international conference of the Association for the Study of Dreams. June: Copenhagen.

Evola, J. (1995). *The Hermetic Traditions: Symbols and Teachings of the Royal Art*. Rochester, Vermont: Inner Traditions International.

Freshwater, D. & Robertson, C. (2002). *Emotions and Needs*. Berkshire: Open University Press.

Garfield, P. (1989). *Pathway to Ecstasy: The Way of the Dream Mandala*. Upper Saddle River, NJ: Prentice Hall Press.

Garfield, P. (1995). *Creative Dreaming*. New York: Fireside.

Gibran, K. (1969). *The Prophet*. Crawley Sussex: Bookprint Ltd.

Grotstein, J. (2007). *A Beam of Intense Darkness: Wilfred Bion's Legacy to Psychoanalysis*. London: Karnac.

Gyatso, G. K. (1992). *Clear Light of Bliss: Tantric Meditation Manual*. Cumbria: Tharpa Publications.

Halevi, Z. (1986). *The Work of the Kabbalist*. York Beach, Maine: Samuel Weiser, Inc.

Hamilton, N. (2006). *PhD thesis*. Leicester: De Montfort University.

Hamilton, N. (2009). *Symmetry in dreams and the psychospiritual awakening process*. Proceedings of IASD Conference, June: Chicago.

Hamilton, N. (2010). *The role of lucid dreams in healing and spiritual awakening*. Proceedings of IASD Conference, Ashville, June: North Carolina.

Hamilton, N. (2011). *Colour, light and dream symmetry—Building blocks of lucidity and evolving consciousness*. Proceedings of IASD Conference, June: Kerbrode, The Netherlands.

Hamilton, N. (2012). *Dreams of awakening*. Proceedings of IASD Conference, June: Berkeley, California.

Hamilton, N. (2013). *The phenomenology of light in the process of spiritual awakening*. Proceedings of IASD Conference, June: Virginia.

Harris, T. (1981). *Journey to the Lord of Power by Ibn 'Arabi*. (T. Harris, Trans). London: East West Publications.

Hartmann, E. (2011). *The relation of imagery to emotion*. Proceedings of IASD Conference, June: Kerbrode, The Netherlands.

Hoss, R. (2005). *Dream Language: Self-Understanding through Imagery and Color*. Ashland: Innersource.

Jacobs, M. (1992). *Key Figures in Counselling and Psychotherapy: Sigmund Freud*. London: Sage.

Johnson, R. (1986). *Inner Work: Using Dreams and Active Imagination for Personal Growth*. San Francisco: HarperCollins.

Jung, C. G. (1926). *Psychological Types*. (H. G. Baines, Trans). New York: Harcourt, Brace & Co.

Jung, C. G. (1956). *Symbols of Transformation: Collected Works of C. G. Jung*. London: Routledge.

Jung, C. G. (1960). *The Structure and Dynamics of the Psyche: Collected Works of C. G. Jung*. Volume 8. Part I. Princeton, NJ: Princeton University Press.

Jung, C. G. (1963). *Memories, Dreams, Reflections*. New York: Pantheon Books.

Jung, C. G. (1964). *Man and His Symbols*. New York: Ferguson Publishing.

Jung, C. G. (1968). *Psychology and Alchemy: Collected Works of C. G. Jung*. Volume 12. Routledge & Kegan Paul.

Jung, C. G. (1969). *Man and His Symbols*. New York: Doubleday Press.

Jung, C. G. (1977). *Mysterium Coniunctionis: Collected Works of C. G. Jung*. Volume 14. Princeton, NJ: Princeton University Press.

Jung, C. G. (1979). *Aion: Researches into the Phenomenology of the Self: Collected Works of C. G. Jung*. Volume 9, Part II. Princeton, NJ: Princeton University Press.

Jung, C. G. (1981). *Archetypes and the Collective Unconscious*. Princeton, NJ: Princeton University Press.

Jung, C. G. (1983). *Alchemical Studies: Collected Works of C. G. Jung*. Volume 13. Princeton, NJ: Princeton University Press.

Jung, C. G. (1991). *Archetypes and the Collective Unconscious: Collected Works of C. G. Jung*. Volume 9, Part I. London: Routledge.

Khan, H. I. (1962). *The Phenomenon of the Soul*, Volume 5. London: Barrie and Rockliff.

Khan, H. I. (1982). *Spiritual Dimensions of Psychology*. New York: Sufi Order Publications.

Khan, H. I. (1982). *The Sufi Message of Hazrat Inayat Khan: The Gathas*. Netherlands: Servire Press.

Khan, H. I. (2003). *The Soul's Journey*. New Lebanon, New York: Omega Publications.

Khan, H. I. (2010). *The Complete Sayings*. New Lebanon, New York: Omega Publications.

Kumar, M. (2009). *Quantum*. London: Icon Books.

Luscher, M. (1969). *The Colour Test*. New York: Random House.

Mallon, B. (2000). *Dreams, Counselling and Healing*. Dublin: New Leaf.

Marlan, S. (2005). *Black Sun*. Texas: Texas A & M University Press.

Maslow, A. (1971). *The Farther Reaches of Human Nature*. New York: Viking Press.

Maslow, A. (1994). *Religions, Values and Peak Experiences*. London: Penguin Books.

Misra, R. (1980). *The Yoga Sutras*. New York: Doubleday Press.

Norbu, N. (1992). *Dream Yoga and the Practice of Natural Light*. (M. Katz, Ed.) Ithaca, New York: Snow Lion.

Novalis. (1997). *Novalis: Philosophical Writings*. (M. Mahoney Stolijar, Trans.) SUNY Press.

Roberts, R. M. (1989). *Serendipity: Accidental Discoveries in Science*. New York: John Wiley.

Roob, A. (2005). *Alchemy and Mysticism*. L.A., California: Taschen.

Sanella, L. (1987). *The Kundalini Experience*. Integral Publishing.

Thurston, M. (1990). *Dreams: An Edgar Cayce Guide*. New York: St. Martin's Press.

Von Franz, M. L. (1974). *Number and Time*. Evanston, Illionois: Northwestern University Press.

Von Franz, M. L. (1975). *C. G. Jung—His Myth in our Time*. Zurich: C. G. Jung Foundation.

Waggoner, R. (2009). *Lucid Dreaming: Gateway to the Inner Self*. Needham, Massachusetts: Moment Press Inc.

Waggoner, R., Hamilton, N. & Middendorf, D. (2013). *Awakening to an expanded reality through lucid dreaming*. Symposium, IASD Conference, June: Virginia, US.

Wangyal Rinpoche, T. (1998). *The Tibetan Yogas of Dream and Sleep*. New York: Snow Publications.

Wangyal Rinpoche, T. (2012). *Awakening the Luminous Mind*. London: Hay House.

Wilber, K. (1999). *Integral Psychology*. Boston: Shambhala Publications.

Wilber, K., Engler, J. & Brown, D. (1986). *Transformation of Consciousness*. New Science Library. London: Shankeley.

Wilhelm, R. & Jung, C. G. (1962). *The Secret of the Golden Flower: A Chinese Book of Life*. (C. F. Baynes, Trans.) First published in London and New York, 1931. Chicago, IL: Mariner Books.

Woodman, M. (1982). *Addiction to Perfection*. Toronto: Inner City Books.

Yau, S. -T. & Nadis, S. (2010). *The Shape of Inner Space: String Theory and the Geometry of the Universe's Hidden Dimensions*. New York: Basic Books.

# INDEX